Psychological and Philosophical Studies of Jung's Teleology

I0095161

This important new volume addresses an underappreciated dimension of Jung's work, his concept of the teleology, or "future-orientation", of psychic reality.

The work, authored by an international group of Jungian scholars, expands upon the socio-cultural, psychological, therapeutic, and philosophical import of this key pillar of the Jungian oeuvre, offering a compelling alternative to current, culturally dominant ideas about how change occurs. The book addresses varied aspects of his teleological thought generally, and its application to the psychotherapeutic endeavor specifically, engaging Freudian, neo-Freudian, and related theoretical orientations in an informed dialogue about the critical issue of the emergent unfolding of subjectivity in treatment.

This is an illuminating read for those interested in the study of Jungian theory, psychoanalysis, social psychology, religion, transpersonal psychology, indigenous wisdom traditions, and philosophical metapsychology.

Garth Amundson is a clinical psychologist in practice in Chicago, Illinois, USA. His past publications include a study of the application of Jungian theory to adolescent psychotic states and the concordance of dimensions of American philosophical pragmatism with Jung's ideas. This is his first edited volume.

PHILOSOPHY & PSYCHOANALYSIS BOOK SERIES
JON MILLS
Series Editor

Philosophy & Psychoanalysis is dedicated to current developments and cutting-edge research in the philosophical sciences, phenomenology, hermeneutics, existentialism, logic, semiotics, cultural studies, social criticism, and the humanities that engage and enrich psychoanalytic thought through philosophical rigor. With the philosophical turn in psychoanalysis comes a new era of theoretical research that revisits past paradigms while invigorating new approaches to theoretical, historical, contemporary, and applied psychoanalysis. No subject or discipline is immune from psychoanalytic reflection within a philosophical context including psychology, sociology, anthropology, politics, the arts, religion, science, culture, physics, and the nature of morality. Philosophical approaches to psychoanalysis may stimulate new areas of knowledge that have conceptual and applied value beyond the consulting room reflective of greater society at large. In the spirit of pluralism, *Philosophy & Psychoanalysis* is open to any theoretical school in philosophy and psychoanalysis that offers novel, scholarly, and important insights in the way we come to understand our world.

Titles in this series:

Eternal Youth and the Myth of Deconstruction: An Archetypal Reading of Jacques Derrida and Judith Butler
by Bret Alderman

Jungian Analysis in a World on Fire: At the Nexus of Individual and Collective Trauma
Edited by Laura Camille Tuley and John R. White

Psychological and Philosophical Studies of Jung's Teleology: The Future-Orientation of Mind
Edited by Garth Amundson

Psychological and Philosophical Studies of Jung's Teleology

The Future-Orientation of Mind

Edited by Garth Amundson

Routledge
Taylor & Francis Group

LONDON AND NEW YORK

Designed cover image: © George Henry Hall (American) – A Pomegranate, Siena (1885). Courtesy National Gallery of Art, Washington, D.C.

First published 2024
by Routledge
4 Park Square, Milton Park, Abingdon, Oxon OX14 4RN

and by Routledge
605 Third Avenue, New York, NY 10158

Routledge is an imprint of the Taylor & Francis Group, an informa business

© 2024 selection and editorial matter, Garth Amundson; individual chapters, the contributors

The right of Garth Amundson to be identified as the author of the editorial material, and of the authors for their individual chapters, has been asserted in accordance with sections 77 and 78 of the Copyright, Designs and Patents Act 1988.

All rights reserved. No part of this book may be reprinted or reproduced or utilised in any form or by any electronic, mechanical, or other means, now known or hereafter invented, including photocopying and recording, or in any information storage or retrieval system, without permission in writing from the publishers.

Trademark notice: Product or corporate names may be trademarks or registered trademarks, and are used only for identification and explanation without intent to infringe.

British Library Cataloguing-in-Publication Data
A catalogue record for this book is available from the British Library

Library of Congress Cataloging-in-Publication Data
Names: Amundson, Garth (Psychologist), editor.
Title: Psychological and philosophical studies of Jung's teleology: the future-orientation of mind / edited by Garth Amundson.
Description: Abingdon, Oxon; New York, NY: Routledge, 2024. | Series: Philosophy and psychoanalysis | Includes bibliographical references and index.
Identifiers: LCCN 2023047969 (print) | LCCN 2023047970 (ebook) | ISBN 9781032536248 (pbk) | ISBN 9781032536255 (hbk) | ISBN 9781003412823 (ebk)
Subjects: LCSH: Psychoanalysis. | Jungian psychology. | Social psychology.
Classification: LCC BF173 .P7767 2024 (print) | LCC BF173 (ebook) | DDC 150.19/54—dc23/eng/20231207
LC record available at https://lccn.loc.gov/2023047969
LC ebook record available at https://lccn.loc.gov/2023047970

ISBN: 978-1-032-53625-5 (hbk)
ISBN: 978-1-032-53624-8 (pbk)
ISBN: 978-1-003-41282-3 (ebk)

DOI: 10.4324/9781003412823

Typeset in Times New Roman
by Deanta Global Publishing Services, Chennai, India

Contents

Contributor Professional Biographies

Garth Amundson, Psy.D., this volume's editor, is a psychologist in Chicago, Illinois, USA, where he practices both independently and in local group practices from a mixed psychoanalytic and Jungian/neo-Jungian perspective. He owned and operated his own group practice between 1999 and 2016 and currently devotes time to researching and writing about philosophical understandings and interpretations of psychotherapeutic beliefs about human nature, purposefulness, and human destiny, as well as clinical supervision. His past publications include two book chapters: *A Jungian Interpretation of the Treatment of Delusions in Adolescence* (in Outpatient Treatment of Psychosis, 2017) and *Jung's Answer to Job: Toward a "Sensible" Mysticism* (in Jung and Philosophy, 2019).

Jody Echegaray, Psy.D., is a candidate-in-training with the C.G. Jung Institute of Los Angeles, California, USA. In this early career interest, he worked to develop technological innovations for the film industry. This expertise is evident in his contribution to the present volume, which addresses the evolution of technological or "machinic" extensions of human striving from an archetypal perspective. Dr. Echegaray has also conducted a mixed undergraduate/graduate-level seminar class at the USC School of Cinematic Arts and Pepperdine University on the challenges and pitfalls of the Hollywood entertainment industry and has conducted research into the uses of film and television in deepening the psychotherapeutic process.

Shane Eynon, Ph.D., is a former psychologist with the US Marines where he served in Afghanistan and state-side treating PTSD and related conditions, and since 2018, is in independent practice in West Chester, Pennsylvania, USA. A Native American, he is an active participant as a lecturer and consultant with educational institutions serving various tribal nations, including the Seneca and Ogalala Sioux. He is also presently serving as President of the International Institute for Psychoanalysis and Psychoanalytic Psychotherapy in Philadelphia, Pennsylvania and is a Clinical Fellow with the International Neuropsychoanalytic Society, with which he is Board Certified.

Dr. Eynon's interest in Jungian theory evolved as an outgrowth of his sense that Jung's transcultural and transpersonal emphases are among the West's most balanced and humble attempts to relate to indigenous traditions. In addition to his chapter in our volume, an expression of this interest is his position as Senior Lecturer with the Centre for Applied Jungian Studies in Cape Town, South Africa, since 2014.

Giorgio Tricarico, Psychologist, born in Milan, Italy, is a Jungian analyst presently living in Helsinki, Finland. He holds a Master's degree in Clinical Psychology from the University of Padua (1996) and attended post-graduate analytical training at CIPA (Centro Italiano Psicologia Analitica; Milan Institute), leading to his becoming a psychotherapist in 2008 and Jungian analyst in 2009. Mr. Tricarico is a member of the IAAP (International Association for Analytical Psychology), and one of the founders of the FEGAP (Finnish-Estonian Group for Analytical Psychology, IAAP member society), where he currently sits as its President. Since 2017, he has served as visiting supervisor for the GAAP (Georgian Association for Analytical Psychology) in Tbilisi, Georgia.

Mr. Tricarico has worked with adult patients since 1998 and lectures and offers seminars internationally on relevant issues in Analytical Psychology. Author of books and articles, he has published two books, *The Labyrinth of Possibility: a Therapeutic Factor in Analytical Practice* (2009) and *Lost Goddesses: a Kaleidoscope on Porn* (2017). The former volume represents the only book-length contribution to the study of Jung's teleology prior to the publication of this present text. Finally, he is also a devoted musician and songwriter.

Mark Winborn, Ph.D., is a Jungian analyst in Memphis, Tennessee, USA. Given the vast extent of his professional affiliations and activities, it is only possible to highlight a few of these here. Dr. Winborn trained at the Jung Institute in Zurich, Switzerland, between 1993 and 1999, and has been a member of their teaching staff as well as an external supervisor since 2014. His involvement as external supervisor and educator is part of his work with numerous Jungian organizations in the USA, the Inter-Regional Society of Jungian Analysts, the Memphis Jungian Seminar, as well as international Jungian institutions such as the Moscow Association for Analytical Psychology in Moscow, Russia. In addition to this, he has been a member of the ethics committee of the International Association for Analytical Psychology since 2016.

Among Dr. Winborn's many publications are the well-reviewed *Deep Blues: Human Soundscape for the Archetypal Journey* (2011), *Interpretation in Jungian Analysis: Art and Technique* (2019), *Beyond Persona with Jungian Analysts: Interviews on Individuation and Beginnings* (2021), and *Jungian Psychoanalysis: A Contemporary Introduction* (2023) as well as a large number of articles and book reviews in esteemed Jungian publications. Finally, he is an avid guitarist with an abiding interest in North American folk traditions, particularly those situated in the Southern United States, and regularly performs in public.

Tosia H. Zraikat, B.Ed. & Master's degree in Transpersonal Psychology, has a richly diverse professional and personal history in spiritual mentoring, qualitative research, meditation, self-hypnosis, creativity, consciousness, myth and symbolism, and dreamwork. She resides in Queensland, Australia, where she is involved in the application of writing to the development of spiritual understanding and psychological well-being, both independently and at the Queensland Renew You Centre for Wellbeing and Longevity. Ms. Zraikat's perspective is notably transcultural and transhistorical, as evident in her certification in Ancient Greek studies from the Coursera program of Wesleyan University and her proficiency in French, Italian, and Russian, in addition to her native English.

Introduction

Jung's Teleology: Its Historical Origins and Place in His Theory

Garth Amundson

Carl Jung portrays psychic reality as unfolding according to the ends of as-yet-unrealized future states of understanding and adaptation, what in philosophical language is called its *teleology* (from the Greek *telos*, "end", and *logos*, "reason"). In 1916 he writes, "…in my opinion the nature of the human mind compels us to take the finalistic view. It cannot be disputed that, psychologically speaking, we are living and working day by day according to the principle of directed aims or purpose as well as that of causality" (Jung, 1916/1961). And later, Jung asserts, "Life is teleology par excellence; it is a series of aims which seek to fulfill themselves. The end of every process is its goal" (Jung, 1934/1970). However, despite these forceful claims, nowhere does Jung systematically define his teleological orientation. This is utterly characteristic of his literary style, and a variation of the adage that the medium is part of the message, namely, that one can discern *what* is being communicated by examining its "how", the form of its communication. For Jung, an idea is first and foremost a happening, a phenomenon that independently descends upon consciousness. This, I think, is why he prefers to theorize and write by the seat of his pants, as it were, from the stream of impressions forcing themselves upon him. To be carried along by the force of an idea does not lend itself to the kind of measured, rigorously consistent logic and cautious restraint we normally associate with psychological theory-making. In Jung's view, one does not "create" a theory; rather, one allows oneself to be appropriated *by* its dynamisms, which arise from sources beyond conscious intelligence. One lends one's ego to the *telos* of its forward-going currents, its aims, to where it is that the idea is "heading". More specifically, Jung believes that ideas, if they are compelling personally and on a collective level, arise independently as symbols of the dynamisms of the unconscious. This is to say that

DOI: 10.4324/9781003412823-1

like all symbols, ideas are living, hence evolving beings. And like all living phenomena, ideas are sapped of their power to move us emotionally when inappropriately subjected to the operations of linear logic, including one-sided demands for clarity that, if achieved, render them intellectually communicable but no more.

Hence, like many of his most important concepts, Jung's teleology exists in the warp and woof of his writings, woven into the immediacy of its particular experiential "universe", and so must be teased out of its enmeshment in other ideas for its meaning and implications to be grasped more completely. This book is our modest attempt to do so while also creatively expanding upon the centrality of teleology to Jung's thought. If we have done our work properly, the power of this idea will remain intact and, beyond this, extend into a series of novel contemplations about psychic purposefulness itself. Toward this end, the *telos* of this introduction is not to simply offer a survey of Jungian thought about the mind's relation to the future, but also to provide readers with a sense of what it means to think teleologically.

This is not the imposing task that it might appear to be on first blush: at every moment (including in dreams) we are creating meaning toward certain ends that we affirm are important and even crucial. This phenomenon is so basic to our humanity and occurs so often that it tends to be "hidden in plain sight", as it were. As such, it is something we only rarely think about, if at all. Beyond the uncontroversial fact that we are goal-oriented creatures, in this introduction I also hope to convey the sense of how Jung leapfrogs from some ancient philosophical observations about how we employ goals to navigate daily life toward what I think of as his own psycho-metaphysical speculations about Being as expressing evolving purposes, speculations that invoke issues such as the meaning of consciousness itself, what its "for-the-sake-of" may be. What follows is my particular perspective on this topic, one dwelling upon the Western, specifically Eurocentric theo-philosophical background of Jung's teleology. This reflects my understanding of Jung as an essentially European thinker who addresses us largely from within the intellectual traditions of the European West. That said, Jung is a trailblazer in drawing upon the myths of diverse non-Euro-Western cultures to aid in his psychological studies, however much he is open to criticism for incorporating these into his preferred European worldview rather than allowing them to stand fully on their own. That is, his hypotheses about the universality of human experience are bolstered by his having studied and personally met those from different indigenous groups worldwide, though generally he interprets these groups' mythologies, including their various notions of causality and purpose, through a Eurocentric lens. Personally, I think this simply attests to the fact that all of us, however erudite or intellectually receptive, cannot begin any encounter the world except by looking at it through our own eyes. The fact that Jung's cultural background and personal psychological defenses limited his understanding of other cultures should be viewed with the conviction that the perfect not become the enemy of the good.

Joseph Rychlak (1991) casts light on Jung's literary style in his account of his teleology, which he notes developed as part of his reliance upon what Jung called a "constructive-synthetic" method of understanding psychological phenomena. As the term implies, this notion of what motivates us is based on the premise that mind is actively involved in constructing the future, and that it does so under the guidance of an innate drive to synthesize disparate dimensions of experience toward a sense of wholeness, unity, or completeness. Jung differentiates this manner of analyzing psychic reality from Freud's modernist reduction of experience to a set of purely personal unconscious conflicts arising in the past. And this premise about human nature shows in Freud's writing style, which is more restrained and cautiously linear than Jung's. Throughout his writings Jung offers compelling general statements about the integrative or synthesizing quality of mind and the way he tried to conform his thinking and therapy practice to this factor. Take as an example the following: "We conceive the product of the unconscious as an expression oriented to a goal or purpose....(and therefore) the aim of the constructive method is to elicit from the unconscious product a meaning that relates to the subject's future attitude" (Jung, 1921/1969, para. 701). Rychlak defines Jung's constructive-synthetic approach as an expression of his belief in an unconscious drive to reconcile conflicting experiences and their diverse aims. This is seen in Jung's concept of what he coined the mind's "transcendent function", its capacity to situate psychological conflicts within the mind's broader, integrative movement toward new, possibly unprecedented states of coherence (Jung, 1958b/1969). Ultimately, this does not "cure" or "resolve" the dilemma but rather transcends its polarities, toward the end of finding new, sustaining meaning within what previously seemed an insoluble collision of opposites. An implication of this view is that psychological symptoms are not only expressions of inner conflicts between clashing desires, but signifiers of some future set of meaningful realizations and adaptations to life striving to break through the ego's natural preference for the pedestrian, the taken-for-granted, and the known. This is implied in Jung's assertion that, as he writes, "(Neurosis) must, ultimately, be discussed as the suffering of a soul that has not discovered its meaning" (1932/1970); and, speaking directly to the futural direction of all psychological problems, he later writes, "Neurosis is teleologically oriented" (1943/1966, para. 40). Further implied in this vision of the *telos* of symptoms is Jung's notion of the "objectivity" of the unconscious and its purposes. We are "visited" or set upon by the dynamisms of the unconscious, often enough in the form of symptoms, this because of the inherently forward-looking direction of mind itself, its constant striving to forecast and/or bring to fruition a "may-be", a possibility, from states of division and conflict.

We might consider Jung's teleological outlook as of form of protest against domination by the faculty of memory itself, which selectively ensconces the forward-going flow of experience in static mental representation. This quality of memory has a highly conservative, "memorializing" function, in which meanings are rendered frozen in time, much like a statue on any Euro-American village green. This "statuesque" quality of memory, its seeming solidity as an object in mind that orients us as experiencing subjects within the movement of time, is essential for our thriving, including that involving possibilities of development toward the future: after all, growth, in all its forms, does not originate in a vacuum but from within the settled facts or "givens" of an established legacy, a psychic inheritance that pays tribute to, eulogizes, or and/or celebrates the past. But herein we see that memory properly exists in a dynamic dialectical relationship with possibility, in the first place so as to exist at all: the memorialized legacy of time, instantiated within the mind's dynamisms as memory, once existed as a movement toward something not-yet-actual. To recall one's past is to remember oneself as imagining a future yet to exist.

Neurosis is symptomatic of disruptions in this past-future dialectic, and hence, in the nature of time itself. We can and often do become unduly and even pathologically dominated by the past, a circumstance that unfolds as we engage in idealizing what we imagine to be its guarantee of structure and certainty. In neurosis, such idealization reveals its dark side, as memory overtakes us with rigidified, constricted vision of ourselves and the world itself. These then become ensconced within our subjective experience of time in static and "monumentalized" forms that are mentally "set in stone", as it were, forcing themselves on consciousness as the unhappy givens of life. By dwelling in the shadow of what has been handed to us by prior experience there is no possibility of experiencing oneself in a revelatory or novel manner, that is, there is no relating to oneself and the world itself as a "happening". Our capacity for innovation, hence personal identity and relation to the world become distilled to a staid collection of fixed traits whose nature we feel we already know. To indulge in a pun, the noble mental statuary reminding us of our relation to time past can easily become "statutory" in the legal sense. Here I am thinking of Sigmund Freud's concept of the law-giving cultural superego, specifically its tendency to impose an enfeebling, one-sidedly backward-looking and fetishistically worshipful relationship to personal and collective history. Here, the cultural "must-be" overshadows and obscures our natural inclination to envision the "may-be".

Anticipating later trends in post-modernism, Jung asserts that values and purposes change throughout the course of individual and group history. This perspective informs his paradoxical understanding of the archetypal images underlying our engagement with reality as eternal yet continually evolving. This evolution occurs, in part, due to the influence of the human being to realize common human purposes (and the urge itself to live purposefully) parochially, within the context of singular, time-bound, "local" strivings. Writes Jung...

> The original structural components of the psyche are of no less surprising a uniformity than are those of the visible body...They are eternally inherited forms and ideas which have at first no specific content. Their specific content only appears in the course of the individual's life, when personal experience is taken up precisely in these forms.
>
> (Jung, 1958a/1969)

In the foregoing, teleology is implied rather than directly stated. However, without too much trouble we can discern his point that the archetypes, while trans-cultural and eternal in and of themselves, seek to express themselves in the domain of temporality. That is, they naturally seek to enter into the realm of space and time and establish residence within the nitty-gritty specificity of everyday human lives. In this way the archetypes evolve toward fuller realizations of their natural ends, evolving teleologically from non-specific, contentless eternal forms to content and context-specific phenomena in daily life. Furthermore, and at the risk of reading into Jung something that he does not mean to say, it would seem that herein we may speculate that the archetypes themselves evolve as they become manifest in the particularity of a given life and its unique historical exigencies. Hence, the timeless archetype of, say, war necessarily expresses itself very differently in the mind of a Ukrainian foot soldier in the current conflict with Russia than in that of an Aztec warrior battling the Spaniard Cortes in 1519. The archetype itself is empty of definite content: it is a potential "space" that becomes "filled in" with a complex amalgam of interrelated parochial personal dispositions, group moral values and allegiances, and so forth.

Jung is not alone among the first modern psychotherapists to assert a future-orientation to mind. Some of the original members of Freud's circle cite the notion of mind as directed toward an as-yet-unrealized future (see Adler, 1921; Maeder, 1910). However, they remain true to the modernist narrative of human development, its purposes and aims, as explainable solely within personalistic, interpersonal, and sociocultural contexts. If Jung had followed their example he would not have been saying anything terribly novel. However, he is critical of what he deemed the limited understanding of time within such modernist narratives, which he finds insensitive to its transpersonal, existential dimension. His constructive-synthetic approach goes far beyond the limits of the personal and sociocultural, to posit a meaningful and possibly redemptive continuity between the individual and a cosmos striving toward the goal of becoming conscious of itself (Jung, 1958). This frankly metaphysical assertion is informed by Jung's insistence that premodern narratives can reanimate and deepen personal and collective modernist consciousness (and we might note that here too he finds a continuity, this time that of an enduring if subtle historical constancy between the discourses of the ancient and contemporary worlds, rather than what is often assumed to be a sharp break between these two eras occurring with the Enlightenment). This stance is the one most "Jungian" dimension of Jung's theory, a view of the psyche that dramatically sets it apart from Freudian perspectives and from most of the core premises underlying normative modernity itself.

This is a metaphysical central pillar of Jung's thought that emerged quite early in his work. Hence, in the 1896 Zofinga lectures, he speaks of this manner of understanding the course and meaning of human life as both a method of inquiry and a reflection of a transpersonal process, one that as such is both external to, and the immaterial intrapsychic foundation of, the human being (1896–1899/1984, para. 142). The priority that Jung ascribes to the mind's future-orientation is one that has long preoccupied near-Eastern and Western thinkers from diverse religious, social, and intellectual sources. Jung's transpersonal teleology, though proximally derived from early 19th century German Romanticism and its rejection of reductive modernist models of the human condition, has a long and complex history predating modernity.

While the fascination with purposes and ends is more prominent in Euro-Western cultures, it is also a not-uncommon feature of many indigenous mythopoeic worldviews. I am no anthropologist, although my limited understanding of indigenous teleologies is that they generally tend to be informed by the notion of time as circular rather than linear, as in the West. Further, they depict human purposes as properly defined from a position of intimate connection and cooperation with Nature. Here Nature is understood as an essentially intelligent and beneficent, if mysterious, guide, one that alerts us to our destinies through dreams, the wisdom of elders, shamanic visions, and revelatory encounters with the rascally spirits of fields and forests. Despite having been reared in Europe, with its Christianized eschatology of creation as progressing toward a defined and final state of fulfillment, Jung takes pains to separate himself from this cultural bias. Hence, Renos Papadopolous (2006) states that, "Jung repeatedly emphasized the *process* of individuation instead of the final product of individuated state itself" (Papadopolous, 2006, p. 31). Jung's vision of Nature as inviting us to become aligned with its perpetually repeating cycles, minus the usual Euro-Western emphasis on an ultimate consummation of time, transcends the limits of his personal background, and is a preliminary although imperfect point of contact with many indigenous concepts of human ends. Hence, for example, he seeks to define his use of the idea of finality (implicit in Eurocentric teleologies) more precisely, by stressing the importance of the *path* of goal-directed query while avoiding the implication that this finally arrives at a fixed, immutable, and unchanging terminus. Writes Jung,

> I use the word finality intentionally, in order to avoid confusion with the concept of teleology. By finality, I mean merely the immanent psychological striving for a goal. Instead of 'striving for a goal' one could also say 'sense of purpose'. All psychological phenomena have some such sense of purpose inherent in them.
>
> (Jung, 1957/1977)

In this volume, Shane Eynon's chapter on the teleology of North American woodlands native societies may help readers think more deeply about this issue, including the benefits and limitations of viewing indigenous and non-Western cultures through a Jungian lens.

In the Western tradition of metaphysics that most directly influence Jung, teleology emerges at least as far back as the ancient mythology of the Middle East with the Hebrews, whose descendants later became known as the *Yehudim* (in English, the Jews). Their *mythos* was a teleology of collective destiny, the protracted, alternately tragic and humorous story of a people ambivalently devoted to the purposes of a god who reveals himself in the unfolding of parochial human history, sometimes beneficently, at other times violently. This, of course, eventually became the mythic basis of the Christian narrative of the deity as revealing himself most perfectly in the personage of Jesus, the Christ, whose appearance among us became interpreted by the early church as signaling the beginning of a trans-cultural (and not solely Jewish) salvific historical movement toward the end of time itself, culminating in the moral victory of good over evil.

It is generally recognized that Plato was the first Western philosopher to systematically spell out a cosmic teleology. In two essays, first in the *Phaedo* (1892/2017) and later in the *Timaeus* (1888/1988), he **set** forth a teleology that is a generative, metaphysically holistic property of the cosmos and individual life, the latter being a microcosmic expression of the dynamisms of the former. Here Plato, addressing us through different literary characters, argues that the movement of individual beings to realize their proper ends reflects the larger processes of the *kosmos* (in Greek, "ordered whole"). These proper ends are oriented toward the penultimate, eternal, and transcendental Form of the Good. In this we see the equation of reason with the Good, an expression of the ancient Grecian captivation by a view of aesthetics as related to geometric proportion and balance, toward a cosmology in which the striving for an arithmetic cohesion and orderliness is the overarching principle binding all things together.

As is well known, Jung is heavily indebted to Plato. His assertion of the mind's future-direction may even be considered a contemporary addition to Neo-Platonic teleology, particularly in the way he applied the Platonic Forms to his concept of the archetypes as eternal, contentless psychic predispositions informing the general structure of our conscious interpretations of reality. Jung's (1916/1967) forays into Gnosticism, the "underground" interpretation of Christian doctrine strongly influenced by Greek Neo-Platonism, are among his unusual and creative uses of this philosophical tradition. Gnosticism is a syncretic product of a vast number of historical influences, including Jewish

Kabbalistic thought and Greco-Roman mystery religions. It is attractive to Jung because it embodies a religious orientation that is also a proto-psychology, yielding an unusual spirituality of inwardness and attention to personal experience in place of adherence to creeds. As such, Gnosticism presages his own syncretic, phenomenological vision of human nature and destiny (Ribi, 2013) and emboldens him in his belief of the continuity between pre-modern and modern models of our nature. Drawing upon the Gnostic wisdom traditions from 100 CE and thereafter, Jung posits that the process of treatment has parallels with the Gnostic account of the fall and progressive return of the alienated soul to its true source in the divine *Pleroma*, the transcendent realm of unity metaphorically "above" the deceptions of the temporal, material world. As such, he sees in Gnostic dualism a transformative telic journey of cosmic fall and redemptive return matching his own sensibilities and concerns.

The second major influence upon Jung's notions of purposefulness is found in his uses of Immanuel Kant's thought, which in many ways is a modernist addendum to Plato. Early in his life Jung became deeply attracted to Kant's writings, stating enthusiastically, "Kant is my philosopher!" (Jung, quoted in Colacicchi, 2021, p. 15). This is understandable because, like Jung himself, Kant was a religious person seeking to affirm the concept of God in a post-Enlightenment, increasingly secular world. Kant begins philosophizing in modernist fashion by outlining the necessary conditions for thought to occur at all, an aspect of which involves an exploration of the limits of what we may reasonably claim to know. This is a "negative" point of departure that is a consequence of the demise of religious certainties brought on by the Enlightenment. Specifically, Kant (1781/2000) argues that we are epistemologically constrained by innate, *a priori* mental categories (humbler, "this-worldly" and "subjectivized" versions of Plato's Forms) that dictate the structure of how we experience and interpret reality, and which we cannot transcend. However, he asserts, the fact that we are capable of reasoning accurately about reality, and that we do so in a manner that consistently conforms to the inborn, *a priori* lawfulness that constitutes the nature of thought itself, provides grounds upon which to affirm the probability, though not the certainty, of an intelligent suprasensible Creator who has authored such a structure to our reasoning. And it is in the affirmation of the relative freedom from brute necessity made possible by the transcendence of the categories, that the modern person may come into accord with the divine, whose essence is unbounded creativity, rather than by unreflectively parroting ancient creeds.

This is a "psychologized" re-visioning of religious life, one in which Christian, particularly Protestant, morality becomes a personal concern that is self-responsibly "worked on" privately rather than thoughtlessly accepted as a matter of loyalty to tradition. This, I presume, is one reason why Kant's analysis is intuitively appealing to Jung. In Kant, the *telos* of human life is to become able to affirm our moral freedom in relation to the natural limits imposed by the givens of the categorical structures of knowledge. Jung appropriates this idea, reframing the Kantian mental categories in his concept of the archetypes, which, similar to Kant's *a priori* cognizing structures, are eternal, unconscious and contentless mental templates propelling us, irrespective of our conscious intentions, toward general modes of comprehending experience. Individuation, his term for the process of becoming the singular human being that one is meant to be, is partly a process of becoming relatively free from the fateful determining power of archetypal forms. Hence, for Jung, achieving this state is a matter of moral fidelity to the unfolding of one's individuality, and as such is the ultimate goal of psychotherapy. As Giovanni Colacicchi (2021) states, while Kant addresses the autonomy of practical reason from necessity in terms of a "consciousness of duty", Jung, he notes, "emphasizes a duty to be conscious" (p. 15). This is to say that one takes up a self-reflexive position toward oneself, toward the end of becoming a defined and differentiated subject. This does not at all mean that one renounces one's grounding in the "givens" of the unconscious, as we often do when we earnestly and one-sidedly seek the dubious neo-liberal goals of "positivity", "self-mastery", or "personal growth", now very much in vogue in therapies such as Positive Psychology. Rather, one engages in a dialogical relationship with the unconscious and its dynamisms, a paradoxical act in which one realizes one's individual destiny (which includes the ability to skillfully discern, interrogate, and sometimes challenge what the unconscious is "up" to) as a function of having given oneself over to its dynamisms. Finally, this would seem to suggest another manner in which the archetypes are not simply fixed in time but evolve; namely, that, in a Kantian vein, these innate cognizing structures can and do respond to our having engaged them dialectically, as self-reflective, conscious agents. As such, they are simultaneously eternal and changeable, metamorphosing in response to our self-responsibly considering the fateful paths upon which they have set us. These are teleological byways upon which we at least have the power to progress at our own pace, self-reflectively developing the possibilities of some elements of what we find along the way and turning away from others. We are "given" a world, not ready-made and complete, but as a general and flexible set of rules within which we may work, a structure within which we can mold the preexisting givens of reality into particular, possibly unprecedented forms.

From the above we see that in considering teleology, as in other matters that capture his interest, Jung's vision of human nature is situated in larger concerns about meaning itself, including questions of personal and collective fate, freedom, and destiny. That said, as a philosophical method of analysis teleology is not confined to such lofty matters. Rather, it is an approach whose perspectives are applicable to understanding *all* dimensions of human life, including the most mundane (which, after all, are the elements out of which a grand penultimate direction in life is constructed). The utterly ordinary decisions we make on a daily basis express the omnipresence of a sense of moving purposefully toward end-points or goals. This is a process that can be studied within the framework of temporality in all its expressions, including the very ordinary. When at the grocery market we might pause for a moment in the produce aisle to consider whether we should buy spinach or head lettuce. We happen to prefer spinach, but our children like head lettuce, and to buy both means that one will eventually rot in the back of the refrigerator. What should we do? Instantaneously a variety of imagined outcomes pass through our minds, a series of hypothesized "if-then" accounts in which vast amounts of information emerge from memory to flood consciousness and become organized with reference to what we project into the future as an ultimately "good" outcome. Perhaps we want to satisfy our children and provide them with a token of our concern for their wishes, in which case we will forego our desire for spinach; or, alternately we may reason that we deserve to treat ourselves for once, knowing that being overly deprived deteriorates our parenting skills, and/or that it is beneficial for children to try new foods. In the latter case, we opt for spinach. In both cases we deliberate with an emphasis upon an abstract concept, arguably a Platonic Form of what is ultimately the best for all concerned, what form of the Good may best fulfill an archetypally determined and future-directed striving toward harmonious balance in the politics of family relationships. Once established, the logical structure of whatever course we settle on as an end determines the unfolding of choices and events "in reverse", as it were, as an as-yet-unrealized future metaphorically "reaching back", *a posteriori*, into the present to organize our thoughts and actions so that they may become organized toward achieving a specific actual form. This is viewed by some, though far from all, philosophers as a veritable creation of something out of "no-thing", the unforeseeable product of an immaterial interpenetration of emotional impulse and lightning-fast anticipatory reasoning. It exemplifies Aristotle's (1983, Book III) category of *final causation*, the concept that what we ultimately intend to accomplish supervenes upon our current experience from the mind's construction of a desired future, to suggest how the diverse elements of experience may be arranged so as to lead to this purely imagined end becoming tangibly or "actually" present over time.

In following the promptings of the mind's future-orientation, we do not simply dispense with the past. In Jung, consciousness is not located "inside" the head but is non-localized, reaching out to effect measurable changes in the world including the nature of time itself. As such, there is every reason to believe that a renewed vision of one's present, as a process moving toward the open horizon of a future may-be, quite literally changes the objective nature of the past (as well as problematizing what we call "objective" reality). This may be called a "retrospective creative teleology". This weighty term simply means that the "actual" meaning of what befell us at a prior time is, to a greater extent than we realize, dependent upon the position of our conscious stance as an observer/interpreter in the *present*. Life, as a progressive revelatory process, does not simply serve up meanings to us while we sit idly by. The "is-ness" of phenomena is, within limits, up to us. We have the option, if we summon courage, of intentionally asserting ourselves toward influencing their *telos*, as Kant and Jung imply in their respective treatises on human freedom. Life's unfolding is bi-directional: it opens, not only toward an as-yet-unactualized horizon of the future, but also toward the as-yet-unactualized significance of the past, which has its own distinctive phenomenological horizon. So, the way forward is simultaneously the way back, and vice-versa. And by progressing in either direction we simultaneously become the authors of certain potentialities within its counterpart. Ultimately, this is to become reacquainted with our immersion in the ontological structure of time itself. Our being as beings-in-time embraces our proper role in defining the "is-ness" of the nature of temporality, which is to say its actual, objective structure, assuming we do not refuse our role as co-creators of reality.

Research into how new possibilities in nature, society, and human consciousness arise continues to add compelling new ways of interpreting Jung's teleology. Prominent among these venues of theorizing are, in philosophy, Emergentism (Broad, 1925) and, in empirical science, quantum mechanics (Planck, 1915; Bohr, 1934/1987). Both these fields are concerned with understanding potentiality in human thought, behavior, and the basic structure of the material world from new perspectives. It is appropriate that I touch on them here, however briefly.

Emergentism originated in England in the 1920s, and ever since has been hotly debated by philosophers and cognitive scientists. In its strong forms it holds that, as D.J. Chalmers (1990) states, a "high-level phenomenon arises from (a) low-level domain, but truths concerning that phenomenon are not deducible even in principle from truths in the low-level domain" (p. 1). In contrast, what he terms weak Emergentism simply explains more sophisticated permutations of phenomena, while unexpected, as nevertheless logically explainable by the elements already present in the conditions giving rise to an end result. While Jung does not directly involve himself in philosophical Emergentism, with which he was probably unacquainted, at different points in his theorizing about the archetypes, he implies that these become actuated in human life in a manner that some contemporary Jungians, such as George Hogenson (2004), believe are interpretable in terms of a strong Emergentism. Among the passages he uses to support his argument are Jung's (1947/1969) suggestive reflections on the forward-going nature of the process of amplifying inner, archetypal images:

> The (archetypal) images are not to be thought of as a reduction of conscious contents to their simplest denominator, as this would be a direct road to the primordial images which I said previously was unimaginable; they make their appearance only in the course of amplification.
>
> (para. 403)

Jung's inconsistent statements about the nature of archetypes do not allow for any single definition of their nature. Yet here he seems to imply that new, archetypally informed and directed realizations are not purely the outcome of fixed antecedent properties of the archetype itself, that is, to what in philosophy is called "simples", that are merely reordered across time in new arrangements. In such a theory the archetypes could not transcend their given, eternal structures, but would perpetually confine us to modes of knowledge of the world that may alter in form but never in their meaning-value for individuals and societies. This latter development requires the addition of human consciousness, such as that occurring in the amplification process, which is always and already embedded in the irreducibly unique concerns of a local *lebens-welt.* Hogenson (2004) claims that in describing the way that archetypes metamorphose into conscious personal and collective symbolic images, "…Jung is not referring simply to developmental change, but also…ontological change" (p. 51). I suggest that this "ontological change" occurs, not only in the maturational *telos* of the person or group, but conceivably in the structure of the archetype itself, as its emergent *potentia* is unleashed through engagement with locally situated human consciousness.

Hogenson's thesis finds support in recent developments in empirical physics. Specifically, the novel findings of quantum mechanics have attracted the interest of interdisciplinary scholars, some of whom find them supportive of Jung's theory of the way in which human creatureliness and the physical world arise from, and remain intimately dependent on, an immaterial substrate of non-localized atomic dynamisms such as photons, electrons, neutrons, atoms, and molecules, all capable of transcending the Newtonian laws governing causality in time and space. These dynamisms are called *quanta*, the exact meaning of which remains uncertain given that thus far we know only what energy *does* but not what it *is per se*. However indeterminate the concept of *quanta* may be, they appear to form the primordial experiential background to human consciousness of reality and shift instantaneously between their purely potential state of waves to particles, a state in which they express themselves in determinate forms in space and time. For example, when attached to an atom electrons exist in their immaterial forms as waves, forming the contentless or "empty" penumbral ground of Being. In this state they do not act upon the world, but are solely potential patterns, abstract numerical possibilities that may spring into existence as localized human thoughts and/or the palpable materiality of the world. In our example, this shift occurs when electrons become detached from nuclei, a state in which they transform into discrete particles. A revolutionary paradigm change occurred in the early to middle twentieth century when one interpretation of this finding indicated that, among other variables, it is the act of engaging in observation of these phenomena of potentiality that determines whether they exhibit wave or particle forms. A startling implication of this finding is that consciousness is not separate from the emergence of the ontological structure of reality. While this view is not universally endorsed by physicists, there are a number of researchers who take it to mean that the objective structure of the world is determined, in part, by the processes of human consciousness (Bohm, 1990; Wheeler, 1987).

This, of course, is quite similar to Jung's contention: in our attending to reality, and according to the perspectives we adopt and questions we ask of it, the cosmos comes into being in specific and novel ways (Jung, 1961/1989, p. 256). D.V. Ponte and Lothar Shafer (2013) understand this cosmic structure as panpsychic, meaning that the cosmos is "mind-like", another element implied in Jung's metaphysical contemplations. While it seems that the meaning of this contention demands that we first define the difference between "minded" and "mind-like", it is clear that some investigators of quantum theory understand Being as emerging, in part, as an expression of the *telos* of human aims and hopes. In this view, we are not only embedded within an emergent reality, but participate in setting this emergence into motion in very particular directions.

We may also note that the theory of the nature of *quanta* in wave form lends support to Jung's reflections on the archetypes as contentless supra-sensible probabilities, existing as metaphysical phenomena, which become manifest within the sensible spatio-temporal domain due to the underlying unity of the knowing human subject with its cosmological origins. Here Jung is working in much the same vein as physicist Wolfgang Pauli, whom he treated for depression and alcohol abuse in 1930. Following the treatment the two men collaborated through correspondence, discussing and refining the similarities in their views. In Pauli's conjectures on the unified field of reality Jung finds a restatement, in the language of physics, of his more philosophical treatment of this matter (1992/2001). Among these is Jung's (1955/1973) controversial theory of synchronicity, what he calls an "acausal connecting principle": that immaterial psychic phenomena may become palpably manifest as mental or physical events (such as premonitions and material manifestations of the activity of mind) outside of Newtonian laws of linear, material-efficient cause-and-effect.

Now let us turn our attention to a brief summary of the contents of the volume's six chapters, each of which explains and adds to a broader understanding of the importance and novel applications of both teleology generally and its importance to Jung.

Our Chapters

Chapter 1 is written by Jungian analyst Mark Winborn. Titled *Coming into Being: Telos in Jung and Bion*, the chapter explores the genesis and unfolding of psychological experience in Wilfred Bion's provocative interpretations of Freudian theory. Using the thought of post-Jungian theorist Michael Fordham and neo-Freudian James Grotstein to serve as conceptual bridges between Jung's and Bion's conjectures on the *telos* of experience, Dr. Winborn's work is a fitting opening chapter, as it provides readers with a "user-friendly" overview of the concept of teleology and its applications in the contemporary psychotherapeutic situation. Of particular help is his description of the uses of these concepts in session, through concrete descriptions of two case studies, toward enabling patients to locate heretofore unrealized possibilities for positive change in their lives.

Specifically, the chapter explores the similarities and differences between Carl Jung's concept of individuation and Wilfred Bion's teleological concept of "coming into being". A particular focus is how Bion's model elucidates the emergence of fundamental levels of psychological engagement with inner life and the world via his concepts of Beta elements, Alpha Function, and Alpha elements, which describe the manner in which what may become conscious interpretations of experience are first generated unconsciously and over time emerge into awareness as telic markers of as-yet-unknown dimensions of the self. Fordham's deintegrate-integrate model of individuation is also introduced as a conceptual bridge linking the teleological emphases associated with Jung and Bion. Later, the work of Grotstein, who was interested in parallels in the theories of both Jung and Bion, is outlined. His concepts of a "transcendent position" and of dreams as functioning to forward the development of the self, acting to "dream into being" dormant facets of mind, represent unusual additions to our grasp of the forward-going nature of our being-in-the-world. Finally, Dr. Winborn's chapter serves as a scholarly counterpoint and alternative to the misperception of some Freudians and neo-Freudians that Jung is not, as I was told by one such critic, "Not a *proper* psychoanalyst". Such assertions are not only indefensible intellectually, I suggest, but also ring increasingly hollow in an era in which theoretical innovators as Jacques Lacan enjoy tremendous popularity among those in our field, despite their sometimes radical reinterpretations of received psychoanalytic wisdom, given that these innovators' works deepen our grasp of the multiple implications of the work of Freud and those in his lineage. By demonstrating the concordance between Jung's teleological orientation and the work of Bion and others, Dr. Winborn provides a venue within which to transcend the doctrinaire and occasionally ugly assertions of any given school of thought to assert "ownership", as it were, of the psychoanalytic tradition. Fealty to the letter of tradition is important, about this there can be no doubt, as it is an "origin story" orienting us to what it is we are doing and why, especially at those points in time immediately after the original founders of ground-breaking movements have passed on. It prevents chaos and sloppy thinking. However, beyond a certain point, such conservatism stifles the forward movement of the creative process and even stands in defiance of the teleology of history itself, which does not stand still but continually expresses itself anew.

The next chapter, my own contribution to the text, is titled *On Truth, Reasonable Certainty, and God: Conviction as Revelatory Process in Peirce and Jung*. It follows somewhat the same line of thought as Dr. Winborn's, albeit from a philosophical perspective. I believe it is of use to those especially concerned with philosophical approaches to Jung. It was written, in part, as a response to the accusation, one I hear not infrequently, that those interested in Jung are in some way anti-intellectual and/or refuse the dictates of reason, specifically that they are a group of New Age pseudo-sophisticates on a fool's errand. I seek to dispel this notion. My focus in this work is on the origins, unfolding in consciousness, and manner of logically evaluating the accuracy of the interpretations of experience we rely upon to guide us through life. I apply this in various ways toward a defense of Jung's essential faith that, over time and on balance, we can and should trust the datum of our lived experience to enable us to fruitfully navigate life, that doing so is not necessarily simple-minded but entirely philosophically defensible and that Jungian theory and treatment is demonstrably able to create conditions in which suffering individuals learn to live freer of neurotic doubt about the direction of their lives.

The chapter describes and discusses the similarities in epistemological and ontological premises of the important first American pragmatist Charles Sanders Peirce, who worked from the late nineteenth into the early twentieth centuries, and Jung toward a fuller understanding of the nature of conviction. In both, conviction, the subjective sense of surety or reasonable certainty about one's interpretation of experience, is analyzed both as a general feature of our navigation of reality, and more specifically as it is situated within religious sensibilities. In their own language, Peirce and Jung argue that productive, fruitful thinking originates in a stance of receptive attention to the natural unfolding of experience, that is, its *telos*, and a willingness to suspend *a priori* judgments about its meaning(s) and truth-claims. Rather, in different ways both men propose that such judgments are most credible when formed a posteriori or "after the fact", based upon our experience what they actually do to enrich our lives. Further, in both Peirce and Jung, the state of being convinced, that is, of "having conviction", has a religious or non-specific "spiritual" dimension. These two seminal thinkers are unique among modern intellectuals in that their epistemologies are grounded in what I call a revelatory metaphysics of cognition, namely, that the processes and final ends of thinking itself are an emanation and signifier of a metaphysical Absolute. Ultimately, both theorists posit that perceptive thinking about thinking can lead us to a clearer understanding of the nature of Being, and the generative, sustaining actions of an intelligent Absolute that is both its source and teleological goal. This figures centrally in their shared optimism: while neither had an easy life nor could be considered traditionally religious, both Peirce and, somewhat more ambivalently, Jung assert that when all is said and done we may have faith that the evolutionary track and final aims of the source of Being are "on our side", so to speak, however circuitous and confusing its course may seem to be at times.

Among other things, I ultimately intend that my contribution suggest a sound (i.e. coherent, intellectually informed, and reasonable) alternative to modern and post-modern cynicism about our capacity to trust the phenomenology of experience, what Paul Ricoeur (1965/2014) calls the "hermeneutics of suspicion". I see this as important because such a narrative can and often does drive psychoanalytic theorizing into a position of implicitly endorsing a position toward being-in-the-world in which the experiencing subject finds him or herself as unable to embrace, much less commit themselves to life in a cosmos in relation to which they feel no meaningful or compelling experiential grounding. Rather, under the influence of an uninterrogated hermeneutics of suspicion, the goal of treatment easily and undetectably becomes to enable the individual to accept their experience of themselves as untethered and adrift in a vast and even malevolent existential absurdity, this being taken as a sign of mature adulthood, good "reality testing", and so forth; as a friend of mine under the influence of several drinks once put it dourly, "a crap shoot". But, with Peirce and Jung, I do not think God gambles with our frailty.

In Chapter 3 by Tosia H. Zraikat, *Jung's Call to Eros: A Personal Journey*, we turn away from the abstractions of the philosophic to investigate the telic movement of Eros as a central element in the *telos* of individuation. Through an admixture of psychological, cultural, and deeply personal venues, the author offers innovative reflections on the energy of Eros, god of connection. Her work addresses the *mythos* of this archetypal deity as operating in the upswell of passion toward the goal propelling us, unbidden, into the realm of relationships, with their generative and transformative potential.

An inner dialogue with deeply felt emotion is intrinsic to Jung's psychology and psychotherapeutic approach and its *telos* of creating and expanding consciousness in the individual. The author discusses how some of her psychotherapeutic work on images and fantasies in therapy with an analyst demonstrated to her the necessary contribution of Eros energy to the unconscious aims and ends of all psychic activity, toward positive change and healing. The chapter ends with some reflections on rehabilitating Eros in the individual and the wider society. Citing numerous significant historical figures, such as Hesiod and Dante, in concert with early and modern Christian theologies, Ms. Zraikat illuminates the action of desire in forwarding the natural teleological movement of the experiencing subject. Her chapter embodies what I think is an essential and nuanced contemplation upon Jung's original forays into the critical importance of the need for personal engagement in the world of the passions, and their function in the progressive unfolding of experience, in any successful psychotherapy.

Chapter 4, *The Ravenous Hydra and the Great Tree of Peace: The Teleology of Indigenous and European Civilizations* by Shane Eynon, adds a needed indigenous perspective to the post-Jungian literature. Dr. Eynon, a Native American psychologist, describes the general perspective on human nature as understood by the indigenous people of the northeastern United States, which includes its vision of community and our responsibility to wisely discern and provide for the well-being of future generations. This is an elevation of communal choice, attained dialogically toward the goal of ongoing peaceful coexistence and unity with the telic and recurring rhythms of Nature, to the forefront of social order. He contrasts this with the Euro-North American hyper-individual *ethos*, and its investment in conquest and domination.

The chapter argues that the various branches of European civilization are driving us collectively toward a social and ecological cataclysm. By examining the underlying collective psychological forces generated within the mythology and cosmologies of European civilization, we can forecast where we are going collectively and identify remedies to these ominous current problems. C.G. Jung provides a compelling and prescient analysis of European civilization based on its foreclosure of fruitful possibilities, an analysis yielding a deeply troubling teleology of apocalypse.

Dr. Eynon outlines the manner in which the Haudenosaunee (commonly referred to as the Iroquois), have developed an entirely different model of civilization that clashes profoundly with European civilization since the start of their process of colonization and the quest for world domination. The Haudenosaunee model of civilization is called the Gayanashagowa (known as the Great Law of Peace), which Europeans envisioned as a democratic confederacy. This civilization places the symbol of the Great Tree of Peace as the central focus of a worldview and cosmology based on collective social harmony with the natural world. The Gayanashagowa's purpose is to balance current human life with the choices made to improve the next seven generations yet to be born.

Central to this chapter is the comparison of aforementioned worldview and its consequent teleological outcomes with that of European colonists from an archetypal stance, specifically identifying the "Ravenous Hydra" as a collective symbol for European civilization's ambitions and identifying its stark difference from the symbol of the "Great Tree of Peace" prominent in Native American culture. This comparison highlights the ultimate *telos* for each worldview and cosmology. The future of Ravenous Hydra, it is argued, will be an apocalypse for both the human world and the Earth, a grim and life-depleting path which a transition toward an alternative vision of humanity can avoid. I suggest that evidence for this is plainly evident in the rapid unfolding of global warming, and the seeming inability of self-described "modern", industrial, and post-industrial nations to be properly sensitive to the roots of this catastrophe in their intractable hostility to Nature.

Our fifth chapter, by Jody Echegaray, titled *Archetype of the Machine*, explores the teleological significance of the rise of computerized or "machinic" technology in Western and, increasingly, world culture through a Jungian lens. The Machine in Jung's collected works is generally referred to as that which stands in opposition to the biological but nonetheless exerts psychic and physical effects. Contemporary science, philosophy, critical studies, popular culture, and the infrastructural basis of our economic and social interactions are saturated by the presence of the Machine – from the fundamental ontological unit to conceptual cornerstones to the underlying engine of change. As such, the traditional bifurcation between the biological and technological has continued to blur, occasioning more points of contact and interpenetration than older oppositional dualities suggest.

Our current cultural, political, economic, and telic horizons seem increasingly threaded with the psychic presence of the Machine, and analytical psychology must somehow engage with the problematics and potential of this unfolding dialogue and dialectic. From the perspective of analytical psychology, one potential avenue offered by this presence is to view it as archetypal. By doing so, we reaffirm the existence and action of psyche manifesting in and through technology, our fascination in it, and our drive toward it. This perspective sees the Archetype of the Machine as representing a telic, evolutive form of earlier archetypes, reflecting many domains of meaning and action inhering in it – one that is neither a merely unipolar counterpoint to the biological nor historically recent.

Dr. Echegaray's chapter offers the reader a timely and non-partisan perspective on the increasing use of AI (Artificial Intelligence) in our daily lives, a development which warrants sustained critical analysis given that it represents an irreversible chapter in the evolution of machinic extensions of human aims. Most refreshingly, his writing avoids two common extremes in our public discourse about this development: hysterical pronouncements of humanity being enslaved or simply rendered irrelevant by computers, and capitalist naïve enthusiasm about the prospects of new technologies to dramatically improve our lives. Rather, his work offers a tempered historical and philosophical stance from which to work out our own conclusions about the potential good and ill of the teleological arc of technological innovation.

Last though not least is Chapter 6 by Jungian analyst Giorgio Tricarico. Entitled *The Dance of Limit and Possibility*, this work is an important qualifier to the text's broadly optimistic stance toward what is possible in the domain of psychological development. Tricarico's contribution embodies a view that is particularly important as an antidote to our modern and postmodern era's often unmodulated belief in the unlimited nature of human striving and the ends it envisions, a historically recent development with roots in the collective and personal grandiosity of Western hyper-individualism. I believe it is also important as an answer to the unwarranted rosiness accompanying the present interest of the general public in Jung's ideas, especially as these are contained in the more superficial and unschooled uses of these by devotees of modern neo-liberal spiritualities composed of hastily and impressionistically assembled mélanges of the ancient religious practices of diverse cultures, among others.

After briefly summarizing some of the main contents of his 2009 book *The Labyrinth of Possibility: A Therapeutic Factor in Analytical Practice*, the chapter focuses on the concept of limit and on its widespread repression in Western culture. Touching on the topics of technology, economics, exploitation of resources, medicine, positive psychology, death, old age, illness, and advertising, it becomes quite evident how the concept of limit is usually repressed, in Freudian terms, and how therefore the idea of possibility itself is generally framed in an omnipotent way, as in the popular and very American belief that "anything is possible", as the saying goes. The aim of the chapter is to reflect upon a more authentic meaning of possibility, which is correctly understood as the transitional space between the certain and the impossible, the potential area where the Jungian concept of individuation resides as well.

In sum, I believe that the foregoing is an important and unusual addition to the post-Jungian literature, addressing the neglected issue of the *telos* of human desire and striving. While much more needs to be said about this dimension of Jung's thought, we hope that our contribution represents a tentative inroad into the exploration of the "for-the-sake-of" of human life.

References

Adler, A. (1921/2013). *The neurotic constitution*. Routledge.

Aristotle. (1983). *Physics: Books III and IV* (Clarendon Aristotle Series and Introduction and Notes) (E. Hussey, Trans.). Oxford University Press.

Bohm, D. (1990). A new theory of the relationship of mind and matter. *Philosophical Psychology, 3* (2–3), 271–286.

Bohr, N. (1934/1987). *Atomic theory and the description of nature. Reprinted as the philosophical writings of Niels Bohr* (Vol. I). Ox Bow Press.

Broad, C.D. (1925). *The mind and its place in nature*. Kegan Paul.

Chalmers, D. (1990). *Strong and weak emergence*. https://consc.net/papers/emergence.pdf.

Colacicchi, G. (2021). *Psychology as ethics: reading jung with kant, nietzsche and aristotle*. Routledge.

Hogenson, G. (2004). Archetypes: Emergence and the psyche's deep structure. In J. Cambray & L. Carter (Eds.), *Analytical psychology: Contemporary perspectives in Jungian psychology* (pp. 32–55). Routledge.

Jung, C.G. (1896–1899/1984). *The zofinga lectures*. Princeton University Press.

Jung, C.G. (1916/1961). *Freud and psychoanalysis*. Collected Works of C.G. Jung, Hereafter referred to as CW (R. F. C. Hull, Trans.) *(Vol. 4)*. Princeton University Press.

Jung, C.G. (1916/1967). *The seven sermons to the dead.* Stuart & Watkins.

Jung, C.G. (1921/1969). *Psychological types. CW (Vol. 1)*. Princeton University Press.

Jung, C.G. (1971). *Psychological types. CW (Vol. 6)*. Princeton University Press.

Jung, C.G. (1932/1970). *Psychology and religion: west and east. CW (Vol. 11)*.

Jung, C.G. (1934/1970). *Psychological commentary on the Tibetan book of the dead. CW (Vol. 11)*. Princeton University Press.

Jung, C.G. (1934/1970). *On the nature of the psyche. CW (Vol. 8)*. Princeton University Press.

Jung, C.G. (1943/1966). *Psychiatric studies. CW (Vol. 1)*. Princeton University Press.

Jung, C.G. (1947/1969). *On the nature of the psyche. CW (Vol 8, pp. 159–234)*. Princeton University Press.

Jung, C.G. (1957/1977). *Symbols of transformation. CW (Vol. 5)*. Princeton University Press.

Jung, C.G. (1958a/1969). *The archetypes of the collective unconscious. CW (Vol. 9)*. Princeton University Press.

Jung, C.G. (1958b/1969). *The transcendent function. CW (Vol. 18)*. Princeton University Press.

Jung, C.G. (1958). *The undiscovered self*. Little, Brown.

Jung, C.G. (1958/1970). *The archetypes and the collective unconscious. CW (Vol. 9)*. Princeton University Press.

Jung, C.G.. (1960/2002). *The transcendent function. CW (Vol. 8.)* Routledge.

Jung, C.G. (1961/1989). *Memories, dreams, reflections (A. Jaffe, Ed. and R. Winston, Trans.)*. Vintage Books.

Jung, C.G., & Pauli, W. (1992/2001). *Atom and archetype: The Pauli/Jung Letters, 1932–1958 - Updated edition*. Princeton University Press.

Kant, I. (1781/2000). *Critique of pure reason* (P. Guyer & A. Wood, Trans. and Eds.). Cambridge University Press.

Maeder, A. (1910). Psychologische untersuchungen an dementia praecox-kranken. *Jahrbuch für Psychoanalytische und Psychopathologische Forschungen, 2*(1), 185–245.

Papadopolous, R. (2006). Jung's epistemology and methodology. In R. Papadopolous (Ed.), *The handbook of Jungian psychology: Theory, practice and applications* (pp. 7–53). Routledge.

Planck, M. (1915). *Eight lectures on theoretical physics* (A. P. Wills, Trans.). Dover Publications.

Plato. (1888/1988). *The Timaeus of Plato* (R. D. Archer-Hind, Ed. and Trans.). Ayers Company Publishers.

Plato. (1892/2017). *Phaedo* (B. Jowett, Trans.). Oxford University Press.

Ponte, D., & Schaffer, L. (2013). Carl gustav jung, quantum physics, and the spiritual mind: A mystical vision of the twenty-first century. *Behavioral Sciences, 3*(4), 601–618.

Ribi, A. (2013). *The search for roots: C. G. Jung and the tradition of gnosis*. Gnosis Archive Books.

Ricoeur, P. (1965/2014). *De l'interprtation. Essai sur Freud*. Media Diffusion.

Rychlak, J. (1991). Jung as dialectician and teleologist. In R. Papadopolous & G. Saymaan (Eds.), *Jung in modern perspective* (pp. 34–53). Wildwood House.

Wheeler, J. (1987). *Cosmology, physics and philosophy* (2nd ed.). Springer Verlag.

Chapter 1

Coming into Being
Telos in Jung and Bion

Mark Winborn

Introduction

This chapter takes its primary title, *Coming into Being*, from a phrase utilized often in the work of Thomas Ogden – coming into being (e.g., Ogden, 2004, 2022). It is likely this phrase was initially introduced into the psychoanalytic lexicon by Sabina Spielrein in her paper, *Destruction as the Cause of Coming into Being*. Speilrein (1912/1994, p. 157) does not rigorously define her use of the phrase but seems to associate it with a felt sense of aliveness, e.g., "The joyful feeling of coming into being that is present within the reproductive drive". 'Coming into being' captures the teleological impulse that is strongly present in the psychoanalytic models of C.G. Jung and Wilfred Bion.

This chapter focuses on teleological themes in both men's work, with a specific focus on the similarities and differences between Jung's concept of individuation and Bion's concept of 'becoming'. More specifically, this chapter examines how Bion's model elucidates the emergence of fundamental levels of psychological experience – via his concepts of beta elements, alpha function, and alpha elements, and reverie. Additionally, Michael Fordham's deintegrate-integrate model of individuation and James Grotstein's concept of the transcendent position will be examined as conceptual bridges linking the teleological themes found in Jung and Bion. Finally, I discuss the implications of Bion's model for the practice of Jungian analysis, proposing that Bion's model provides a complementary conceptual lens that articulates a level of transformation that is only implicit in Jung's model of individuation.

Teleology

Teleology is the explanation of phenomena by the purpose they serve rather than through the identification of the causes of the phenomena. In

DOI: 10.4324/9781003412823-2

other words, a teleological perspective asks what purpose a psychic phenomenon serves and where is it moving to. According to the Britannica editors (2023), teleology originates from "Greek *telos*, 'end', and *logos*, 'reason', i.e., explanation by reference to some purpose, end, goal, or function. Traditionally, it was also described as final causality, in contrast with explanation solely in terms of efficient causes". According to Papadopoulos (2006, pp. 29–30):

> Teleology refers to the approach that considers phenomena in terms of their *telos; telos,* being the goal, end, purpose and fulfillment … This means that in approaching psychological phenomena, one can either trace them back to their 'origin' into one's own history (reductive method) or endeavor to relate to the purpose and meaning they have in terms of the person's goals and future orientation (constructive method).

In speaking about psychoanalysis, Peltz (Peltz, 2015, p. 654) asserts, "There is no teleology in this method other than a faith that the primacy of emotional encounter will lead us to the essence of what's happening in the spiraling process of discovery". However, I propose that an 'emotional encounter leading us to the essence of what's happening in the spiraling process of discovery' is a teleological statement. Like Janus, the two-faced Roman god who is always facing both the past and the future, the teleological perspective in psychoanalysis adds a forward-looking vision, i.e., where psyche is moving, complementing a backward-looking vision, i.e., where the individual comes from. A teleological orientation is central to the Jungian and Bionian perspectives.

Teleology in Jung

Papadopoulos (2006, p. 29) indicates that evidence of Jung's teleological approach can be observed as early as his Zofingia lectures. According to Samuels et al. (1987, p. 148) a teleological orientation, "characterises Jung's observation about the unconscious, neurosis, and most especially individuation". Alvarez (1992, p. 175) indicates, "The prospective, forward-looking and aspiring element in human nature has always been important in Jungian analytic theory". Jung refers frequently to the teleological thrust he observes in the psyche, e.g.:

- Now, since the psychic process, like any other life-process, is not just a causal sequence, but is also a process with a teleological orientation (Jung, 1953/1966, para. 210).
- Life is teleology par excellence; it is the intrinsic striving toward a goal, and the living organism is a system of directed aims which seek to fulfill themselves. The end of every process is its goal (Jung, 1960/1969, para. 798).
- Neurosis is teleologically oriented (Jung, 1953/1966, para. 54).

Sharp (1991), Jacobi (1973), and Samuels et al. (1987) all highlight Jung's somewhat interchangeable use of the terms purposive, synthetic, finality, and constructive with teleology and teleological, e.g., "By finality I mean merely the immanent psychological striving for goal. Instead of 'striving for a goal' one could also say 'sense of purpose'" (Jung, 1916/1948, para. 456). Jung's overlapping use of terminology is also present in this passage, "We conceive the product of the unconscious … as an expression oriented to a goal or purpose", and that, "the aim of the constructive method … is to elicit from the unconscious product a meaning that relates to the subject's future attitude" (Jung, 1921, para. 701–702). Papadopoulos (2006, p. 30), indicates that Jung's use of teleology suggests "an impossibility of complete knowledge in a definitive way, as knowledge is related to a future purpose and goal. This means that, in effect, Jung's epistemological teleology locates knowledge in the very process of generating itself". As will be discussed later, Papadopoulos' description of Jung's use of teleology is quite close to the teleological vision present in Bion's model.

Transcendent Function

The teleological thrust in Jung is strongly represented in his concept of the transcendent function (Jung, 1916) which Jung proposes as the internal mechanism by which opposites of psychological experience are transformed via a higher synthesis into a new third quality of experience. More specifically, it is a psychic function that is activated when a tension between psychological opposites is constellated, especially the tension between consciousness and the unconscious. Jung's concept of the transcendent function is intimately connected with his concepts of psychic energy, tension of opposites, symbols, and individuation. Some of these connections are outlined in the following passage:

The shuttling to and fro of arguments and affects represents the transcendent function of opposites. The confrontation of the two positions
generates a tension charged with energy and creates a living third thing
... a movement out of the suspension between opposites, a living birth
that leads to a new level of being, a new situation. The transcendent function manifests itself as a quality of conjoined opposites.

(Jung, 1916, para. 189)

Thus, in Jung's theory, when a tension of opposites is established (i.e.,
opposing psychological positions, particularly between unconscious
and conscious), this results in the activation of the transcendent function, which in turn supports the union of opposites, i.e., the potential
movement toward a new psychological state – the transcendent third.
The transcendent third has been described as paralleling Hegel's dialectic process in which a synthesis emerges from the tension between
a thesis and anti-thesis (Solomon, 1994). The activity of the transcendent function is expressed via the symbol which facilitates the transition
from one psychological attitude or condition to another. Miller (2004,
p. 60) indicates that the transcendent function, "firmly established the
teleological, purposive view of the unconscious". Similarly, Corbett
(1992, p. 396) indicates that "The transcendent function enables such
movement toward wholeness to occur ... Its function is to express the
telos-goal of the personality".

Jung emphasizes that his use of the term 'transcendent function' does not
have a metaphysical connotation, "by 'transcendent' I do not wish to designate any metaphysical quality, but merely the fact that by this function a
transition is made possible from one attitude to another" (1921, para. 828).
The inter-relationship between the transcendent function and individuation
is emphasized by Miller (2004) and von Franz (1971). According to Miller
(2004, p. xi),

The transcendent function is the core of Carl Jung's theory of psychological growth and the heart of what he called 'individuation', the process by which one is guided in a teleological way toward the person he
or she is meant to be.

Or, as von Franz puts it (1971, p. 84), "The principium individuationis is
naturally this transcendent function".

Individuation

The teleological element in Jung's model is most fully developed in his concept of individuation which Jung saw as the ultimate goal of the analytic process. Individuation conveys "the idea that psyche aims each of us in a particular, teleological direction" (Miller, 2004, p. 60). Individuation refers to an ongoing, progressive process of coming into the fullness of one's own being. Jung defines individuation as, "becoming an 'in-dividual,' and, in so far as 'individuality' embraces our innermost, last, and incomparable uniqueness, it also implies becoming one's own self. We could therefore translate individuation as 'coming to selfhood' or 'self-realization'" (1953/1966, para. 266). He also conceptualizes individuation as the process by which the Self is synthesized with the rest of the personality, "The goal of the individuation process is the synthesis of the self" (1959/1969, para. 278).[1]

Jung sees individuation as a process rooted in our instinctual repertoire, "The dynamic of this process is instinct, which ensures that everything which belongs to an individual's life shall enter into it" (1952, para. 745). While Jung saw individuation as a naturally occurring process, whether experienced unconsciously or consciously, he conceived of it as a process of maturation that was deepened and accelerated by the analytic process (Jung, 1959/1969, para. 270). Jung also saw individuation as a process which is activated during the second half of life, after leaving the parental home and establishing one's family, occupational identity, and achieving some degree of financial stability, i.e., tasks typically undertaken during the first half of life which Jung referred to collectively as the hero's journey and associated with the establishment of a firm ego foundation.

Jung describes a conscious engagement with the individuation process as occurring through the confrontation between the individual's conscious and unconscious positions. He saw the transformation associated with individuation as depending upon symbols generated through this confrontation,

> But if the individuation process is made conscious, consciousness must confront the unconscious and a balance between the opposites must be found. As this is not possible through logic, one is dependent on symbols which make the irrational union of opposites possible.
>
> (Jung, 1958/1969, para. 755)

Jung defines a symbol as follows:

> By a symbol I do not mean an allegory or a sign, but an image that describes in the best possible way the dimly discerned nature of the spirit. A symbol does not define or explain; it points beyond itself to a meaning that is darkly divined yet still beyond our grasp and cannot be adequately expressed in the familiar words of our language.
>
> (1960/1969, para. 644)

Jung also conceives the individuation process as closely connected with the realization of the Self,

> In the last analysis every life is the realization of a whole, that is, of a self, for which reason this realization can also be called 'individuation'. All life is bound to individual carriers who realize it, and it is simply inconceivable without them. But every carrier is charged with an individual destiny and destination, and the realization of these alone makes sense of life.
>
> (1953/1968, para. 330)

Upon entering the second half of life, Jung observed there was often a diminishment or loss of meaning in these extraverted life accomplishments which also frequently resulted is some form of malaise, depression, or anxiety. Jung referred to the onset of these symptoms as the "neuroses of the second half of life" (Jung, 1977, p. 108) but he also referred to this life phase through various archetypal themes, e.g., 'the dark night of the soul', 'the night sea journey', or the 'Nekyia' (an ancient Greek cult-practice in which the dead are consulted about the future). Jung saw this phase as a necessary introversion of libido necessary for the individuation process, e.g., "The Nekyia is no aimless or destructive fall into the abyss, but a meaningful *katabasis* [descent into the lower world] ... its object the restoration of the whole man" (1934, para. 213). Jung saw the dysphoria, diminishment of meaning, and loss of psychic energy associated with the focal pursuits of the first half of life as providing the stimulus for a turning inward which he associated with the individuation process during the second half of life.

Teleology in Bion

A note of introduction to Bion's conceptual language; he is intentionally vague in providing labels for his concepts as well as what we should be looking for in these concepts. Bion did this to create concepts that would remain grounded in experience rather than having a fixed meaning.

Becoming

Wilfred Bion, like Jung, articulates a prospective aspect of psyche which takes the form of 'becoming', most specifically the effort of the mind to 'come into being'. Speaking in language that could easily be mistaken for Jung's description of individuation, Sandler (2005, pp. 75–76) indicates that

> Becoming ... may be seen as steps toward becoming who one is ... Becoming may be seen as a continuous process during a life cycle. It is becoming who one is in reality; a marriage of an internal couple. This couple is made up of the person and its true self.

Although Bion intentionally left many of his concepts unsaturated and often wrote cryptically, Symington (2001, p. 195) captures the essence of Bion's references to 'becoming':

> What generates the 'individual psychological birth' is a creative act. This is what brings the person into being. It implies that if this does not occur, then a person does not come into being. Wilfred Bion's writings are sprinkled with references to the difference between being a person and being just like a person ... it is a creative act that brings the person into being. What existed before was a number of bits or fragments, and the creative act welds them together into a person ... Bion's clinical technique aimed to assist in bringing this about.

For Ogden (2004, p. 864), 'becoming' is intimately tied to the analytic process:

> Psychoanalysis centrally involves the analyst's getting to know the patient – a deceptively simple idea – and the patient's coming to feel known by the analyst, as well as the patient's feeling that he is getting to know himself and the analyst ... In this experience, the patient is in

the process of more fully coming into being and the analyst is getting to know the person who the patient is becoming.

In the following passage, Parsons (2023, p. 414) expands on Ogden's position:

[Ogden] is thinking about what it means to grow up. Psychic development is something analysts know about: developmental stages, maturation of object relationships and so on. But Ogden is not thinking of this either. He is thinking about 'the problem of growing up, of coming more fully into being'. Ogden phrases 'the problem' of it like this: The need to grow up constitutes an intense, unrelenting force within us that leads us to hurl ourselves against the walls of internal and external constraints in our effort to achieve increasing depth and breadth of who we are and who we might become.

Clearly, there are strong parallels between Jung's concept of individuation and Bion's concept of 'becoming', with both concepts possessing strong teleological implications.

"O"

"O" is perhaps Bion's most ambiguous concept and Bion intended for it to be ambiguous. Bion thought of "O" as an experience, somewhat similar to the way Jung uses the term 'numinous' to refer to experiences of the transcendence, the divine, and the Self. Bion (1965, 1970) defines "O" as absolute truth, ultimate reality, the experience of the numinous, the fundamentally unknowable. Tennes (2007) highlights Bion's concept of "O" as the psychoanalytic concept which best expresses the ontological otherness that serves as an objective ground of being, informing our individual subjectivity.

For Bion, coming into contact with "O" is an essential aspect of 'becoming' and therefore an important element of the teleological thrust in Bion's model of the psyche, much like Jung conceptualizes individuation as being a process of becoming a unique individual as well as establishing greater engagement with Self, e.g., "A key element in Jung's work ... stems from the notion that the Self (comparable to O, ultimate reality) has a purposive, prospective, creative aspect" (Beyda, 2012, p. 77). Bion (1965, pp. 158–159) describes the relationship between 'becoming' and "O" as follows,

Of particular concern to the analyst in his function of aiding maturation of the personalities of his patients … transformation in "O", or… from K [Knowledge] to "O" – that involves 'becoming' – is felt as inseparable from becoming God, ultimate reality, the First Cause.

Sandler (2005, p. 52) offers a more succinct statement of the process, "To analyse equals the "pursuit of truth-O", of becoming, of turning transformations in K into transformations in O".

Thinking and Dreaming

Both Jung and Bion articulate models of transformation in their conceptual frameworks. For Bion, this takes place largely in his theory of thinking (Bion, 1993, pp. 110–119). Bion frequently refers to 'thinking' in his writing (e.g., 1962b, 1992, 1993), but his idea of thinking is not synonymous with cognition or intellectual acts. He uses the word 'thinking' as a shorthand term for the capacity for being through reflective embodied experiencing of emotion. Hence, emotional experience is the foundation from which the capacity for increasingly complex forms of reflection emerges. In Bion's model, there is no dichotomy or opposition between emotional experience and thinking in the way Jung refers to feeling and thinking as functions operating in opposition (Jung, 1921).

Dreaming in Bion's model is also directly tied to his concept of 'becoming'. Dreaming, in Bion's model, not only refers to the nocturnal act of dreaming but also refers to unconscious psychological work that someone does with their emotional experiences. It is through this work that we attempt to 'dream ourselves into being', even while awake. We have no direct experience of the waking dream; we can only recognize it through the behavioral and narrative derivatives that filter into our conscious thoughts and actions. In Bion's model of dreaming, the emphasis shifts away from the meaning and symbolic content of dreams and refocuses our attention to the process of dreaming as an experience (or non-experience) of being. Note the teleological parallel between Jung's model of individuation and Bion's idea of 'dreaming ourselves into existence'. Bion's model of dreaming builds a bridge which allows a Jungian perspective on dreams to coexist with a psychoanalytic perspective on dreaming (Winborn, 2017a).

In Bion's model, the work of analysis still involves the work of understanding symbolic content, which reveals unconscious meanings, but analysis also becomes a process of metabolizing unsymbolized aspects of experience which have never been conscious and never been repressed because they have never risen to the level of a thought (referred to elsewhere as non-representable or unrepresented states – e.g., Levine et al., 2013; Winborn, 2017b). Only by working at this level can those experiences become available for reflection and symbol production. This element of Bion's model articulates a level of experience which is only alluded to in passing in Jung's model. In Bion's model, the focus shifts to the qualities of a patient's patterns of speech – alive or impoverished, the way patients inhabit their bodies, the specificity of their feeling states, or the level of differentiation of experience. Shifts in these qualities point to an increased capacity to digest or metabolize experience and ultimately to greater coherence of Self.

Bion relies on four concepts to outline the process of the transformation from unrepresented, unsymbolized experience into psychological experience available for symbolic productions: beta elements, alpha function, alpha elements, and reverie (Bion, 1963). Beta elements are raw bits of unmetabolized, undigested proto-experience which are precursory to sensory, psychic, affective, or somatic experience. These bits do not have meaning and are not sufficiently formed or coalesced to be reflected upon but will often be utilized in projective identifications, enactments, and overt actions. Because beta elements operate outside awareness and have not yet been represented, they are not available for thought, reflection, or learning and are not subject to repression or suppression. The existence of an over-abundance of beta elements is most frequently associated with patients referred to as pre-symbolic, often associated with situations where there were early developmental traumas and environmental failures. In our current age, such psychological conditions are present in a large portion of patients encountered in analytic practice.

Alpha elements are experiences which have become sufficiently coalesced to be reflected upon. They are produced from the impressions of experience which have been made storable and available for dream thoughts and for unconscious waking thinking. Alpha elements do not yet have meaning but are capable of being worked with as psychological events by an individual, analogous to the way in which words can be grouped together to form sentences and paragraphs which have narrative meaning. Alpha elements become building blocks of experience which have the potential to become connected together to form dream thoughts. For Bion, dream thoughts are the components of dreaming conceptualized as occurring both during sleeping and waking states unless the capacity to dream has been disrupted. Or, as Ellman (Ellman, 2010, p. 524) puts it,

> The accumulation of alpha elements creates the apparatus for thinking thoughts – in other words, thoughts exist prior to a thinker who thinks the thoughts and the ability to think thoughts actually 'creates' the thinker," thus the creation of alpha elements by the alpha function is directly linked to 'becoming.'

The alpha function refers to the capacity of the analyst to contain elements of their psyche and the patient's psyche while engaging in reverie about the patient's beta elements experiences in order to facilitate their transformation into alpha elements. For the patient to learn from experience, the alpha function of the analyst must operate with an awareness of the proto-emotional experience of the patient until the patient develops sufficient alpha function to participate in the process as a mutually constellated alpha function. Interpretations generated from the analyst's alpha function are not intended to give the patient understanding or meaning per se, but rather to help the patient recognize these experiences, develop a language for describing and remembering them, and to facilitate the organization of a previously unorganized experience.

The alpha function is similar to the transcendent function except, in Jung's model, the transcendent function operates to generate symbolic material and functions intrapsychically, while in Bion's model, the alpha function operates intersubjectively and on the level of the pre-representational. We can think of the alpha function as operating on a more fundamental level of transformation than the transcendent function – the level of very small, almost imperceptible shifts which transform unintegrated elements of experience into usable bits of experience. These transformed bits become the building blocks of larger shifts involved with the symbolization process of the transcendent function and the capacity to individuate. It is likely that the alpha function and the transcendent function of the analyst work in conjunction but are engaged with transforming different levels of experience. Civitarese and Ferro (2013, p. 200) and Grotstein (2007, p. 271), conceptualizing along similar lines, propose an 'alpha-megafunction' operating on a similar level of experience as Jung's transcendent function. Bion's model and the concept of non-representational states expand the Jungian perspective on the general categories of experience which might be encountered in an analytic session, adding non-represented, non-repressed unconscious elements to more familiar categories of experience, symbolized, non-symbolized/concrete, and repressed unconscious.

The term 'reverie' was adopted by Bion (1962a) to refer to a state of mind that the infant requires of the mother – a state of calm receptiveness to take in the infant's own feelings and give them meaning – a state which also has application to the analytic situation. For Bion, reverie is the primary way of accessing, perceiving, experiencing, and working with the states and experiences he describes as beta elements. Reverie is opening to one's own internal stream of consciousness and unconscious promptings – opening to ideas, thoughts, feelings, sensations, memories, images, urges, and fantasies with the assumption that what arises from the analyst's background psychic and somatic activity will potentially be useful to transforming beta elements into alpha elements (Bovensiepen, 2002; Winborn, 2014). Reverie involves being receptive on many levels to the experience and communication, both explicit and implicit, of the other person's presence in the room. It also includes sensitivity to the emerging analytic third (Ogden, 1994) in the reverie field.

Case Example – Transformation of Beta Elements - The Ballerina

The following case illustrates the transformational process of converting beta elements (non-represented experience) into alpha elements (represented experience) through the alpha function of the analyst. The patient was a 61-year-old woman: a retired successful business executive who was intelligent, attractive, slender. For the entire first year of her twice-weekly analysis, she had come into the room in a studied, graceful manner reflected in how she walked, sat, and even in how she maintained a certain graceful posture with her legs neatly crossed as she lay on the couch. As I watched her and took her in over those months, I frequently had the thought, "*This is how a ballerina must appear if she entered analysis*". At one point in the analysis, the patient brought up a feeling of stiffness between the two of us. I acknowledged that I too felt a certain stiffness and reserve in our interactions. I described to her how I noticed her style of movement and how it seemed to me that she never appeared fully relaxed with her body or un-self-conscious of her posture. She agreed that she could recognize herself in my description but hadn't been consciously aware of doing it. As she reflected further, she said, *"There's always something that feels coiled in my mind, but I don't know what it is or why it's there"*. In other words, she connected my words about her posture and her subtle bodily tension with a state in her mind. However, prior to this moment, she had never reflected on the state as having any significance – it was just a given in her psychic state. This theme came up again in the next session and I made the interpretation – *"I believe your posture is a way that you came to hold yourself together, both inside and outside, and that there is a feeling you will fragment if you don't maintain tension in your body and in your mind this way"*. Since that time, without further discussion, her posture gradually relaxed, and she began to think with less rigidity. My conceptualization of this process is that her posture reflected an undigested beta element for which there had previously been no recognition, no name for the experience, no meaning for the patient, and no identified psychological function. By holding, reflecting upon, and digesting this postural manifestation for over a year, which culminated in a spoken observation and then interpretation, I provided the alpha function for the bipersonal field we shared. The patient's subsequent capacity to remember this experience, reflect further upon it, think more fluidly, and release much of the somatic tension in her posture suggests the beta element had been transformed into a usable piece of experience which Bion refers to as an alpha element. It seems clear to me that this state of mind-body tension was not attached to a particular complex because it was continuously present in all of our sessions rather than emerging during the activation of a specific complex.

The Grid

Bion organized and summarized his model of 'thinking' and 'becoming' in a template he referred to as 'The Grid' (Bion, 1989), and as such it can be considered Bion's most complete teleological position. The grid incorporates his various ideas on how thought progresses along increasingly more complex and differentiated lines as a reflection of the interactive processes of 'learning from experience' and 'becoming'. The organizing principle of the grid involves the nature of thought: the vertical axis of the grid refers to the development or evolution of thought *per se*, while the horizontal axis refers to "thinking about the thoughts by an apparatus of thinking known as the mind" (Grotstein, 1981, p. 515). The major categories of the grid can be considered an extension and elaboration of Freud's two principles of mental functioning (Freud, 1911), which Jung's (1956) theory of two kinds of thinking parallels closely. As (Ellman, 2010, p. 538) elaborates on the grid:

> The evolution of human thought proceeds along a genetic axis (i.e., the vertical axis of the grid); thoughts emerge out of the sensory impressions (beta elements) being transformed by alpha function to produce alpha elements. After this transformation, those alpha elements become suitable for experiencing, dreaming, and being thought about at a conscious level. At a fundamental level, Bion's grid attempts to explain how thoughts grow in complexity, sophistication, and abstraction. Levels of complexity are associated with the sophistication of thoughts that can be 'grown.'... The vertical (genetic) axis of Bion's grid shows development of thought. Progress should be thought of in terms of increasingly competent reality testing ... The horizontal (systematic) axis shows development in the realm of communication.

According to Ellman (2010, p. 240), Bion's model:

> involves a way of understanding the work of psychoanalysis as the facilitation of the development of the emotional and cognitive abilities necessary to support a way of being that is an ongoing creative and transformational process of 'becoming who one is'. For Bion, the letter "O" symbolizes the fundamental article of faith that there is an experience and an experiencer, and that there exists an ultimate or absolute truth which is unknowable.

Comparing Bion and Jung

Both Bion and Jung both articulate a prospective aspect of psyche. As mentioned earlier, for Jung this is reflected most fully in his concept of individuation and for Bion this took the form of 'becoming', most specifically the effort of the mind to 'come into being' (Ogden, 2004, 2022). Grotstein notes the parallel between Jung and Bion in terms of the teleological thrust of the psyche,

> I think they both [Jung and Bion] were going in the same direction, in a kind of poetic language which indicated what we see and know is limited by our senses. There is a coherence beyond. I think that's one of the principal things that unites Jung with Bion, that there is something beyond, before, and in the future.
>
> (Grotstein in Culbert-Koehn, 1997, p. 18)

Bion's teleology is without a specifically delineated goal other than the transformation of unmetabolized experience into elements of experience that can be reflected upon. Bion's approach provides a complement to the Jungian model of transformation which has more specific and higher-ordered outcomes associated with the concepts of the transcendent function and individuation. A primary focus for Bion is on recognizing and gathering up small bits of unintegrated experience rather than uncovering, finding meaning, or narrating. Other higher-order processes, such as discovery of meaning, individuation, or improved relational capacity, will become more likely as these unintegrated bits of experience become more cohered as larger units of psychologically usable experience. In this regard, Bion's model is operating on a level of experience that precedes the process of symbolic activity typically focused on in Jungian analysis and therefore expands the range of psychological experience which can be recognized and addressed in the analytic process.

The experience of transcendence is intimately tied to the teleological focus in Jung and Bion. Grotstein identifies transcendence as an area of overlap between Jung and Bion, "Another place of correspondence is his concept of … I call it transcendence, he [Bion] calls it transformations. There I think Jung and Bion are going along parallel tracks" (Grotstein in Culbert-Koehn, 1997, p. 16). Transcendence refers to levels of experience which move beyond the personal and solely subjective. Jung uses a variety of terms to address this level of experience; 'archetypal', 'collective unconscious', 'objective psyche', and 'self.' An example of such transcendence can be found in Jung's description of the Self:

> I usually describe the supraordinate personality as the 'self', thus making a sharp distinction between the ego, which, as is well known, extends only as far as the conscious mind, and the whole of the personality, which includes the unconscious as well as the conscious component. The ego is thus related to the self as part to whole. To that extent the self is supraordinate. Moreover, the self is felt empirically not as subject but as object.
>
> (1959/1969, para. 315)

Elsewhere, Jung indicates:

> But as one can never distinguish empirically between a symbol of the self and a God-image, the two ideas, however much we try to differentiate them, always appear blended together, so that the self appears synonymous with the inner Christ ... Anything that man postulates as being a greater totality than himself can become a symbol of the self.
>
> (1958/1969, para. 231–232)

Bion chooses the term 'O' to represent all that is infinite in contrast to finite, all that is unknowable in contrast to known, and all that supersedes personal experience (Bion, 1965). He refers to state of union with 'O' as 'at-one-ment' (1965, p. 163). Sandler (2005, p. 834) clarifies Bion's position, i.e., that we cannot know "O" but through an experience of a transformation resulting from contact with "O" – it contributes to the ongoing process of 'becoming', "Knowledge belongs to the conscious realm; evolving and becoming, emanations of "O" and to be at-one ... belong to the realm of the ultimately unknowable, but 'be-able' – that is, existent".

While an embrace of the unknown but experienceable does not feature as prominently in Jung's writing as in Bion's, this attitude is present in Jung, e.g. "Doctor and patient thus find themselves in a relationship founded on mutual unconsciousness" (1954/1966, para. 364). Elsewhere, Jung addresses the unknown more specifically:

> The unconscious is not simply the unknown, it is rather the unknown psychic; and this we define on the one hand as all those things in us which, if they came to consciousness, would presumably differ in no respect from the known psychic contents, with the addition ... of the psychoid system, of which nothing is known directly.
>
> (1960/1969, para. 382)

Bion felt that only by approaching the analytic session with this frame of mind can the analyst discern what is emerging in the field, and in relation to "O", rather than defaulting to a categorization of experience based on concepts, terms, and patterns previously experienced. This stands in contrast with Jung's discussions of Self, archetype, and collective unconscious where he elaborates at length on the many associations he identifies between transcendent aspects of experience and the patterns found in myths, fairytales, alchemy, and religion.

Fordham as Bridge Between Jung and Bion

The dialogue between Jung and Bion would certainly not have continued beyond Bion's attendance at Jung's Tavistock lectures in 1935 without the pioneering efforts of Michael Fordham. He was the first significant figure in analytical psychology to explore the developments that had emerged in psychoanalytic theory and practice in the decades after the split between psychoanalysis and analytical psychology in 1914 when Jung resigned as President of the International Psychoanalytical Association. Fordham was a child psychiatrist at the London Child Guidance Clinic from 1934 through the years of World War II. During that time, he was searching for better methods of working with severely disturbed children but Fordham felt the tools provided by his Jungian training were insufficient on their own. Fordham discovered the resource he was seeking when he was exposed to the work of Melanie Klein, in particular *The Psychoanalysis of Children* (1948) which he reports reading "with amazement and emotional shock" (Fordham, 1993, p. 65). Fordham also eventually became exposed to Bion's work, which he incorporates extensively in *Explorations into the Self* (1985). Summarizing that exposure, Fordham says, "It has seemed to me that Bion has presented much matter which needs to be assimilated by analytical psychologists" (1985, p. 2). Elsewhere Fordham (1998, p. 191) states, "Bion's extraordinarily rich but difficult thought has a curious familiarity, which I believe derives from a similarity with many of Jung's formations".

Primary Self and the DeIntegrate/Integrate Model of Individuation

Many Jungian analysts continue to view individuation as a process primarily occurring during the second half of life. However, beginning in 1944, Michael Fordham proposed a revision of Jung's model of individuation (Fordham, 1994). Fordham referred to this as the deintegrate-integrate process (Fordham, 1971). Fordham's perspectives on the existence of a primary self in infants and the interactive nature of the emergence and development of the self-structure is now strongly supported by contemporary developmental research, such as Stern (1985) and Beebe and Lachmann (2002).

Fordham was significantly influenced by Bion's concepts of beta elements, alpha elements, and alpha function in developing his extension of Jung's theory of individuation into infancy; a process he termed the 'deintegration-integration of the primary self' (Fordham, 1985). As Astor (1995, p. 53) puts it,

> Fordham suggested that before there was an ego there was a primary self. This primary self he thought of as integrated, a psychosomatic potential waiting to unfold in interaction with the environment. The primary self expressed itself through actions which brought it into contact with the environment.

Deintegration is the process Fordham utilizes to identify the way the infant interacts with the mother as well as the infant's means of unpacking their own experience of the self through interactions with the mother or caregiver. As described by Astor (Astor, 1995, pp. 50–51),

> Parts of the self which deintegrated, Fordham called deintegrates. A deintegrate of the self would retain characteristics of wholeness. A deintegrate could be an instinctual act, such as the hungry baby's cry – i.e., it would be contributing to the organism's biological adaptation – or it could be the creation of an image with potentially symbolic meaning.

Integration is the process by which deintegrates which have been adequately met by their external object world (or mother) are taken back in by the infant and experienced as part of their self. Note the similarity between Bion's description of the alpha function of the analyst in the conversion of beta elements into alpha elements and Fordham's description of the role of the caregiver in terms of the deintegrate-integrate model of individuation.

Fordham provides a fuller summary of the deintegrate-integrate process in the following passage:

> Deintegration and reintegration describe a fluctuating state of learning in which the infant opens itself to new experiences and then withdraws in order to reintegrate and consolidate those experiences. During a deintegrative activity, the infant maintains continuity with the main body of the self (or its centre), while venturing into the external world to accumulate experience in motor action and sensory stimulation … Such a concept of the self brings a new dimension to both depth psychology and developmental psychology, for it is now conceived to be a dynamic structure through whose activity the infant's emotional and ego growth takes place.
>
> (Fordham, 1988, p. 64)

Fordham continued to think of the self as an archetype but came to question Jung's description of the self as the archetype of wholeness and instead came to focus on the dynamic-interactive functions of the self (Fordham, 1985, pp. 23–33). It is the interactive-dynamic aspect of the self as organizer that Fordham emphasizes. Fordham differentiates his perspective on the self from Jung's in the following manner,

> My thesis of self postulates, besides an unchanging self, a stable representation in consciousness, the ego. The ego grows out of the interaction between deintegrates and the environmental mother, and her extensions. The interaction produces many self representations, the most stable and prominent of which is the ego.
>
> (Fordham, 1987, p. 363)

Combining Fordham's view of the self with the way in which Jung mainly, but not exclusively, wrote about the Self as an archetypal idea, it is possible to arrive at a concept of Self which is ultimately mysterious and yet manifests itself in the life of the individual in ways which form the basis for personal identity.

Fordham's deintegrate-integrate model of individuation is much closer in description of process and outcome to Bion's model of transformation via alpha function than Jung's model of the transcendent function. He also acknowledges the influence of Bion's (1959) concept of 'attacks on linking' in the development of his concept of 'defenses of the self' (1974). Fordham's dedication to a pluralistic, integrated vision of analytic theory and practice can be discerned in the title of one of his last books, *Freud, Jung, Klein: The Fenceless Field* (1998). In this volume, Fordham (1998, p. 192) outlines eight areas in Bion's theoretical system which find correspondence in Jung.

There are also clear parallels between Fordham's model of infant experience and development and Wilfred Bion's work on beta elements (consisting of primitive somatic experience, affects, and sense impressions). Beta elements are acted on by the alpha function of the mother (or analytic clinician) as she receives, contains, digests, and interprets the baby's experience. The beta elements are gradually transformed into alpha elements which ultimately are available for transformation into the symbolic function via dreams, fantasies, and personal narrative. Fordham described these experiences as deintegrates, especially the intolerable affective-sensory experiences of the infant, as being equivalent to Bion's concept of the beta elements which required the mother's calm maternal reverie, her alpha function, to generate meaningfully integrated experiences from these deintegrates/beta elements. Therefore, Fordham saw the infant's mind as becoming structured, first through the mother's metabolization of the intolerable experience, then through the activity of the infant's primary self, then later through the archetypes and the activity of the ego as it begins to form. Therefore, Fordham proposes that the primary self becomes known to the infant through its deintegrates, with the most significant deintegrate of the self being the ego (Astor, 1995, pp. 51, 54). Ultimately, I propose that Fordham's deintegrate-integrate model of individuation and his introduction of the 'primary self' create a bridge between the teleological models in Jung and Bion and permit a conceptual dialogue between these complementary teleological views.

Grotstein as Bridge Between Jung and Bion

As indicated earlier, Grotstein was also interested in areas of correspondence and complementation between Jung and Bion. Grotstein's proposes a 'transcendent position' (Grotstein, 1997, 2000) which moves beyond Melanie Klein's (1946) 'paranoid-schizoid' and 'depressive' positions, just as Ogden has proposed a developmental organization preceding Klein's 'paranoid-schizoid' position, namely the 'autistic-contiguous' position (Ogden, 1989). In Grotstein's conceptualization, the transcendent position is necessary to account for the experience of "O" and to speak of psychological experiences that go beyond part-object and whole object functioning:

> Thus, I believe that another position, which I call the transcendent position, is required to accommodate the conception of transformations and evolutions in "O" ... In the transcendent position, the object dissolves into the ultimate, ineffable Subject. There is no object in the transcendent position. "O" not only involves a transformation and evolution from the paranoid-schizoid and depressive positions, it also involves a resonance with a total subjectivity ... In the transcendent position, the individual must forsake the presence of the object in order to look inward into his or her own subjectivity. Thus, in the transcendent position one experiences the quintessence of subjectivity that transcends (for the moment) object relations.
>
> (Grotstein, 1997, p. 10)

Also significant among Grotstein's contributions is his elaboration of Bion's model of dreaming as a way of transforming experience combined with a guiding psychic presence similar to Jung's idea of self (Jung, 1959). Grotstein elaborates a model of dreaming that reflects a dialogue between parts of the psyche interacting to do the work of dreaming into existence, i.e., the dreamer who dreams the dream, and the dreamer who understands the dream (Grotstein, 2000). In Grotstein's words:

> The Dreamer Who Understands the Dream is as mysterious as the Dreamer Who Dreams the Dream. It is the self in relationship to "I". A self in association with a Divine Self seems to be able to experience the Truth of a dream – as the Truth within a dream.
>
> (Grotstein, 1979, p. 118)

Grotstein's description has elements quite similar to Jung's description of the activity of the Self and the relationship between the Self and the ego:

> The term 'self' seemed to me a suitable one for this unconscious sub-strate, whose actual exponent in consciousness is the ego. The ego stands to the self as the moved to the mover, or as object to subject, because the determining factors which radiate out from the self surround the ego on all sides and are therefore supraordinate to it. The self, like the uncon-scious, is an a priori existent out of which the ego evolves. It is, so to speak, an unconscious prefiguration of the ego. It is not I who create myself, rather I happen to myself.
>
> (Jung, 1958/1969, para. 391)

Grotstein's integrative model articulates the integration of symbolic mean-ing with lived experience.

Two Case Examples – A Broader Teleological Model
Case Illustration 1 – Mary

My first case illustration is a patient I began seeing while practicing as a young psychologist and throughout my training as a Jungian psychoana-lyst during the 1990s. She was one of the cases I presented as part of my requirements for graduation from analytic training. Mary was a nurse in her 40s who appeared to be very conscientious and competent in her job and well-liked by co-workers, friends, and acquaintances. Mary indicated that her reason for seeking treatment was connected to her difficulties in forming relationships and an absent sense of self. At the time I was seeing Mary, I was primarily using a combination of classical and developmental Jungian approaches, focusing on dreamwork and working within the transference/countertransference dynamics. I was working under the assumption that Mary's symbolic capacity was adequately developed for Jungian dreamwork, and I did not yet have an awareness of Wilfred Bion's model of the psyche – particularly his intersecting concepts of beta elements (i.e., unformulated-unrepresented experiences), alpha function, and alpha elements. The broader category of non-representational states (Levine et al., 2013) had not yet emerged in analytic literature. In other words, I did not have access to a conceptual framework that would have helped me recognize and respond to Mary's experiences from a different teleological perspective than the higher-ordered symbolic perspective outlined in Jung's model. Retrospectively, I can see that I would have needed the teleological perspective outlined by Bion; one which can engage with less developed experiences that have not yet been represented in the psyche and made available for symbolic thought.

The early phase of treatment felt rather productive given my idealized view of analysis at that time. In many respects Mary appeared to be an ideal 'Jungian' patient: she journaled daily, dreamed prolifically, and would often produce several pages of thoughts about her dreams. It was only later that her absence of affective connection to the material became more apparent to me. Mary eventually acknowledged that she derived no sense of usefulness or understanding from the dreamwork. She was operating within the role of the compliant patient and was bringing in dreams because I had suggested it. My recollection of her past dream images never resulted in an affective response from Mary, i.e., her own imagery never became symbolic for Mary.

At one point Mary offered the following self-description that depicts the empty void and isolation she experienced: "*There is a big empty dark room inside of me, and that's all that's there. I'm in the middle sitting on the floor. And my room is empty ... There is not a door that leads out or in. And I'm stuck because there isn't even anything in my brain to occupy me. So I'm not among the living dead. I'm among the dead - dead*". In her mind she had recurrent images of one or more Pac Man figures. Invariably, the role of the figures would be to "*gobble up*" thoughts and feelings, making them unavailable for experience or discussion. Episodically, Mary would lose consciousness during sessions, remaining unable to communicate for ten to fifteen minutes at a time. Retrospectively, Mary's needs would have been better met by an approach focused on her non-representational states (beta elements), rather than the traditional Jungian metapsychology in which I was being trained.

Mary described her father as angry, yelling a lot, and frequently absent. Throughout her childhood, her mother was very labile and would become unpredictably enraged. Mary also indicated that she experienced no warmth from her mother. Mary's mother had several psychiatric hospitalizations, including insulin shock therapy, for depression. During these periods the children were cared for by relatives.

Mary reports that she was very isolated and scared as a child, with few friends and little exposure to adults other than occasional visits with relatives. She felt ignored much of the time, and in one session she made the following observation: "*It always seemed so hard to figure anything out* because *there was never anyone there to ask a question or offer advice*". As a child she had an ongoing fantasy that adults could read her mind; a feeling that sometimes continued in adulthood. At thirteen she was molested by the grandfather of some children she was baby-sitting. She left home at eighteen; living on the streets for a year.

When Mary began treatment, she was experiencing intense hypnagogic hallucinations (e.g., ceilings melting, shapes coming out of the wall, figures appearing in her bedroom), transient dissociative episodes, hypervigilance, sleep disturbances, difficulty with intimacy, lack of assertiveness, infantile feelings, and fear of loss of control. She also disliked physical touch and experienced intrusive mental images, such as images of sexual assault and beatings, and disturbing somatic experiences, such as numbness on the inside of her thighs, someone holding her underwater, or sensations of hands touching or grabbing her. Mary would intermittently become self-injurious and experience fleeting suicidal thoughts.

My conceptualization of Mary's psychic structure centered around a negative mother complex, an absent father complex, and a child complex constellated in conjunction with the negative parental complexes. I also identified what I termed an Osiris complex to describe Mary's disconnection of experiences. For example, in one tearful session she said, "*I didn't know my eyes were leaking till my hand got wet*". While my assessment of her fundamental lack of integration and connection was accurate, at the time I could only conceptualize these elements as dissociated fragments, once part of a larger whole. I was unable to consider these elements of experience as never belonging to a larger whole. I realized at the time that Mary did not form connections between her thoughts, feelings, sensations, and behaviors but I conceptualized the disruption in terms of complex theory and limitations in the development of Mary's ego-Self axis, but did not account for the non-representational aspects of her experience.

Clearly, there are many characteristics associated with Mary's case that can be viewed through the lens of a dissociative response to trauma. It is also clear that as an infant she experienced significant disruptions in the relationship with her primary caregivers. However, there is a great deal of material in Mary's case that points toward the kind of emptiness, lifelessness, and disruption in representational capacity that is highlighted in literature on non-representational states. In Mary's case, I attempted to frame her pre-representational experiences through the representational framework of an Osiris complex which focuses on something dismembered rather than something not yet formed. Had I had the conceptual framework of non-representational states I could have engaged with her experiences differently. I likely would have been able to relinquish my efforts to 'discover meaning' and instead focus on permitting representations to form in my reverie – eventually giving shape, color, and language to her experiences lacking representation. My difficulties in adequately engaging Mary's experiences illustrate the need for an alternative teleological model, such as Bion's; one which is oriented around the experience of 'becoming' through the transformation of unformulated elements of experience into experiences that can be utilized for higher-ordered representational and symbolic processes.

Case Illustration 2 – Andriy

In contrast, I began seeing Andriy fifteen years after the analysis with Mary ended. During the interim, I became familiar with Bion's model of the psyche, and the concept of non-representational states had appeared in the analytic literature. While there are significant differences between the life experiences of Mary and Andriy, there were also similarities in terms of the level of their psychological organization. Andriy, like Mary, had multiple traumatic experiences in his life, and like Mary he also presented intense affective states that seemed to lack psychic representation and could not be engaged, at least initially, through symbolic processes. Therefore, much of my early interactions with Andriy did not focus on dream interpretation, amplification, or interpreting the analytic interaction from an 'as if' position (Jung, 1950/1976, para. 1418). These activities involve working with psychological experience which has previously been represented in the psyche and which rely on the presence of an adequately developed symbolic capacity. Instead, my early efforts were to facilitate the development in Andriy a language of experience – e.g., making observations to him about shifts in his tone of voice, posture, physiology, sensory perceptions, and affective states. I would offer descriptive possibilities for his various experiential states that were often inchoate for Andriy, as well as help him establish linkages between these shifts in experiential states and various areas of his life – an approach I discuss in greater detail elsewhere (Winborn, 2023). Over time this approach also facilitated the development of Andriy's reflective function (Knox, 2004), an important element of symbolic capacity.

When I began with Andriy, he had seen two therapists prior to arriving in my consulting room. Even though he was dissatisfied with his experience with his first therapist, he remained with her much longer than he desired because he was afraid he would fall apart if he left. He also remained in several jobs much longer than he wished because he felt he could not summon the emotional resources to face his fears and leave the situation. This theme has been expressed in our relationship through his ambivalence toward his felt dependency on me. At times, particularly during the first years of our work, Andriy felt torn between his need for me, and our sessions, to prevent him from falling apart, and his fear that he would become so dependent upon me that he would be unable to leave, as he did with his first therapist and several jobs.

Andriy had just turned 46 when we began our therapeutic work. Andriy presented with a long history of anxiety and depression. He was plagued with the feeling his life was always on the edge of a precipice; always imminently on the verge of unraveling, imploding, or falling apart, i.e., that he would die, lose his marriage, or fail in his business. Andriy also constantly felt his body would betray him by failing to function properly, e.g., fears of being unable to sleep, eliminate properly, or function sexually. He also experienced pronounced social anxiety, feeling he was always on the verge of doing or saying something that would reveal his ugliness, lack of understanding, or strangeness, or that he would be made fun of or humiliated. He often experienced these same anxieties with me, reporting feelings of shame about what he was thinking or feeling, even when he had not yet verbalized it.

Andriy emigrated with his parents from an Eastern European country of origin to the United States when he was approximately five years of age. He learned English more quickly than his parents and often served as a translator for them in their new environment. He also has the memory of serving as peacekeeper or mediator between his parents when they argued.

Andriy describes his relationship with his mother as conflictual; a conflict he primarily associates with her persistent, demanding approach to his development as a musician. He describes his father as rather removed (a distance Andriy attributes to avoidance of conflict with Andriy's mother), primarily focused on work and projects, particularly renovations to their home. He has memories from his early life, in his country of origin, of his father constantly warning him how much danger was present there. Later, he recalls his father delivering ominous monologues about the state of the world and the ongoing dangers for people of their cultural-religious background. Andriy often links his anxieties and fears to his father's anxious interpretation of the world. Two other periods of time are especially salient in his memory. He often refers to a period during his middle school years in which he was bullied by a group of male classmates, episodes which Andriy feels he somehow participated in creating the setting for. The other salient experience which Andriy referred to often during the first years of our therapy was his involvement with a fraternity during his university studies. He was ostracized during his four years in the fraternity and eventually became a target of overt ridicule by some of its members.

When Andriy initially entered therapy, I was struck by the sense of anxiety and impending devastation that permeated his being. Every breath and movement seemed labored. For months, his speech was fragmented, halting, and disrupted – often punctuated with deep sighs or self-directed curses muttered under his breath. His thoughts would begin to careen tumultuously almost as soon as he began a sentence; the words he initiated frequently being overtaken by competing thoughts or efforts to suppress forbidden thoughts. It was often difficult to follow the semantics in Andriy's efforts to verbalize his distress. The dissonance and rhythmic disruption of his speech communicated as much as, if not more than, the content of his speech. Andriy perpetually existed in the realm of 'catastrophic chaos' where 'nameless dread' predominates. I often found myself in my own confused, swirling mass of thoughts and sensations as I struggled with his incomplete sentences and fragmented feeling states. I often felt an urge to fill in the 'blanks' for him, to create some order in the chaos, to somehow 'structuralize' his experience through sheer force of will. Frequently it was difficult to take in his obsessive rumination without falling into his feelings of hopelessness and helplessness. In many early sessions, I felt my best option was to listen quietly, find some anchor point for my own mind, and attempt to contain the fragments of experience and sensation that poured forth in fits and starts.

What follows are excerpts from our first therapeutic session, which took place nine months after an initial intake was done to place Andriy on my waiting list.

A: *"Umm, umm, umm ... I was looking at the picture of the electric chair on the cover of Time magazine. Just the picture was horrifying. I don't really remember what we talked about last September. Can you remind me?"*

(I summarize the main themes he had outlined during our intake session.)

A: *"Good summary. My first therapist was passive. I think I was just looking for comfort. Now I have ... a wife, a house, a baby, a business ... but I never expected to have any of that stuff. Sixteen years ago, I thought my life was already over. Now I'm kind of optimistic".*

Me: (Recalling Andriy's deep sense of hopelessness from our initial intake session nine months earlier) *"Optimism is hard won. I imagine it hasn't come naturally for you".*

A: *"Yeah ... death is ... seems more a driving force ... Destruction ... Hope may be a better word than optimism".*

(I ask how it was ending with his previous therapist who he continued to see while on my waiting list.)

A: *"When I had the first therapist, I was always thinking of leaving ... I felt like I had a choke chain on that prevented me from leaving ... This is the first time I've made a conscious decision to leave a therapist ... passivity ... fragility ... hopelessness ... lack of maleness ... all seem to go together. I asked my first therapist why she didn't speak more. She said she felt like I was hanging on her every word ... that was true ... My own thoughts would get paralyzed".*

As I reproduce this dialogue from my notes, I recognize that I wrote down our exchange in a way that sounds much more organized than I experienced it, perhaps reflecting my own need to create narrative order from something that emerged in a more fragmentary way.

The next session begins with Andriy saying:

A: "I got so busy this week ... Not wild about the 8:30 am time slot" (refer-ring to the time that became available for him).

Me: "Wednesday at 4 pm may open soon if you'd like to consider that".

A: "Yeah ... Well, I ... I ... this time I was telling myself I wanted to talk about ... women and relationships. But I'm kind of anxious".

Me: "It's difficult to decide about the time to meet". (In this intervention I am aware of Andriy's ongoing affective states which create cogni-tive disruption, making all decisions, not just this decision, difficult and experientially dangerous).

A: "Yeah ... I have a hard time making decisions. Elena (his wife) *points that out ... I've got lots of anxiety about getting enough sleep ... anxiety attacks ... the world feels like scary ... stressful place and things would unravel if I don't get enough sleep. I'm worried about my bodily func-tions – like my bowel movements fifteen years ago ... Now I have anxi-ety about maintaining an erection ... and then marriage will unravel ... or other areas of my life unraveling ... Things are fragile ... hanging in the balance ... something small can send me on a big head trip ... Even social discourse feels potentially out of control ... because I don't know what I'm going to say next and ... I could say something horrible or stupid. My father goes on and on about death. But I'm not allowed to talk about it ... I've always felt alienated and alone. I don't feel manly and I wanted to be cool – one of the guys".*

Here I shift to a segment from a session six months into our work together. Andriy has just returned from a trip visiting his parents. He begins,

A: "Umm ...umm ... (sigh) ... well ... umm. I don't know why this is so hard to talk about this. Just reading what I wrote after last session – You are that friend, confidant, guide, mentor I never had".

Me: "It's difficult for you to say that."

A: "Yeah ... self-conscious ... Afraid ... I have this intensity of longing I hide from myself most of the time ... Makes me feel squeamish ... naked ... exposed".

Me: "How alone you've felt growing up and going through life, having to process everything on your own".

Andriy asks whether I've seen the movie St. Vincent and I indicate that I have.

A: *"The scene where Vincent teaches the kid to fight ... Nobody did that for me ... I was that paralyzed ... just like in my dreams. Like the Jews during the Holocaust who dug their own graves ... One time I was fixing my bike in the driveway and a kid kept harassing me. I went to ask my dad for help, but I didn't tell him why. The kid backed off a little when my dad came out, but the kid kept saying shit and my dad just ignored it and never said anything to me about it".*

Me: *"You felt he was ineffectual or indifferent?"*

A: *"I don't know. Maybe the latter. It was depressing and disturbing. Maybe I felt shame ..."*

Me: *"You wanted him to handle the kid and then tell you how to handle it in the future".*

A: *"Yeah, to be Bill Murray (the actor who played Vincent in the movie). We were all sleepwalking. We all failed. He failed. I failed to tell him what I needed from him ... I think it took a lot of courage for me to go get him at all. It had been going on for a couple years ... And I had never said anything to anyone ... I was even in the closet with it to myself. This was about the same time as the lunchroom incidents (when Andriy was being bullied at school). I was also taking piano lessons with my mom. I was initially my mom's protector from my dad ... Then as I got older, I started taking things out on her. By around age eleven or twelve, I switched to clarinet. I took pleasure in getting her enraged. A power struggle. I think when I was defending her, I ended up feeling used. About power and resistance".*

Me: *"I can see how the interactions with Elena would play into that scenario. And how that need to resist with her takes on a feeling of survival".*

A: *"Right. It does even sometimes with our daughter".*

It is only during the past year that Andriy's deep sense of dread and the fragmentation of his speech and self-experience have begun to abate. In addition to our work together, his increased sense of cohesion and the development of some sense of self-agency began with a return to music. He took up playing a new instrument and found an instruction program that facilitated an experience of ongoing improvement and continuous feedback about his progress. Gradually his hope and self-confidence have increased sufficiently that he sought out better office space and took on two employees as well as arranging to bring in an intern. He also has incorporated daily exercise and has come to enjoy singing. Recently he has confronted his social anxiety more directly by initiating more business-related phone calls and posting messages on social media, both of which he had been frightened of doing in the past. Additionally, he has grown interested in reading about the Holocaust, which he had actively avoided in the past due to his father's insistence that, as a child, he watch terrifying footage of the Holocaust to warn him of the dangers of being Jewish. In his childhood, he was tormented by the question, *"If they knew they were going to be killed why didn't they fight back?"*, which tied into his own felt history of helplessness and powerlessness. Now, as an outgrowth of his reading, when he is feeling overwhelmed or scared, he often says to himself, *"This isn't a concentration camp"*. Rather than being an attack on himself, as he might have done in the past, this phrase has become a way of grounding himself and reminding himself that his subjective perception of his situation is often not how his world is. He is even able utilize this phrase with a bit of grim humor in a way that helps him reconstitute.

In a recent session, Andriy said:

A: "I have more energy now than I did twenty years ago".
Me: "Yes a lot of your energy was taken up by feeling your world was about to crater around you".
A: "Yes. That sucked up a lot of energy. Things are going well with my daughter too. We do music a lot together. I feel quieter, calmer, less rushed – like stepping out of a loud party into a quiet room … I feel more confident about the business. More optimistic. It kind of tracks along with the guitar progress, seeing gradual, steady improvement over several years. Getting body and mind in alignment".
Me: "That speaks to the part of you that always felt your body was on the verge of letting you down, or not working".
A: "Yes".

In a recent session, Andriy reported the following dream:

I was outside. It was snowy and icy, like a blizzard. I felt lost or disoriented. But then a man walks by, like a primitive ice fisherman, an aboriginal. He was naked and covered in ice but was translucent. I could see the muscles and blood moving under his skin. I woke up wondering how he could survive under those conditions.

Rather than interpreting the 'meaning' of Andriy's dream, Andriy's dream can be understood as a reflection of his overall psychosomatic state at that moment, as well as providing a representation of the various psychological transformations that have occurred during his time in analysis. While Andriy's alter-ego in the dream, the ice fisherman, is naked and covered in ice, nonetheless he is clearly human, with muscle and blood moving beneath his translucent skin. Perhaps just as significant, Andriy is aware of the iceman's resilience, i.e., his ability to survive, even under arduous circumstances. The appearance of the iceman reflects an amalgam of smaller transformations of beta elements into alpha elements, culminating in an image that can be represented, remembered, and reflected upon – a movement from nebulous, overwhelming unrepresented states to affectively rooted images that can be engaged with psychologically.

Conclusion

As I have proposed in this chapter, a teleological perspective facilitates a forward-looking focus on where psyche is moving rather than an exclusively backward-looking, causal perspective that focuses on repairing psychological trauma or resolving internal conflicts. This review of teleological elements found in the psychological models of C.G. Jung and Wilfred Bion examines the contrast and complementation between the two models. The case examples were selected to highlight the contrasts between Jung's model and Bion's model. Jung's teleological model focuses on higher-ordered symbolic processes which underlie his concept of individuation. While Bion's model addresses higher-ordered symbolic processes, it also provides a conceptual framework for recognizing and engaging with lower-ordered proto-experiences needing representation before they can be utilized in dreaming and waking background dreaming. Bion's concept of 'becoming' offers a flexible teleological model which complements Jung's concept of individuation and expands the potential range of patients who can participate in an analytic process.

Fordham's deintegrate-integrate model of individuation and Grotstein's transcendent position concept provide additional conceptual bridges, facilitating further integration of the teleological models of psychic transformation offered by Jung and Bion. An analytic position embracing and integrating both models enhances the analytic clinician's capacity to recognize and engage the widest range of psychological experience; both higher-ordered, symbolic experience and unformulated, unrepresented, sensory-affective-somatic experience.

Note

1   Jung did not capitalize the term 'self' in his writings. However, it has become commonplace in Jungian literature to present 'self' in its capitalized form 'Self'. This convention will generally be utilized in this chapter. The primary function of this practice is to make a distinction between the use of 'self' in ordinary daily language and to distinguish Jung's use of the term from other psychoanalytic authors, e.g., Winnicott, Kohut, Kernberg, Khan, and Jacobson. The capitalized 'Self' is specifically used to designate the primary organizing structure of the individual psyche but also to convey Jung's conceptualization of the Self as possessing a transcendent aspect which connects the experience with something beyond the personal psyche, often referred to by Jung as 'the God-image'. However, later in this chapter, Fordham's modifications of Jung's theories of Self and individuation will be presented. Fordham chooses to utilize the lower case 'self' when discussing his concept of 'primary self'. See Gordon (1985) for a fuller description of the use of 'self' in analytical psychology and other psychoanalytic models.

References

Alvarez, A. (1992). *Live company: Psychoanalytic psychotherapy with autistic, borderline, deprived and abused children*. Routledge.

Astor, J. (1995). *Michael Fordham: Innovations in analytical psychology*. Routledge.

Beebe, B., & Lachmann, F. (2002). *Infant research and adult treatment*. Lawrence Erlbaum.

Beyda, A. (2012). Review of the mystery of analytical work: Weavings from Jung and Bion by Barbara Stevens Sullivan. Routledge, 2010. *Fort Da, 18*(2): 73–79.

Bion, W.R. (1959). Attacks on linking. *International Journal of Psycho-Analysis, 48,* 308–315.

Bion, W.R. (1962a). *Learning from experience*. Karnac.

Bion, W.R. (1962b). The psycho-analytic study of thinking. *International Journal of Psycho-Analysis, 43,* 306–310.

Bion, W.R. (1963). *Elements of psychoanalysis*. Karnac.

Bion, W.R. (1965). *Transformations*. Karnac.

Bion, W.R. (1970). *Attention and interpretation*. Karnac.

Bion, W.R. (1989). *Two papers: The grid and caesura*. Karnac.

Bion, W.R. (1992). *Cogitations*. Karnac.

Bion, W.R. (1993). *Second thoughts*. Karnac.

Bovensiepen, G. (2002). Symbolic attitude and reverie. *Journal of Analytical Psychology, 47*(2), 241–257.

Britannica, the Editors of Encyclopaedia. (2023, June 7). Teleology. *Encyclopedia Britannica*. Retrieved June 17, 2023, from https://www.britannica.com/topic/teleology.

Civitarese, G., & Ferro, A. (2013). The meaning and use of metaphor in analytic field theory. *Psychoanalytic Inquiry, 33*(3), 190–209.

Corbett, L. (August 23–28, 1992). Therapist mediation of the transcendent function. In M.A. Matoon (Ed.), *The transcendent function: Individual and collective aspects. Proceedings of the twelfth international congress for analytical psychology* (pp. 395–401). Daimon Verlag.

Culbert-Koehn, J. (1997). Between Bion and Jung: A talk with James Grotstein. *The San Francisco Jung Institute Library Journal, 15*(4), 15–32.

Ellman, S. (2010). *When theories touch: A historical and theoretical integration of psychoanalytic thought*. Karnac.

Fordham, M. (1971). Primary self, primary narcissism and related concepts. *Journal of Analytical Psychology*, *16*(2), 168–182.

Fordham, M. (1985). *Explorations into the self.* Society of Analytical Psychology.

Fordham, M. (1987). The actions of the self. In P. Young-Eisendrath & J. Hall (Eds.), *The book of the self* (pp. 345–365). New York University Press.

Fordham, M. (1988). The infant's reach. *Psychological Perspectives*, *21*, 58–76.

Fordham, M. (1993). *The making of an analyst.* Free Association.

Fordham, M. (1994). *Children as individuals* (revised version of a book originally published in 1944 as *The life of childhood*). Free Association Books.

Fordham, M. (1998). *Freud, Jung, Klein: The fenceless field.* Routledge.

Freud, S. (1911). Formulations on the two principles of mental functioning. In *SE12* (pp. 213–226). Hogarth Press.

Gordon, R. (1985). Big Self and little self: Some reflections. *Journal of Analytical Psychology*, *30*(3), 261–271.

Grotstein, J.S. (1979). Who is the dreamer who dreams the dream and who is the dreamer who understands it? *Contemporary Psychoanalysis*, *15*(1), 110–169.

Grotstein, J.S. (1981). Wilfred R. Bion: The man, the psychoanalyst, the mystic. *Contemporary Psychoanalysis*, *17*(4), 501–536.

Grotstein, J.S. (1997). *Bion's transformation in 'O' and the concept of the transcendent position.* http://www.sicap.it/merciai/bion/papers/grots.htm.

Grotstein, J.S. (2000). *Who is the dreamer who dreams the dream? A study of psychic presences.* Analytic Press.

Grotstein, J.S. (2007). *A Beam of intense darkness: Wilfred Bion's legacy to psychoanalysis.* Routledge.

Jacobi, J. (1973). *The psychology of C. G. Jung.* Yale University Press.

Jung, C.G. (1916). *The transcendent function: CW* (Vol. 8, pp. 67–91). Princeton University Press.

Jung, C.G. (1916/1948). *General aspects of dream psychology: CW* (Vol. 8). Princeton University Press.

Jung, C.G. (1921). *Psychological types: CW* (Vol. 6). Princeton University Press.

Jung, C.G. (1934). *Picasso: CW* (Vol. 15). Princeton University Press.

Jung, C.G. (1950/1976). *The symbolic life: CW* (Vol. 18). Princeton University Press.

Jung, C.G. (1952). *Answer to job: CW* (Vol. 11). Princeton University Press.

Jung, C.G. (1953/1966). *Two essays on analytical psychology: CW* (Vol. 7). Princeton University Press.

Jung, C.G. (1953/1968). *Psychology and alchemy: CW* (Vol. 12). Princeton University Press.

Jung, C.G. (1954/1966). *The practice of psychotherapy: CW* (Vol. 16). Princeton University Press.

Jung, C.G. (1956). *Symbols of transformation: CW* (Vol. 5). Princeton University Press.

Jung, C.G. (1958/1969). *Psychology and religion: CW* (Vol. 11). Princeton University Press.

Jung, C.G. (1959). *Aion. CW* (Vol. 9). Princeton University Press.

Jung, C.G. (1959/1969). *The archetypes of the collective unconscious: CW* (Vol. 9). Princeton University Press.

Jung, C.G. (1960/1969). *The structure and dynamics of the psyche: CW* (Vol. 8). Princeton University Press.

Jung, C.G. (1977). *C.G. Jung speaking: Interviews and encounters.* Princeton University Press.

Klein, M. (1946). Notes on some schizoid mechanisms. *International Journal of Psychoanalysis*, *27*(3–4), 99–110.

Klein, M. (1948). *The psychoanalysis of children*. Hogarth Press.

Knox, J. (2004). From archetypes to reflective function. *Journal of Analytical Psychology*, *49*(1), 1–19.

Levine, H., Reed, G., & Scarfone, D. (Eds.). (2013). *Unrepresented states and the construction of meaning*. Karnac.

Lopez-Corvo, R. (2005). *The dictionary of the work of W.R. Bion*. Routledge.

Miller, J. (2004). *The transcendent function: Jung's model of psychological growth through dialogue with the unconscious*. SUNY Press.

Ogden, T.H. (1989). On the concept of an autistic-contiguous position. *International Journal of Psycho-Analysis, 70*(1), 127–140.

Ogden, T.H. (1994). *Subjects of analysis*. Aronson.

Ogden, T.H. (2004). This art of psychoanalysis: Dreaming undreamt dreams and interrupted cries. *International Journal of Psycho-Analysis, 85*(4), 857–877.

Ogden, T.H. (2022). *Coming to life in the consulting room: Toward a new analytic sensibility*. Routledge.

Papadopoulos, R. (2006). *The handbook of Jungian psychology: Theory, practice, and applications*. Routledge.

Parsons, M. (2023). *Coming to life in the consulting room: Toward a new analytic sensibility* (Ogden, Thomas H. Trans.). Routledge, 2022, ISBN: 978-1-032-13264-8. *International Journal of Psycho-Analysis, 104*(2), £29.99, 413–423.

Peltz, R. (2015). What is deep? *Rivista di Psicoanalisi, 61*, 645–662.

Samuels, A., Shorter, B., & Plaut, A. (1987). *A critical dictionary of Jungian analysis*. Routledge & Kegan Paul.

Sandler, P.C. (2005). *The language of Bion*. Karnac.

Sharp, D. (1991). *C.G. Jung lexicon: A primer of terms and concepts*. Inner City.

Solomon, H. (1994). The transcendent function and Hegel's dialectical vision. *Journal of Analytical Psychology, 39*(1), 77–100.

Spielrein, S. (1994). Destruction as the cause of coming into being. *Journal of Analytical Psychology, 39*(2), 155–186.

Stern, D. (1985). *The interpersonal world of the infant: A view from psychoanalysis and developmental psychology*. Basic.

Symington, N. (2001). *The spirit of sanity*. Karnac.

Tennes, M. (2007). Beyond intersubjectivity: The transpersonal dimension of the psychoanalytic encounter. *Contemporary Psychoanalysis, 43*(4), 505–525.

von Franz, M.L. (1971). The role of the inferior function in psychic development. In M.L. von Franz & J. Hillman (Eds.), *Lectures on Jung's typology* (pp. 67–88). Spring Publications.

Winborn, M. (2014). Watching clouds together: Analytic reverie and participation mystique. In M. Winborn (Ed.), *Shared realities: Participation mystique and beyond* (pp. 70–96). Fisher King Press.

Winborn, M. (2017a). Jung and Bion: Intersecting vertices. In R.S. Brown (Ed.), *Re-encountering Jung: Analytical psychology and contemporary psychoanalysis* (pp. 85–112). Routledge.

Winborn, M. (2017b). The colorless canvas: Non-representational states and implications for analytical psychology. In E. Kiehl & M. Klenck (Eds.), *Anima mundi in transition: Cultural, clinical and professional challenges. Proceedings of the 20th IAAP congress – Kyoto* (pp. 430–439). Daimon Verlag.

Winborn, M. (2023). Working with patients with disruptions in symbolic capacity. *Journal of Analytical Psychology, 68*(1), 87–108.

Chapter 2

On Truth, Reasonable Certainty, and God

Conviction as Revelatory Process in Peirce and Jung

Garth Amundson

For Jung, conviction leading to action is a central tangible expression of the forward-looking nature of the psyche, the endpoint of its authoritative bidding that we fulfill what Heidegger calls our "ownmost" destiny. This is something that the *Zeitgeist* of modernity demands of us. However, for all its promise, it is a deeply ambivalent gift. Having swept away the ritual structures of ancient eras, modernity beckons us toward an ontic clearing in which we may work out singular visions of life. But the demands of ownmost-ness also flood us with dread – of alienation, of guilt, and, fundamentally, of desire itself. Unprecedented freedom from bygone creeds has a severe dimension, since it produces an existential ultimatum to which few of us can respond confidently or with resolve. Hence, the thoughtless and inauthentic retreat to what Martin Heidegger (1927/1962, p. 38) terms "average everydayness" – the domain of going along to get along, an expression of our primordial state of enrapturement by an unself-reflective social "they" – that is emblematic of our time. Jung puts it thus:

> Man can live the most amazing things if they make sense to him. But the difficulty is to create that sense. It must be a conviction, naturally; but you find that the most convincing things man can invent are cheap and ready-made and are never able to convince him against his personal desires and fears

> (Jung, 2000, p. 90).

This chapter is concerned with the theme of conviction that I see as informing Jung's oeuvre. It is one which I think may even be construed as at its very core. Specifically, he asks, how do we arrive at a dependable sense of clarity about the meaning and course of life? What is the process through

DOI: 10.4324/9781003412823-3

which we come to feel deeply, in our "heart of hearts", that some idea, goal, or aspiration – and, by extension, life itself – is "worth it"?

The crisis of late modernity, as Morris Eagle (1984) states, is no longer found in Freudian-esque mass outbreaks of aggression, but in the vacuity and passionlessness of individual human souls. Jung believes that driving what he calls the "psychic epidemics" of our age is a collective lack of ennobling experiences of *participation mystique*, of being carried forward toward an as-yet-unthought future by a supramundane and numinous creative Will bridging individual being and the transpersonal. On this score he waxes critical of Freud's psychotherapeutic stance: while uniquely able to identify what it is we should be free *from*, psychoanalysis simply sloughs off the question of what it is we are to be free *for*, he asserts.

To aspire toward an end that we deem both good and possible is hardly imaginable minus a belief that our experience is able to more or less accurately impart the topography of Being. However, particularly among modern educated persons, including those steeped in Freudian thought, it is largely taken for granted that we exist encased, as it were, within dense layers of cognitions that function so as to alter, distort, and/or deceive us as to the nature of our motives and aims, up to and including the very ontological basis of our subjectivity itself, as well as the nature of the world, conceived to be an alluring but uncannily inaccessible object "outside" of, or distinct from mind. Of course, there are profound epistemological rationales, starting in the modern era with Rene Descartes, for such a historically unprecedented conclusion about mindedness. These perspectives are of unparalleled importance for any discipline, such as psychotherapy, founded upon a theory of mind, and forward impressive arguments against the notion that mind and world are continuous. That said, one cannot help but notice that in the course of living, when things "count", we engage the world *as if* to implicitly affirm that our experience is structured so as to be revelatory or, to use Martin Heidegger's (1927/1962) term, "disclosive" of truths that are quite literally and authentically "there" to be discovered. This conviction is one of many, usually unconscious, "ontological commitments" we may settle upon to inform and direct our reasoning and suggest choices for how to traverse life. Of all such commitments, it is one that I believe is singularly unavoidable. That is, it is an experiential "given" that we *must* affirm, however unconsciously, so as to navigate experience in even the most rudimentary way.

Of course, the fact that in daily life our immediate experience often deceives and misdirects us would seem to vindicate the skeptical modernist epistemological narrative. However, I suggest that a broad view of the arc of our personal and collective histories makes this conclusion far from certain in any absolute sense. On the contrary, we might consider that human beings show a remarkable capacity to discern and act adaptively (read "wisely") in relation to the topography of both inner and outer realms, not without hesitance and missteps, but eventually and on balance, that is, in the "long run". When all is said and done, we "find our bearings", "get it right", and regularly "make it through" even the most arduous difficulties, including those emerging from the abyss of the unconscious, which we not only endure but overall tend to turn to good. The mysteries of the intrapsychic *topos* are baffling and disorienting indeed. But we should not forget that even the psychoanalytic endeavor, which is steeped in the modernist episteme, stands upon the observation that we can and overall do usefully engage its dynamisms, in daily life and psychotherapy, by first surveying what William James (1890) calls the "stream of consciousness" (p. 239), a dimension of what we call "experience". In a Freudian treatment, this is undertaken by relaxing our compulsive tendency to impose an antecedent structure upon experience, and let our thoughts wander here and there, as they come. Analysis begins with the unpremeditated contemplation of experience, an exercise in learning how to check the mind's neurotic quest for mastery, and "just look". Viewed thus, our conscious engagement with painful symptoms is understood as able to lead us somewhere. That is, they do not disappear (which is why it is not credible to apply the medicalized term "cure" to define the ends of any depth psychological endeavor) but evolve toward an ameliorated experience of ourselves and our future prospects. Framed in this way, we might say that in **Sigmund Freud's oeuvre** it is not resistance to the unconscious but rather a refusal of the disclosive teleology of *conscious* experience, of its particular revelatory phenomenology, that threatens to undermine our psychic adjustment and happiness. This is to say that experience *leads* us somewhere satisfying and measurably beneficial to our being if we follow it attentively and with an attitude of receptivity. And this, in turn, seems to strongly suggest a real epistemological (and, as I will argue, ontological) continuity between experience and the structure of Being, of that which is authentically and truthfully real, including the objective structure of the unconscious. Hence, even in a classical psychoanalysis, despite its origins in the modernist "hermeneutics of suspicion" (Ricoeur, 1965/2014), treatment begins, proceeds, and culminates according to a *de facto* phenomenological *ethos*, for the simple reason that as a human activity it *must* do so. Just as regularly as people find their experience meliorated and enriched by agreeing to the rule of "freely associating" to the spontaneous arising of their thoughts in psychoanalytic treatment, so too the veracity of what may be called a "hermeneutics of trust" is supported by the fact that, for vast swaths of humanity, following religious promptings or "instincts" "pays off" in experience, and does so as dependably as most of their other judgements about the world. *Contra* modernist narratives of the tragic and even absurd inevitability of our entrapment within a divided subjectivity, warring with itself and an objectionable objective world, this would seem to imply that our experience of symptoms is not only or even primarily a brittle bulwark against the unconscious. Instead, these may be viewed as productively continuous with its dynamisms, given that it is only possible to fruitfully engage the latter by teasing out and nurturing the growth of the germinal meanings we find in the former. It is for this reason that Jung posits that we do not so much resist as misunderstand the communications of the unconscious, which engage the ego via the primal vitality of symbolic images, often appearing as inexplicable and uncanny symptoms, rather than through the categories of linear reason characteristic of consciousness (Jung, 1912/2003). The symbols of the unconscious situate themselves, often forcefully, in awareness, where their reparative teleology may be integrated into daily life by developing skill at interpreting the themes they impart. This is a central reason that Jung (1958/2011) insists on the need to nurture a defined ego position toward unconscious dynamisms, so as to engage these dialogically. This is an affirmation of the truth-imparting phenomenology of consciousness, one implied though largely absent in Freud in explicit forms.

Arguably, motivating the widespread contemporary premise that we cannot grasp anything beyond the boundaries of subjectivity, conceived of as a lonely island divided both against itself and the world, is a deep suspicion of pre-modern religious truth-claims. For this reason, modern intellectuals typically reject the notion that epistemology has any real or meaningful continuity with ontological or metaphysical postulates (assuming they allow that ontology and metaphysics are even worth our attention, which more than a few do not). This goes beyond simply asserting that the structure of Being is ineffable, that is, that it finally eludes representation in thought. In pre-modern epistemes the ineffable nature of ultimate reality is regularly asserted and even celebrated. Rather, major intellectual trends in modernism go beyond this, to posit that we are not only barred from cognizing a metaphysical dimension of Being, that is, of capturing it in linear logic, but that we cannot plausibly claim that such a dimension can be experienced in *any* way. Derived from this premise is the modern (and now post-modern) era's skepticism about what an act of interpretation purports to achieve. I suggest that the modernist move to divide epistemology from meaningful, credible ontological and metaphysical speculation is part of a larger attempt to redefine pre-modern, largely religious visions of the world as irrelevant, and thus deny them a place at the table of discussion about human nature, social and cultural challenges, and meaning itself. This divisiveness is worsened by those holding metaphysical (usually traditionally religious) convictions of the nature of the world, who often contribute to their own irrelevance by simply doubling down, minus explanation or reasoned argument, on the credibility of personal experience; lacking the language to forward a reasoned argument for their convictions, they are able to do no more than stubbornly stand by the assertion of feeling enriched and even redeemed by their religious commitments. Understandably, modernist intellectuals see this as further evidence of the indefensible, even delusional nature of such convictions, and the accuracy of their narrative of the existentially alienated subject.

But, however vague, inarticulate, and/or defensive these appeals to feeling enriched or redeemed by religion may seem, I suggest that here the faithful are actually "on to something" that can be spelled out and defended in formal philosophical terms. That is, I think that, in their own way, the ordinary religious believer somehow grasps that in this matter everything rests on the trustworthiness of that ill-defined thing we call "experience". And here I suggest we need to give these adherents some credit: while in the modern West there remain pockets of religious believers who rely primarily on ensconced theological doctrines to frame their ontological commitments, it is worth noting that most accept the modernist elevation of personal experience to a position of authority superseding ancient canon. That is, they are intellectual pluralists, by and large, affirming the truth of their preferred canon while also accepting of the idea that this cannot and should not be forced on others, and that ultimately each of us must work out our own vision of "salvation", be it other-worldly, this-worldly, or an admixture of the two. Hence, the fundamental question for the majority of both religious and non-religious persons in this pre-modern and modern/post-modern debate seems to center upon the nature of experience. Specifically, to what extent is it reasonable to affirm that personal experience is a credible signifier or "pointer" to a trans-egoic, supramundane Absolute?

Of course, the foregoing is the site of a major divergence between Freudian and Jungian models of mind, one that is itself a microcosm of the larger Western cultural transformation from pre-modern, largely religious, to modern secular hermeneutical narratives. Because of his personal history of compelling, essentially mystical experiences which he took as expressing a transsubjective reality, Jung is decidedly supportive of the authenticity of religious and metaphysical truth-claims. However, he is also acutely aware of the gulf between pre-modern and modern views of such contentions. Hence, in the fields of psychotherapy and psychological anthropology, Jung seeks a more tempered and creative dialogue between pre-modern religious belief and modern/post-modern secularism. Toward this end, his position attempts to embrace and synthesize both the pre-modern, largely religious affirmation of an unbroken thread between human life and the Absolute, and the modern allegiance to subjectivity, specifically, the sanctity of what we call "inner experience". From this he evolves a psychological metaphysics of experience, the metaphysical dimension of which is framed, not within doctrinal or theological assertions, but in an intelligent and quite modern appeal to the revelatory flow of immediate experience. His oeuvre is one that defines the experiencing subject as situated in a pregnant, ontologically suggestive continuum with a hypothesized Absolute, the supramundane Source of our capacity to accurately cognize and traverse Being's *topos*. This is an Absolute that by and large expresses itself subtly, in the gradual unfolding of experience. Jung asserts that it is by attending with an attitude of belief to the forward-going progression of experience that we may traverse experience more productively, a position toward psychic reality grounded in what I call an implicit theo-ontological "hermeneutics of trust". For most religious orientations toward experience, except those imbued with a self-other and/or intraspsychic dualism (and these are a minority among world faith traditions), this is an ontological commitment to the concept that our experience of the world is revelatory of truth, because it displays the intentions of an intelligent Absolute. Related to this view is the belief that our immediate experiential engagement with both the world of the non-self and the "inner" world of our own thoughts, while opaque, paradoxical, and even baffling, is ultimately a reliable avenue to truth. Across non-dual religious traditions, the epistemic dimension of this stance is a generic ontological persuasion that personal experience is essentially continuous with the nature of its objects; and, related to this, the belief that this intelligent Absolute addresses us within the structure of

Being, via its immanent and temporal "objects", toward the goal of enabling our flourishing.

In non-dualist theisms, this state of fulfillment evolves via an intense, alternately loving and testy give-and-take between the deity and human beings. Framed in Heideggerian terms, we might define this as a mytho-poeic "call and response": the Absolute regards our being-in-the-world as important, and therefore, strives to initiate a dialogue with each of us, "speaking", as it were, through the unique circumstances of our lives. That said, one need not have the slightest metaphysical impulse or adhere to a theistic metaphysics to sense that Being "calls" to us, to use Heidegger's term. The fact of being in such a revelatory discourse may be reasonably inferred from our ordinary manner of traversing life: our interpretations and the actions they suggest create objective effects that immediately gain ontological autonomy. From this ontic position they address us, as it were: we act and there follows an effect, one that turns to face us as an autonomous interlocutor and, more often than not, dependable scout or guide to the existential landscape we aim to traverse. This is a metaphysical restatement (and inferential elaboration) of what we mean by "learning from experience"; and no one learns anything who is unwilling to suspend certain precious *a priori* biases and simply attend to the stream of consciousness. In Heideggerian language, this means to let things show themselves as they are and hence *may be*, in the lighted, disclosive "clearing" of Being's ongoing self-revelation (Heidegger, 1927/1962). To repeat, this dialogical stance toward the world's ontic structure does not presume, much less demand, the hypothesis of an Absolute interlocuter. However, the utterly ordinary event of mentally processing the datum of sensate experience in a way that facilitates our ability to wisely steer a course through the world's ontological structure *may* be supplemented by what I will call an onto-theological "metaphysics of wonder" at the ordinary fact that mind and world are conformed to one another so elegantly and, on balance, reliably. Intrapsychically, this is much like the way the dream functions in its role as addressing the ego, which is why Jung understands dreams as guides, benevolent advocates, or stubborn opponents of our egoic agendas. The thoughtful religious person has developed skill at attending to such communiques. This implies a willingness to let Being "state its case" via the contextual "total situation" (Dewey, 1938, p. 66) of our immersion in the life of the world, its progressive teleological self-disclosure, as opposed to preemptively forcing experience through an intellectual obstacle course of foregone conclusions and ready-made, often facile objections. In this, where one starts makes all the difference in terms of the conclusions one eventually draws: to be genuinely religious, whether by allegiance to a specific doctrine or less discriminately "spiritually" inclined, is to initiate query from a compelling sense of benumbed awe in the face of the sublime and uncanny intelligence of Being. This evocative aesthetic of bedazzlement by the world transcends the concrete facticity of one's status as a naked ape that craves solace. All this to say that to the person predisposed to a theocentric or religious consciousness, the notion of the Absolute is a provocative addition to the datum of experience.

In this chapter I argue that a theo-philosophical stance toward experience is legitimized by its observable effects on how we actually navigate the world. That is, we live better – more compassionately, productively, and confidently – when supported by the conviction of being related to an intelligent and creative Absolute. Reasonable minds will disagree as to why this is so. Our present, dominant Western mythos simply presumes that this is a relic of bygone eras and another fateful indicator of the all-too-human willingness to deny reality, one best debunked through appeals to what are taken as the self-evident facts of reason (usually bolstered by scientific logic or modernist philosophical or psychological dualisms, such as, in psychoanalysis, Jacques Lacan's divided subject) and dismissed. In contrast, the typical religious believer, however ill-equipped to respond to the self-certainty with which these critiques are often leveled, can frequently do no better than insist upon their experience of having been enabled to live a better life by virtue of their faith commitments.

So, what should we think about God and religious or "spiritual" beliefs generally? This chapter is an attempt to lend credibility to religious and "spiritual" persons' appeals to experience to justify their metaphysical commitments and the sense of conviction that is attached to these. My argument is teleological, specifically, one that considers the way thoughts evolve in consciousness – the datum of our unfolding experience – as pointing to something latent within and also beyond itself. It implies a position requiring the suspension of disbelief, and thoughtful observation of the stream of consciousness in a manner allowing the phenomenology of experience to speak for itself. Such a stance presumes that biases and presumptions be mentally "bracketed" (Husserl, 1913/1973) and temporarily put to one side, as much as possible. To be clear, this is not a narrowly "religious" methodological orientation toward experience; rather, I argue that it is precisely how *all* productive thought naturally proceeds. Related to this is another dimension of a hermeneutics of trust, namely, the conviction that the structure of our experience is fundamentally conformed to the nature of Being. Evidence for this is easy to come by in the course of life. We human beings are remarkably adept at correctly cognizing the nature of the world. While we constantly wrestle with the many things in our experience that are confounding, we tend, over time, to accurately grasp their natures and turn them to good. I suggest that this means something beyond the fact that we are endowed by nature with unusually large frontal lobes.

And here we get to the teleological basis of Jung's theory of human nature. His concept of the "forward", futuristic thrust of human life asserts that our experience is continuous with Being itself, and that through sensitivity to this ontological continuity we may come to know who it is we are "meant to become", as Friedrich Nietzsche states. Perhaps because, like Jung, I see no good reason to confine our thinking about the Absolute to any single category of experience, in this chapter I apply pragmatist philosophical concepts to illuminate Jung's understanding of how it is we come to experience an abiding certainty about the nature of the world. The pragmatist tradition brings a logical rigor to Jung's poetical but often imprecise ideas, including a devotion to the scientific method and its standards of public verifiability, falsifiability, and hesitance to forward conclusions that clash with our empirical experience of reality. This does not mean that a pragmatic metaphysics idealizes immediate experience as a "direct pipeline" to sure knowledge. Rather, it affirms a disclosive continuity between experience and its ultimate Source, an idea reconcilable with the concept that we must infer beyond experience to arrive at reasoned convictions.

To this end, I use selected aspects of the ideas of pragmatism's founder, Charles Sanders Peirce (1839–1914), to tease out just what it is I think Jung tries, in his meandering way, to say[1]. Peirce's philosophy is ideally suited to my approach because it is both the most logically rigorous of all pragmatist theories, which supplement Jung's internally contradictory account of his metaphysics, and mirrors his thoroughgoing adherence to "spiritual" perspectives. These men use quite different venues through which to explore the structure of our cognizing activity: Peirce through an exacting semiotic theory, and Jung through a mytho-poeic cultural anthropology. However, they are in many ways a natural pair, intellectually, in that both conceive of our ability to navigate reality as a reflection of its supramundane ground. Their respective writings and lectures address large swaths of human nature and endeavor, expansive observations which unite the two under the umbrella of faith in the epistemological trustworthiness of lived experience as ultimately pointing us toward the awareness of our immersion in a purposeful metaphysical *mise-en-scène*. To be clear, in what follows I do not seek to assert anything beyond a mutually illuminating general concordance between their positions: in many respects, Peirce and Jung offer very divergent understandings of human nature and its relation to Being. However, although different types of theoreticians, in their distinct ways both posit a dynamically evolving Absolute as the generative source of our capacity to fruitfully judge and steer a course through experience. Further, both assert that the ontological nature of this Absolute may be credibly inferred by disciplined attention to our how we arrive at judgements about reality.

For both Peirce and Jung, the process of translation from pre-reflective to reflective thought exists as a creative, even playful dialogue between an inchoate primordial chaos and determinate form. The energic thrust in this to-and-fro tango arises from a synthetic and synthesizing All-in-All, the cultural symbols of which Jung (1916/1957) defines as transcending duality. Here, the definiteness of its manifestations in thought is a function of its continuity with the murky abyss of pre-consciousness. We experience this as a metamorphosing "presencing" of Being within experience, to borrow a Heideggerian term.

Being's "presencing presence" operates beyond simple polarities to yield our experience of the world. Hence, the particularization of objects of experience co-occurs as the other side of the perpetually changing, open-ended mutability of Being, making it possible to recognize identity through change and, conversely, change through identity. To say this differently, Being and time are mutually "possibilizing" (Kearney, 2001). As such, they form a unified phenomenological field enabling us to cognize, "re-cognize", judge, and navigate the world.

Peirce's Metaphysics: a Semiotics of Evolving Knowledge of God

Peirce is most widely known for his semiotic epistemology, his theory of the way that conceptual signs form and become registered as instrumental mental phenomena enabling us to effectively navigate reality. He is not widely thought of as a metaphysician or religious thinker, but rather as a logician;

in fact, his corpus contains only one essay devoted exclusively to metaphysics, *A Neglected Argument for the Existence of God* (Peirce, 1908/2020), published late in his life. However, many commentators (most prominently Raposa, 1989) argue convincingly that metaphysics is *the* underlying guiding theme in his oeuvre, a consistent if usually implicit motif throughout his work, from his fledgling intellectual efforts as a Harvard undergraduate until his death (Orange, 1984).

Peirce's approach to metaphysics is part of his devotion to the scientific method as our best, most dependably revelatory method of correctly inferring the nature of the world. That is, he believed that we can and should rely upon scientific logic, with its reliance upon the empiricism of sensate experience and criterion of public verifiability and falsifiability, to correctly interpret and fruitfully engage experience. An aspect of this commitment is found in his metaphysical realism, namely, the presumption that there are objectively real elements of the world that are palpably "there" to be discovered. Among these metaphysical "reals" is God or the Absolute, the being of which is obscure but inferentially knowable via the datum of lived experience. Peirce's commitment to science does not mean that he posits that only trained scientists can correctly grasp the nature of the Absolute. Rather, he asserts that we are all *de facto* scientists in some way, in that we share in the universal capacity to employ what he, in a 1905 lecture, calls "critical common-sensism" (5:402 n.3.). The rules of the scientific method are merely formally codified examples of the manner in which all fruitful thinking proceeds, he asserts. For this and other reasons, Peirce optimistically proposes that the next stage in the development of human religious consciousness is a uniting of our concepts of God with the methods and findings of science.

With this in mind, let us explore Peircean metaphysics, beginning with his semiotic theory, which I explain with reference to the way he incorporates this into a larger, "spiritual" viewpoint.

Peirce's thought is daunting in its complexity, and, despite its obsessional rigor, many of its elements admit of multiple, sometimes contradictory interpretations. This need not be judged a mark against it: these qualities allow it to be creatively played with or "mused" over, to use a Peircean term, toward the realization of novel perspectives, the origins of which are a holistic network in which the fact of change exists in a co-dependent and co-creative relationship with the fact of constancy. As I will explain, Peirce's philosophy is a grand and dense architectonic, a veritable philosophy of everything, in which the lawful regularity of Being is discernable, not because it is static and unchanging, but because it is continually alterable and emergent, hence capable of producing utterly original phenomena. In Peirce, it is the phenomenon of change that (counter-intuitively) renders the objects of experience definable in their particularity: more exactly put, alteration and novelty are only perceptible against a backdrop of stability and regularity, what Peirce calls the habit-taking tendency of the cosmos. That is, we find the world intelligible because it evolves in new forms and directions, a mutative symphony of emergent possibilities yielding new expressions of orderliness and coherence that become instantiated as regularly recurring qualities of Being. So, burgeoning new phenomena coalesce into determinate and repetitively "habitual" forms, and in this way act as stable, established ontological molds enabling still further procreative changes to unfold, in a perpetually evolving dialectic.

Peirce's mature semiotic episteme defines our capacity to know and traverse reality as made possible by a triad of what he defines as signs, objects, and interpretants. This "triadic" epistemology is a result of his reinterpretation of Immanuel Kant's categories of knowledge, the intrinsic properties of mind which allow us to rightly cognize objects in the world and navigate life in a practically fruitful manner, what pragmatism calls the adaptive "instrumental" use of thinking. Kant identifies twelve categories of knowledge that serve as the non-specific, innate predispositions of mind rendering specific objects in the world cognizable. These exist in four properties: quantity, quality, relation, and modality (each of these existing as possibility, existence, and necessity) (Paton, 1936, pp. 295–299). Peirce reduces Kant's categories to three groups, Firstness, Secondness, and Thirdness, which I will describe below, each of which contains different relationships between signs, objects, and interpretants (Peirce, 1903). In a marked departure from Kant, Peirce defines the three categories as existing along a developmental trajectory from unbidden primordial immediacy to abstract or "symbolic" generalities, abstract and lawful regularities that we apply to navigating the topography of Being.

Put simply, a sign is a signifier of some phenomenon, what he defines as its object. Anything that mediates an object to experience is acting as a sign, be this language, a physical change in the environment, a behavior, and so on. Signs signify only when they evoke an interpretation of the object, that is, a certain understanding of the perceived object; in this sense, they are more properly defined as the "media" or vehicles of a given interpretation. Peirce, who is heavily influenced by Darwinian theory, proposes an evolutionary teleology of signs. Specifically, he says that the function of an interpreting sign-vehicle starts as an intrusion upon pre-reflective experience, an idea I take as a phenomenological reframing of the general psychoanalytic concept of "the unconscious". This primordial intrusive event evolves over time into more nuanced, constrained, and determinate cognitions. These serve to enable our navigation of the world in progressively more sophisticated because "transcendentalized" forms (that is, forms that are increasingly abstracted from, though always connected in an unbroken continuum with, the concrete objects and circumstances initially evoking them).

Peirce obsessively refined this epistemic viewpoint throughout much of his life. In the final form of his semiotic theory, emerging between 1906 and 1910, he concerns himself with the processes involved in understanding the world as it actually exists, apart from the judgements of any individual cognizing subject. This reflects his metaphysical realism, which he devises in part from his immersion in the medieval-era scholasticism of Duns Scotus (Almeder, 1973). It is a view grounded in the conviction that our interpretations ultimately refer back to metaphysically real objects, which are the way they are, that is, the way they exist in reality, independent of our conjectures. Understanding this clarifies Peirce's employment of mediating interpretants in his thought. For Peirce, we cognize partially, a reflection of our limited capacities as finite creatures. However, a knowledge of the *ding-an-sich* (thing-in-itself) is possible, at least in principle, through what he calls the efforts of a dedicated "community of inquirers" following a logically correct method. Important to bear in mind here is that Peirce rejects what he takes as the Kantian premise that the mediate nature of experience implies the intrinsic unknowableness of objects in and of themselves, an idea Kant sets forth in his famous distinction between our experience of phenomena and the epistemically inaccessible "noumenal" realm of Being. As John Smith (1987, p. 78) states, for Peirce there is no "experience of experience", but only experience: or, stated philosophically, the phenomenal and noumenal realms of experience are mediated by the innate categories of interpretation, within which they are continuous with each other. Although we do not now see things as they are, in and of themselves, but through the mediation of signs, these signs are not corrupted versions of the "really real". Rather, what we cognize, semiotically, are actualities that are meaningfully related to metaphysical reals with which they are continuous, the creative Source of which we one day "will know, even as we are known", as the Christian apostle Paul teaches.

However, I hasten to add that Peirce's brand of realism is quite unique, even idiosyncratic. It is the product of his attempt to create an evolutionary architectonic unifying realism with a qualified constructivism – the independence of objects of perception from thought, expressed phenomenologically in their resistance to our attempts to interpret them in unlimited ways, with the fact of the creatively generative action of thinking in recasting, reforming, and revising the actual nature of these objects vis-a-vis their meaning within our transactions with reality. Hence, Peirce simultaneously maintains a vision of the objective nature of reality as, within limits, relative to human interpretation "in general", as he put it. This is another aspect of Peirce's thought about which it is difficult to establish clarity, as he offers diverse and opaque statements of his views on realism versus idealism. Carl Hausman (1993) attempts to clarify this matter by arguing that Peirce presents us with what he calls a "weaker kind of realism" (p. 147) than those found in objectivist and materialist philosophies, which Peirce dismisses outright as mechanistic. Rather, says Hausman, this is an episteme that defines the developing processes of cognition as progressing toward a final point of convergence with what Peirce calls "the final object of inquiry", an Absolute existing as an ideal limit on, and penultimate goal of our cognizing. This is not the ideal object asserted by Kant's transcendental idealism, which exists as an inferred, fixed and immaterial absolute that we reason, through deduction, *must* exist to allow for the very possibility of thought itself. Rather, Hausman says, it is one that Peirce understands as a continually evolving "actual inexhaustible actuality", one whose determinative and limiting function over thinking exists in dialectical unison with a boundless indeterminacy that allows and invites development, including the spontaneous emergence of innovation and novelty. Together, these qualities form a co-dependent and mutually defining unity of fixity and change that is the ontological basis of all development in the structure of Being. It is for this reason that Peirce sees the final, ideal object of truth toward which cognition aims as a "may-be", one that is not determined in advance but rather is partly constituted by the intrusion of chance events into the processional, forward-moving flow of life: "at any time an element of pure chance survives and will remain until the world becomes an absolutely perfect, rational and symmetrical system, in which mind is at last crystallized in the absolutely distant future", as he states (Peirce, 1891). In the Peircean episteme regularity and alterability, including changes generated by chance, are mutually conditioned in an ontological evolution that in Buddhist metaphysics is called "co-dependent mutual arising". Among other things, this is a dynamic and prolific interface of stability and metamorphosis, co-constructive factors in our experience of the world's intelligibility acting to instantiate what we might call an infinitely productive "coherent indeterminism" (or, conversely, an "indeterminate coherence"). Peirce's atypical realism is also partly indebted to the Platonic concept of ideal forms, which he reinterprets as evolving transcendental categories of experience that are consummated in temporality. As Peirce states in a talk called *The Logic of the Universe*, "we must suppose that the existing universe, with all its arbitrary secondness, is an offshoot from, or an arbitrary determination of, a world of ideas, a Platonic world …" (1884b/1934, p. 6.194). And, expanding on Plato, he notes that the *way* these eternal forms develop is through the minutiae of human lived experience, our phenomenological entanglement in the actual fabric of the world's worlding.

Herein we find the basis of Peirce's denial of necessitarianism, the notion that the cosmos develops according to a mechanistic, predetermined program. Rather, he asserts, the cosmos is capable of real spontaneity (Peirce, 1892). He vetoes the idea of a necessary outcome to the flux of creation based upon the ontological illimitability and fecundity of the Absolute object of knowledge, a property in which human mental processes also partake, albeit to a lesser degree. This is the ontological ground of freedom as a constituent of Being, and which humans experience in their capacity to discern possibilities not immediately "given", or even contradicted, by the datum of experience.

Peirce argues for our qualified but real participation in the (in principle) unbounded freedom and potentiality of the Absolute. He arrives at this assertion by analyzing the relationship of the concepts of infinity and possibility. One of these arguments concerns the veiled presence of the infinite within our experience of the passing stream of thoughts. Regarding this, Hausman points out that, "Peirce says that consciousness does not embrace a present idea in a finite interval of time. If it did, we could have no access to past ideas, for each idea would be contained within limits" (p. 180). Peirce applies the concept of mathematical infinitesimals to explain this idea, one which Isaac Newton and Gottfried Wilhelm Leibniz formalized as the "infinitesimal" in calculus. Somewhat like Georg Wilhelm Friedrich Hegel, Peirce sees in the concept of infinite divisibility the generative power of "nothingness" or "negation": the more we divide a number, the more doing so generates ever smaller, also infinitely divisible fractions thereof. Applied to the process of thinking, what we experience as the discrete intervals in the temporal sequence of thought are infinitesimals, infinitely divisible "bracketed" moments in a continuous, uninterrupted mental stream that in principle is uncreated and unending. And it is this illimitability that allows for human freedom from brute necessity.

In this we may gain another angle on the intimate connection of Peirce's epistemology to his ambitious cosmology: the processes of human thought reflect the evolutionary processes of the cosmos itself, one which he characterizes as occurring under the principle of what he calls an *agapic* progress toward truth (from the Greek *agape*, the mutual love of God and humans). This points directly to his implicit religiosity, which is an innovative metaphysic of the final unity of the transcendentally ideal and the normative, parochial habits and practices of humans. Hence, Peirce's developmental phenomenology of thinking is transpersonal: thought evolves both "within" the individual (I use the term only nominally, as he denies the notion of an ontologically discrete, self-contained subject) and also extends beyond the bounds of private experience, to an originary ontological Source that expresses itself in all phenomena, including thought itself.

This is a scientized mysticism of sorts, one emerging organically from the forward-looking optimism of a young Euro-North America, a future-directed attitude inculcated with the devout eschatological sensibilities of the Pilgrims. Hence, for example, Peirce sees humans as singularly graced with the ability to progress toward an objective knowledge of the cosmos. This includes knowledge of the nature of God, what he also calls the Absolute, as the penultimate object of our knowledge and generative source of our desire to know. Peirce portrays God as an evolving process rather than a static essence. In the domain of mind this metaphysical process is reflected in the spontaneous telic emergence of thoughts from the pre-reflective (what we may also call unconscious or preconscious) flow of experience of what he calls "Firstness". Put simply, Peirce asserts that the unbidden impulsions of Firstness emerge spontaneously from the abyss of preconsciousness. More poetically, Alfred North Whitehead (1929), whose theorizing is indirectly indebted to Peircean semiotics, defines this as the dark "penumbral" flow upon which experience rests, an undifferentiated, protean stream that is both utterly independent of, and also the very ground of consciousness.

Some commentators assert that it is incorrect to think of Peircean Firsts as objects of *immediate* experience because they are incapable of becoming objects of reflexive awareness.

For example, Joseph Randall (1978), argues that Peirce defines Firsts as beyond conscious representation, and therefore, as not actually experience-able. Expanding on Randall's analysis, I would say that the inaccessibility of Firsts means that their existence is inferred, on the assumption that thoughts must begin somehow and at some moment. Peirce is unclear about this point. For example, he often refers to Firstness as "felt", that is, as undifferentiated, pure *quale*, which is as much as saying that one is aware of having an affective experience of a First. However, I can agree with Randall's analysis, which seems to astutely distill Peirce's central notion from the often unduly complex and confusing nature of his manner of expression. If we accept Randall's interpretation, Firsts are hypothetical, inferred to begin as cognitively unrep-resentable objects existing in states of singularity, that is, as monads subsisting in isolation from their relation to other objects. For example, when we encounter fire, we take it in passively, as an individual, self-contained mental unit that "makes an impression" upon us, as it were, in the way that a piece of paper is "im-pressed upon" or imprinted by a stamp. But this impression is not conscious, rather, it is entirely pre-reflective. Therefore, for Peirce, thinking originates, not as a process consciously represented or determined but as "undergone", to use John Dewey's (1934/1958, p. 44) term, that is, inscribed upon us by Being itself.

From the primordial encounter with objects in the mode of Firstness, which cannot be integrated into consciousness and so are "un-recogniz-able", as it were, thought matures into concrete, hence, more differentiated perceptions of simple correlations between distinct phenomena, which Peirce calls "Seconds". At the level of Secondness, the interpretant triad evolves in complexity, such that it functions as a semiotic connecting principle conveying information about the *unifying* elements between the objects of knowledge, co-occurring dyads Peirce called "indexes". We perceive that, say, fire is accompanied by smoke, a basic two-way relation communicated to experience via indexical sign-interpretants. After recurring experiences of co-occurrence, such knowledge is encoded as a dependable Second, existing as a reflexive habit of thought. Together, the modes of First and Secondness exist as successive phases in a process that independently and intrusively "comes to mind". Having no other, contrasting object against which to bring their individual qualities into a state of differentiated clarity, Firsts fail to register in experience. But with the addition of dyadic relationships in Secondness, an experience of surprise and even shock may occur, as objects abruptly announce themselves in awareness, in what I take to be a kind of revelatory "a ha" moment. Seconds have import as brute physical associations but cannot be defined as having (or conveying) meaning *per se*, which only becomes possible in the self-reflexivity of Thirdness.

Indexical co-occurrences attain the status of self-reflexive meaningfulness when they mature into enduring experiential touchstones, acting to synthesize a variety of what initially seem to be wholly autonomous experiences. This unfolds in Peirce's category of Thirdness, in which we become capable of discerning connections between disparate dyadic indexes and weave these into wholly abstract, self-contained ideational networks. I think of these networks as semiotic galaxies existing with the vast universe of thought, integral aggregates, similar in some ways to Jung's (1947/1954) concept of unconscious complexes, whose diverse elements gravitate toward specific organizing themes. So too in Peirce's episteme: Thirds exist as harmonizing symbols, "dense" blendings of signs applicable across a range of circumstances, and whose connections are perceived in the abstract, as pure concepts. As the conclusion of the progressive broadening (or "transcendentalizing") of experience, Thirdness synthesizes the raw, undifferentiated emotive impact of indices in the mode of Firstness, and its elaboration in the encounter with the elemental dyads of Secondness, into abstract, "portable" representations of our being-in-the-world Pierce calls "generals", "laws", or, sometimes, "symbols". Our use of Thirds comprises the basis of our ability to navigate reality with a degree of real freedom. Hence, in our example fire may become an ascendant principle imparting certain important value-laden needs and experiences: home life (the hearth as familial gathering place), a compelling passion ("burning desire"), the birth of consciousness ("enlightenment"), and/or life itself.

Peircean sign theory serves as part of an inventive argument for the existence of an Absolute suprapersonal intelligence[2], existing as a telic movement of inquiry into the hypothesized ultimate origins of thinking, one progressing from doubt to reasonable certainty. That is, we might frame Peirce's episteme as a daring attempt to answer the question, "Where do our thoughts come from?". His response is a neo-scholastic (Scotian) argument from causation: we may form a reasonable guess by following the perpetual regression of linked chains of signs backward to a hypothesized source. To explain: signs initially interpret objects "immediately", to use Peirce's term, meaning that only elements of the object relevant to forming a certain interpretation, in the form of an unanalyzed impression, are conveyed to the perceiver. We do not conceive of the object in its totality, but through the constraints of a stage-specific interpretant. In the mode of Thirdness, our ability to form general (symbolic) cognitions is dependent upon being able to follow "chains" of signs toward this opaque but ultimate, ideal end: any given sign can interpret an object only because it is related to some other sign, which in turn interprets another object via another sign, and so on. If we could trace these sign-chains over many eons, well beyond the existence of the human species and, in fact, in a manner that would somehow finally traverse infinity, we would arrive at their metaphysical generative source: in Peircean terms, the general of all generals; in mathematical terms, the set of all sets; or, to the Kantian, the penultimate category of all categories.

Now, I should note that one important interpretation of Peircean teleology (with which I tend to agree) is that such an ideal end of inquiry is inconceivable and unattainable. A distinction between reality and actuality is relevant here: for Peirce, the ideal exists as a "real" endpoint that informs, and guides thought in the realm of the "actual" but is itself unrealizable in any total or final sense by virtue of the fact that it is infinite (Hausman, 1993), that is, a limitless *potentia*. In this we may see that Peirce (like Aristotle, upon whom he relies for certain ideas but cites only rarely) ascribes a dual role to these metaphysical objects, in that they act to inform the content of thought and a forward-going course for its unfolding, while they draw us toward them as thinking's penultimate goal. Hence, according to Peirce, the final object of our striving to know is also the originary Source of our capacity to think at all, as well as what Henri Bergson (1911) calls the *elan vital* (vital energy) propelling our wish to comprehend reality. In terms of our daily navigation of the world, if Peircean ideal objects of thought did not exist in their function as the metaphysical well-springs of our thinking, then it is difficult to account for the fact that we can meaningfully cognize and engage reality in even the most rudimentary way. We could not begin to conceive of experience apart from some concrete triadic interpretant at the level of Secondness. Therefore, for Peirce, the reality of a hypothesized Absolute may be inferred from the generalizability of symbolic consciousness. From this premise he asserts that the universe is a vast semiotic network, a veritable signifying puzzle, emanating from an intelligent Absolute mind that invites us to grasp its nature, and whose existence we may recognize, inferentially, by thinking systematically about the nature of thinking itself[3]. This Real object is "really" knowable, but ineffable and unobtainable in experience "actually".

In this integrative *telos* of co-constructive regularity and innovation, Peirce's well-known concept of abductive inference plays a crucial role. As we have seen, Peirce builds upon the notion of causation and progressive development by suggesting that the cooperation of human beings is also required to realize real change within spatio-temporal being. He proposes that this occurs specifically through the operation of what he called abductive logic, which, along with deduction and induction, he defines as one of the three methods of inferential reasoning through which we engage the world (Peirce, 1903/1934). For Peirce, it is abduction alone that is capable of unprecedented new insights into the structure of reality, whereas deduction and induction are confined to analysis of what is already given in experience. That is, only abduction functions according to the dictates of futurity and the possibility of novel ideas and insights. He states that it is "the only logical operation which introduces any new idea ... Deduction proves that something must be; induction shows that something actually is operative; abduction ... suggests that something may be" (Peirce, CSP 5.171). In this context, to say that something "may be", what William James calls a "live option" (James, 1897/1956), is to approach it with the logic of discovery rather than proof, one whose genesis exists as what we commonly refer to as a "hunch" or a "gut feeling". Rather than seeking out reasons in support of an already established hypothesis, abduction "makes an inference from effects to causes, from observations to their best explanations" (Niiniluoto, 1999, p. 39). As such, it is "an ampliative inference, which at best gives some credibility (or epistemic probability) to the conclusion" (Ibid., p. 39), that is, an inference that "amplifies" our comprehending of experience.

Without entertaining the logical audacity of our hunches, there could be no new learning or innovation, given that discovery proceeds by positing new, non-normative meanings from the givens of experience. Abduction is a form of reasoning "backward", or *a posteriori*, from an observed phenomenon to a fact believed to explain it, an antecedent factor not directly disclosed in experience. It is a form of reasoning considered fallacious in classical logic because it infers causes from effects. However, it is also a form of reasoning that is omnipresent in our daily lives. Despite its counter-logical form, it tends to "work" in the real world, not consistently (we regularly make minor and sometimes major mistakes in judgement) but dependably enough to make it a central means by which we accurately cognize reality. Implied here is the idea that we are constantly engaging reality based on a fundamental faith in its coherence and truth-disclosive nature;

and, further, that we are continuously compelled to do so in order to traverse the most mundane problems. For example, I observe that a door which was closed an hour before now stands open, an example of an immediate perception or First (a door) leaping immediately ahead to a Second (a door in relation to a passageway). Instantaneously and reflexively, I infer backward, so to speak, and form a governing hypothesis about an antecedent causal event: someone must have opened the door, a generalizable Third. Important to note here is that I have no way of proving this inference. A current of wind, ghost, or sudden change in the earth's gravitational field could also have opened the door. I may seek to verify my abductive conclusion objectively, perhaps locating a housemate who confirms that it was they who opened the door. But even then, I accept their statement on faith: after all, they may be deceiving me, suffering a memory lapse, or maybe they actually opened the door at some point in time but that this is not the true cause of the door's having **been open** when I saw it.

However, when it comes to abduction, "the proof is in the pudding", that is, an instrumentally productive, though in principle unprovable semiotic Third. This *de facto* metaphysical realism is unavoidable, as we cannot negotiate any experience without acting "as if" we see the world *just as it is*, that is, truthfully, whatever else we assert to be our theory of knowledge. We engage Being practically by acting with trust in its coherence, which I say is a *de facto* religious attitude – the evidence of things unseen, hoped for, or wagered to be actual, to paraphrase the apostle Paul. Now, it may seem to be a gigantic, unjustified leap from abductively reasoning that someone opened a door to, say, the premise that an intelligent deity creates and sustains life. However, in Peirce's episteme the latter is, in principle, no more or less certain than the former. Ultimately, each conclusion can only be judged by the degree to which acting on its truth-claims enable us to gracefully traverse experience; that is, whether it bears fruit pragmatically by smoothing the way from doubt to reasonable certainty and enables us to fashion verifiably positive, perhaps innovative pathways through existence.

To realize the hidden potentialities within experience via abduction requires a deconstruction of our usual habits of reasoning, the preliminary step to what Peirce (1908/2020) calls "musement". Musing is a distinctly creative and future-directed cognitive activity. It bears similarities to psychoanalytic free association, as well as to Jung's (1921/1990) description of intuition, the free mental play with certain possibilities implied although not explicitly present or "given" within an experience. Musement is an experimental form of thinking within which abduction may apprehend meaningful content: it is grounded in futurity and is the sole manner of cognizing that expresses the future-orientation of psychic reality. Abductive thought requires tolerance for uncertainty, paired with trust in the essential reasonableness, and perhaps benevolence, of the *telos* of unfolding world-historical processes. Within abduction are key elements in the phenomena of faith, hope, and the courage to "hang in there" so as to continue to sportively manipulate the constantly emerging stream of mental contents, minus any clear understanding as to "who" or "what" generates this process and where it may lead. Metaphysically construed, it is also an expression of trust in the essential coherence and "good will" of a cosmos that makes such a form of thinking possible. It is revelatory and therefore radically "anti-doctrinal", shedding the false assurances of veridical accuracy found in all manner of "isms", which Peirce believes rely solely on static mental representations of past experience reapplied, mechanically, to new circumstances.

Similarities in Jung and Peirce's Revelatory Metaphysics

As one might infer, a full comparison of Jung's and Peirce's epistemes would require several hefty volumes (and maybe a lifetime of research). Here I only wish to tentatively "flesh out" the underlying unitive spirit of Jungian and Peircean thought by touching upon two areas of general concordance between their theories. These are their shared status as authors of "scientific-metaphysical" visions of human nature and endeavor, and the role of play and "musing" or freely associative thinking in the realization of new possibilities. In what follows I dwell largely, though not exclusively, on the similarities between their thinking. To reiterate what I noted earlier, I do not wish to assert a facile and preemptive unity between their ideas, which clearly diverge in many respects. By no means are they saying, "the same thing differently", though I think they share a quite similar general stance toward experience and the structure of reality itself, one which I will now try to tease out.

Jung and Peirce's Revisions of Kantian Epistemology: Toward a Scientific Metaphysics

Arguably, underlying Jung's conception of how we know and engage the world is his theory of archetypes: the innate universal cognitive templates, what Jacobi (1959) defines as inherited, non-specific mental possibilities of representation of universal human experiences that predispose us to interpret the world as we do. To achieve an epistemological/metaphysical grounding of knowledge in the flow of experience, both Jung and Peirce look to Kant's epistemology, his theory of the innate categories of experience he also intended to serve to justify the conviction of a suprapersonal source of Being.

As noted above, both Jung and Peirce reinterpret the Kantian categories to serve their purposes, a difference between their efforts being that Jung, unlike Peirce, misunderstands key dimensions of Kantian thought. I will have more to say about this later. For now, let us explore their uses of Kant, with an eye to framing how the amazing endurance in human experience of religious resolve may be shown to be intellectually and, indeed, *scientifically* credible, not simply by appeal to notions of "intuition", as important to discovery as it is, but also according to the standards of evidence and verifiability of the scientific method itself. As we will see, this is a concept of science extending beyond the material and efficient domains of analysis idealized by modernity, to include metaphysics, a branch of the "queen of sciences", philosophy. In this understanding of what constitutes science, the metaphysical is analyzed using an admixture of natural science buoyed by formal analysis of the cognitive processes enabling reasoned inferences about the suprasensible, which supersedes nature as given and so is a closed book to methodologies confined to the study of material processes.

Natural science offers us a way of understanding the world. As such, it is founded upon certain epistemological principles and assumptions which are necessary to justify any claim that we are accurately reasoning about reality. Neo-pragmatist Sami Pihlstrom (2003), in his critical review of pragmatist uses of Kantian transcendental idealism, suggests that we may think of Peirce's appropriation of Kant as yielding what he calls a "scientific metaphysics" that he says, "naturalizes the transcendental". In this context, I take this to mean a science based on an epistemology that conceives of scientific thinking, which is focused upon our lived or "natural" experience of the world, as made possible by the inherited innate categories of knowledge of which Kant spoke, *a priori* modes of experience and thought transcending the parochial particulars of experience to produce general or "symbolic" knowledge of the kind that supports human thriving. Kant presents his epistemology in the form of an argument based in reasoning about the conditions for the possibility of cognizing objects in experience: that is, he seeks to explain how uniquely human forms of "knowing", which transcend the concrete fixity of particulars as well as the limits of time and space, is possible. He argues that to comprehend this we must reason backward (or abductively, to use Peirce's term) to infer some property of mind that must necessarily exist apart from and prior to experience. He concludes that this property exists as various *a priori*, eternal modes of encountering experience enabling us to cognize abstractly, free from bondage to the constraints of environmental "givens".

Pihlstrom argues the interesting point that Kant's popular reputation as a "pure" idealist, one conceiving of the categories as ontologically separate from and wholly antecedent to lived experience, is not entirely true to the logical methodology of his theory. It is not that this interpretation is wrong, as far as it goes, but that it does not delve far enough into its nuances. Specifically, it is a view that neglects the subtle and in some ways counterintuitive manner in which Kant presents his mature argument for the epistemic categories. Let us put this in historical perspective: upon finding that his initial arguments for transcendental idealism in the *Critique of Pure Reason* were misconstrued by his contemporary Berkely as supporting a kind of solipsism, in which the "outer" or "objective" reality of objects is subjected to fundamental doubt, Kant issued a revised account of his views in a second edition (Kant, 1781/2000). In that revision is his attempt to move beyond what he took as the either/or of two misconceptions about his view of how we comprehend objects: naïve realism (sensory experience or what he deemed "empirical intuition" as directly revelatory of things-in-themselves) and an equally naïve unqualified denial of any possibility whatsoever of confidently asserting the existence of things-in-themselves, which easily translates into pessimism about even the most rudimentary empirical truth-claims generated by thought, sometimes to the point of asserting a blanket skepticism about the datum of experience.

Kant's counter-argument to these unsatisfying models is highly original, provocative, and radical even by contemporary standards In it he focuses upon the impossibility of extracting/abstracting the ontic category of spatiality from objects, asserting that it is our mental representations themselves that endow spatiality with actual, objective being. I understand this to mean that because our empirical acquaintance with space is necessarily relative to our observational position, it cannot be said to exist solely in objects-in-themselves (unlike, say, color). However, neither does Kant opt for a radical idealism to explain our intuition of space, as Berkeley believes he does. Rather, he asserts, the objective being of space inheres in its property as a formal, *a priori* category of knowing, and in this way acts as an onto-logical domain bridging observer and observed object with the result that spatiality comes into being *as a function of being perceived by an interpret-ing subject.* This strikes me as a prescient anticipation of both the findings of quantum physics and the more general post-modern concept of certain dimensions of reality as co-constructed, within limits, via our conscious-ness of them. Writes Kant:

> One must note well this paradoxical but correct proposition, that nothing is in space except what is represented in it. For space itself is nothing other than representation; consequently, what is in it must be contained in representation, and nothing at all is in space except insofar as it is really represented in it.
>
> (1781/2000, pp. 374–375)

Following this, Kant asserts:

> Every outer perception therefore immediately proves something real in space, or rather *is itself the real*; to that extent, *empirical realism is beyond doubt,* i.e., to our outer intuitions there corresponds something real in space.
>
> (1781/2000, p. 375; italics mine)

John Brady (2018) explains this element of Kant's episteme by noting that for Kant:

> Matter is sensation. This is not just an arbitrary stipulation, or skeptical confession that we cannot go from the existence of sensation to the exist-ence of external matter. *Kant means it quite literally.* If space is an ideal formal frame of experience, 'external objects' just become those objects of 'outer sense' who are defined by being composed of sensation that is organized within the ideal frame of space. Thus, the spatially organized objects of empirical intuition, as representations marked and composed of sensation, are as real as real can be.
>
> (No page number available; italics mine)

Nick Stang (2016) cites another premise of Kant's idealism that is relevant to this topic, specifically, his assertion that real phenomena in the world impress themselves experientially upon consciousness. He uses this to make the more general point that Kant does not seek to instill anything like a fundamental skepticism about the situatedness of mind in a real world that acts upon it through what he terms "affection". He states that Kant insists:

> that his idealism is merely formal: he has argued only that the form of objects is due to our minds, not their matter (cf. Kant's Dec. 4, 1792, letter to J.S. Beck (Ak. 11:395)). While the form-matter distinction in Kant's philosophy is a complex matter in its own right, Kant's point seems to be that the matter of experience, the sensory content that is perceptually and conceptually structured by space and time, and the categories, respectively, is not generated by the mind itself, but is produced in our minds through (what he called) affection by mind-independent objects, things in themselves ... Thus, Kant can claim that only the *form* of experience is mind-dependent, *not its matter*; the matter of experience depends upon a source outside of the mind.
>
> (No page number; italics original)

In sum, both the above quoted commentators try, in their own ways, to disabuse us of the habit of interpreting Kant as promoting a radical mind/world dualism, a manner of seeing his writings that I believe may reflect our modernist (and post-modernist) compulsion to doubt experience more than an agenda central to Kantian epistemology. Pihlstrom is thinking in the same general vein as Stang when he makes the elegantly practical and characteristically pragmatist observation that Kant, like all of us, I suggest, begins to reason about how we know what we know with the assumption that there actually *is* something called "experience" which we "have" of the world in the first place. Experience is a given, and the necessary point of departure for all thinking. We cannot even doubt the truthfulness or accuracy of experience minus the belief that we have experiences, and that these may direct us toward a clear grasp of the world. Pihlstrom writes:

> Kant himself took something contingent and natural for granted ... (H)e did not attempt to provide an answer to the skeptic from a neutral, universal, universally accepted standpoint. He took as given the contingent fact that we *have* experiences of an objective world and then tried to

determine the necessary conditions of the possibility of such experiences ... Indeed, (therefore) why shouldn't we, as Peirce taught us, stop doubting as philosophers what we do not doubt as human beings?

(Pihlstrom, 2003, pp. 159–160)

Hence, a scientific metaphysics is one that, as Pihlstrom writes in the above quote, begins from a presumption of "something contingent and natural". And what is "natural" in this context is human experience itself, our existential status as beings that begin our interpretive activity from a position of immersion in a world always and already there. Only Kant's affirmation of this, in principle, entirely unprovable assumption allows him to proceed to construct his complex transcendental metaphysics. Hence, in this view, Kant's epistemology stands or falls upon the humble foundational assumption that we really *do* have experiences, and that these experiences are revelatory of what Husserl (1936/1970) calls a *lebens-welt* ("life-world"), one whose nature is discoverable. This is not a process of discovery to be construed "naively", as a simple assertion of direct correspondence between sensation and objective reality, but through a correct understanding of the inherent structure of cognizing itself. From this it follows that, in Kant, experience is a mediated but essentially trustworthy experience of *an objectively real world*; and that the existence of the innate epistemic categories should not be conceived as obstacles to believing our interpretations of the world but are in fact what *allow* a basically trustworthy empirical experience (as Brady states, of its spatiality) to occur at all. Hence, in this sense Kant indirectly supports Peirce's claim that experience, however baffling, is, on balance, trustworthy, and in this he comes as close to proposing a Peircean weak metaphysical realism as is possible without actually warranting the title of realist. In daily life, this understanding of cognition is expressed in a simple resolve to trust the essentially truth-disclosing nature of immediate experience and be guided, as it were, by our hunches and intuitions. To reiterate a central pragmatist thesis, our best and, ultimately, only evidence that these are truthful is that they "pay dividends" instrumentally; that is, that they tend, by and large, to "pave the way" and "get us somewhere" instrumentally and self-evidently useful to our thriving.

This clarification of Kant's categories is relevant to other dimensions of Peirce's oeuvre, as described earlier. Peirce does not discern the implied phenomenology in Kant that Pihlstrom identifies, and so toiled for years to reconstruct the Kantian categories so as to make them compatible with the *de facto* phenomenology of his metaphysical realism. However, if we believe Pihlstrom's interpretation of Kant, this may not have been entirely necessary, given that there is already an implicit if highly qualified weak realism in Kant's theory of the categories. Citing implications of Susan Haack's (1992) analysis of Peircean realism, Pihlstrom notes that Peirce engages in this project as part of his desire to found the empiricism of scientific reasoning upon a sound philosophical basis. Pihlstrom cites Haack's summary of her position to illuminate the centrality of realism in Peirce's scientific metaphysics:

> If laws and general types were not real, but were figments of the mind, Science (sp) would indeed be ... a (Wittgensteinian) 'put-up job'; and it is hard to see how one could defend even a modest idea that, whether or not it succeeds, science legitimately aspires to find out how things are. If laws and general types are real, however, there is something for the classifications we devise and the laws we postulate to get right or wrong.
>
> (pp. 42–42)

A final implication of the foregoing is that metaphysical realism, which often strikes modern minds as a naïve if not self-deceived throwback to medieval scholasticism, is in fact necessary for science to exist in any credible form (Pihlstrom, 2003, p. 157).

Like Peirce, Jung relies heavily upon Kant's episteme to explain and argue for the veracity of his theories. This is particularly evident in his use of the Kantian categories to forward his notion of the presence of innate psychic archetypal formations as the primal "lenses" through which we engage the world. Philosophically, Jung's argument for the archetypal basis of our constructions of reality is an application of Kant's argument from the subjective conditions of knowledge to the inferential hypothesis of a property of mind that is not bound to the limits of the merely given, material *quanta* of experience. Jung adheres to the transcendental idealism of Kantian thinking, including what is widely presumed to be the unqualified nature of Kant's verdict that the *a priori* epistemic categories bar us from comprehending the *ding-an-sich*, the thing as it is "really". He argues that archetypal ideas may be interpreted as examples of the Kantian categories: like the categories, the archetypes are immaterial structures empty of content. Hence, there are no directly inherited memories passed on *in toto*, as Lamarckianism holds[4]. Rather, Jung posits archetypes as contentless forms or mental templates allowing us to cognize the world and dictate the innate structure, including the limits, of our cognitions. The archetypes cause certain objects in experience to stand out as "bracketed" in consciousness, to use Husserl's term, when encountered. These immediately strike us as figural, that is, as "figuring" prominently in our final symbolic processing of a total experiential situation. Hence, they are analogous to the emotionally evocative Seconds described by Peirce, which burst forth upon awareness. An archetypal situation is activated, or "constellated", to use Jung's term, according to particular classes of circumstances in which some aspect of life in the world confronts us.

Implied in Jung's thinking of how archetypes are expressed in daily life is the intimate relationship of the *a priori* archetypal predispositions to the phenomenology of a particular lived experience. For example, when in the presence of someone we find sexually desirable, we are immediately flooded with physiological arousal accompanied by fantasies, the specific content of which derive largely from our singular personal history. Further derived from personal sources is the intensity, scope, and import of these fantasies, which our novel developmental histories render idiomatic and unique, our "ownmost". That said, the *fact* of being predisposed to sexual arousal is transpersonal, hence, an archetypal property of mind existing as a Peircean "general", an impersonal law of human nature. This is a key Kantian notion, namely, that the transcendental categories of knowing are revealed temporally in, and may be inferred from, "localized" particulars. Like Kant, Jung asserts that we can and should nurture the self-reflexivity and freedom of a conscious position in relation to the imperious potency of archetypes, so as to avoid being drawn helplessly into fateful patterns of thought and action. Consciousness, when able to flexibly apply a variety of generals to the analysis of a problem, forwards what Jung **calls** the *telos* of the individuation process. As a result, one progresses a bit closer to realizing certain unique potentialities heretofore dormant within the unconscious or only provisionally formed in consciousness.

Now, many commentators find Jung's understanding of Kant to be logically muddled, at times, based on misreading his ideas, and thus, as failing to justify the notion that archetypes predispose us to certain forms of experience. Among the most severe of these criticisms is that Jung conflates the Kantian categories of the noumenal and phenomenal modes of knowing, that is, what Kant deemed the realm of the "concepts of pure reason" with lived experience of phenomena. In doing so Jung incorrectly implies, without qualification, that direct or "empirical" knowledge of things-in-themselves is possible, which these critics assert is not Kant's conclusion, as well as a contradiction of what Jung himself elsewhere claims to be the case (Bishop, 1999; deVoogd, 1984; Hayman, 1999). Put in Kantian language, Jung is held to account for collapsing the categories of phenomenal experience and the in-itself unknowable noumena, thus as much as saying that things that Kant deemed without absolutely verifiable being are directly and immediately knowable. Now, I believe these critics are essentially correct in accusing Jung of misunderstanding Kant on this score. However, it strikes me that Jung's impressionistic and imprecise understanding of the categories need not be framed only as valueless error and dismissed. That is to say, Jung's use of Kant *is* erroneous, but not in the global sense asserted by his critics, nor in a way that renders his mistaken collapse of the noumenal and phenomenal entirely without merit, inasmuch as this is suggestive of the "deeper" reading of Kant outlined previously. Instead, I suggest that his application of Kant to argue for his archetypal psychology is rendered more plausible when we consider the aforementioned, more thoroughgoing reading of Kant, which, as I have noted, reveals that the philosopher's assertion of the impossibility of direct empirical knowledge of objects in the world is actually quite qualified, restrained, and ultimately does allow for an enduring trust in the phenomenology of experience. To state this more exactly, Jung's fundamental error consists in failing to comprehend the nuances of Kant's concept of the relationship between the phenomenal and noumenal domains. However, he correctly infers that Kant's understanding of the relation of the knowing subject to the external world allows us to affirm, in a qualified manner, that there is an indirectly but convincingly knowable world that is always and already "there". As I noted above, Kant simply and straightforwardly asserts that there must be actual objects in the world that actually *do* activate the phenomenon we call "experience". His intention was to spell out the formal conditions of being "minded" that allow for experience to take in and respond to these "really real" objects. Kant never sought to enforce epistemologically unwarranted skepticism about whether we can know the world as it is, apart from the *cogito*. In his own funny way, Jung seems to read Kant correctly on this score. However, he errs in presenting this insight in an unsophisticated manner, by recklessly projecting a pervasive and naïve strong metaphysical realism onto Kant's epistemology that Kant himself explicitly opposed. Yet, despite this misinterpretation, Jung's faulty knowledge of Kant enables him to play creatively with the theory, to "muse", in Peircean terms, free from the demand to arrive at an adamantine, objectively "correct" grasp of its tenets. In doing so, I believe that he also inadvertently stumbles upon the genuinely phenomenological or "naturalized" genesis of Kant's categories described by Pihlstrom. That is to say that Jung arrives, through a kind of intuitive groping about in a state of partial ignorance, at the same, logically defensible reading of Kant that Pihlstrom arrives at through his more informed and objectively credible reinterpretation of the philosopher's work. This extends to Jung's (1961/1989, p. 256) assertion that human self-reflexive consciousness quite literally calls the objective world, including its **spatio-materiality**, into being, a notion that he did not develop with reference to Kant, but which certainly agrees with Kant's provocative and little-known belief that spatiality springs into being the moment it becomes represented mentally.

Understood thus, Jung's improper grasp of the relationship of the Kantian phenomenal and noumenal realms illustrates Peirce's concept of the self-correcting nature of induction, presumably including inductive reasoning that starts with a clearly erroneous premise (Mayo, 2005). However, for Peirce, induction is not self-correcting simply because of its methodology. In addition, one must genuinely desire to know the truth, as he states: "If you really want to learn the truth, you will, by however devious a path, be surely led into the way of truth, at last" (Peirce, 5:582). In common parlance, one's "heart must be in the right place". Jung's mistaken grasp of this dimension of Kantian thought seems to derive from his wish (one he perhaps "felt" somewhat indiscriminately more than thought) to revise Kant's theory in such a way as to ground the transcendent categories in a metaphysically real, phenomenally discoverable life-world. I suggest that the fact that here he distorts Kant's episteme does not necessarily mean that he was not "on to something". Of course, the intrusion of this, probably unconscious ambition into Jung's interpretation obstructed the presentation of his theory of archetypes by creating conceptual unclarity, as well as the impression that he is an unintelligent or careless scholar. However, a more charitable view of Jung's error is suggested by Peirce's theory of the process of how knowledge develops. As outlined earlier, for Peirce, the realization of new truths begins with the advent of undifferentiated, purely qualitative Firsts forming spontaneously in pre-consciousness. These metamorphose over time into Seconds, which thrust themselves upon experience as novel realizations of logical relations between distinct but unrelated nuclei of meaningful relations. In Secondness each semiotic nodal unit exists in its own particular, localized semiotic world, and, as such, lacks generalizability. It is here that I think we may cite some analogies to what Jung describes as the process of intuition, one of the four innate means by which individuals are predisposed to interpret and judge experience (the other three being thinking, feeling, and sensing). Jung first outlines his concept of the four modes of knowing in *Psychological Types* (1921/1990), an early work whose theories rely heavily upon his application of the Kantian categories. Intuition, as one of Jung's neo-Kantian preexistent approaches to reality, is an epistemological mode that begins in a vague sense of some new meaning as having "dawned", unbidden and unexpected, upon ego-consciousness (1921/1990, pp. 30). Like the other three modes of knowing, intuition can be outer-directed (extraverted) or inner-directed (introverted). Jung thinks of intuition as sometimes able to transcend the givens of merely egoic understanding, because it is unusually permeable to discerning the teleological direction of certain events in the external world (in its extraverted form) or potential new understandings or collective shifts in worldview emanating from the unconscious (in its introverted form) (1921/1990, p. 79). This is the origin of the "hunch", consisting of an evolving feeling of some larger, as-yet-incomplete but developing significance growing of its own accord in experience. Like Peirce, Jung understands thought as originating in an ill-defined, vague set of compelling but indeterminate impressions; he describes intuition as embodying the telic nature of this meaning-making process in unusually pure form. If followed faithfully on the path from ill-defined feelings to coherent concepts, intuition yields new symbolic understandings of reality. This is somewhat like Peirce's notion of the emergence of Thirds, in which scattered dyads of meaningful relations have coalesced and become meaningfully related to one another in a state of overarching unity. As in Jung, Peirce sees this as the domain of symbolic thinking. While Peirce's understanding of symbols is unlike Jung's in important respects, both posit these with reference to Kant's transcendental idealism: in Peirce, generalized Thirds transcend the limits of space and time and so can be applied to analyzing vast swaths of phenomena beyond the concrete limits of the merely given; also like Jung, Peirce believes an immaterial Absolute to be the metaphysical origin and final goal of human symbolic engagement with the world.

There is more to say as we consider the role of intuition in the development of science, and particularly the "scientific metaphysics" that I suggest Peirce and Jung seek to legitimize. As we may recall, Peirce defines science as proceeding to make new discoveries through a formally systemized use of this universal manner of knowing, which is to say that, as Albert Einstein (1931/2009) suggests, "Imagination is more important than knowledge. For knowledge is limited to all we know and understand, while imagination embraces the entire world, and all there ever will be to know and understand" (p. 97). Interestingly, in this statement, Einstein, one of the modern era's most important and original scientists, implies what Peirce and Jung understand as the teleological nature of genuinely original thinking, and its origins in states of curious uncertainty and bafflement supplemented by an underlying sense of some larger realization in the offing. It seems to me that Einstein's category of imagination, Peirce's theory of abduction, and Jung's concept of intuition share a common belief in the preeminence of *a posteriori* reasoning in the scientific endeavor, and all of life. And, lest we forget, science, at least in principle, is founded upon the conviction of the generative and truth-revealing interplay of error and truth. That is to say, while of course the practicing researcher seeks correct conclusions about phenomena, "pure" science does not quibble unduly over the fact that we regularly misread and misinterpret phenomena. Rather, it understands error as being as important as the event of having successfully uncovered some new truth in the process of discovery. This is not only because error impels us to reformulate our hypotheses so as to arrive at better formulations, but also because "missing the mark" is potentially revelatory of surprising new truths not immediately or even directly logically related to an experimenter's initial interests. Of course, the person who imposes a dubious hypothesis upon the datum of experience may be falsely "reading in" conclusions that are objectively not there to be had. However, often enough such a person may also be "reading beyond", however clumsily, what is given in their approach to the datum. This is an act, witting or not, of creatively discerning some factor not straightforwardly suggested when the issue under investigation is assumed to contain within itself, as it immediately presents, all that can be thought of and concluded regarding its nature.

This is what is meant by the American idiom, "thinking outside the box". Put differently, to read "beyond" is to grasp some object of experience as more than a collection of parts. What is discerned in this way may be an inference, result, or final verdict that is actually "there" to be discovered, including those existing only as possible implications, but which require the presence of a self-reflecting mind to coax them to the moment of birth. These are diverse kinds of realizations requiring the action of imagination, abductive inference, or intuition (call it what we may) to elicit them from embeddedness in the evidence as given. And this, I suggest, points to the revelatory potential of mind as embedded in the processes of an emergent world, in what Peirce sees as a transsubjective movement toward the final limits of truth, the immanent, here-and-now evidence of which is found in the knowing subject's ability to tease out and bring to light embryonic possibilities in the known world that otherwise would never have been realized.

Hence, understood in a Peircean sense, Jung's mistaken use of Kant may be grasped as one of the chance disruptions in reality by which new discoveries occur. The "intuitive function", as he calls it, was well known to him, given his own proclivity for thinking beyond apparently veridical "facts", by employing a process of imaginatively inferring what is *not* directly conveyed by undue adherence to the security of Occam's *Razor*, which states that the best, most likely truthful conclusions are the logically simplest, which in practice typically means the most "self-evident". In contrast, intuitive thinking is vitally important to realizing new knowledge, because it infuses thought, formally scientific and otherwise, with the singularly human capacity to transcend and problematize the seeming fixity of the seemingly plainly obvious, as Kant argues. In Jung, intuition is perhaps the most innately creative of the different epistemic modes, a reason for which is that its psychic tap root is the function of mind as, within limits, discerning and "calling forth" new realities that could not come to be without the active presence of the human observer. The transcendence of reason allows us to see reality as more than the sum of its parts: likewise, intuition, as one of Jung's categories of reasoning, starts with the objectively factual but infers some larger scheme of meanings hidden within its folds. This includes realizations which may be entirely unprecedented and initiate the creation of new objective facts that would never have existed minus the intervention of a human being having become consciously engaged in contemplating what lies beyond reality's givens. In this way we are all "sub-creators" of Being, as neo-pragmatist Giovanni Maddalena (2015) states in his neo-Peircean account of what he describes as creative "gestures". Related to this is Peirce's Christianized belief in the ontologically exceptional nature of human creatureliness, a belief more or less shared by Jung, as evident in his foregoing contemplations on the singularity of human consciousness. Implied in their oeuvres is an anthropocentric theme of the Absolute as having set humans in a unique position of self-reflectively engaging the world, and in doing so furthering the transpersonal work of cosmic (*agapic*) evolution.

I suggest that intuition, as a function of mind that transgressively breaks through the limits of the given to enable new discoveries and novel objective facts, is inherently "disruptive", in the same way that Peirce referred to new discoveries as formed when the habit-taking nature of reality is disrupted by the outbreak of chance events. It seems to me that intuition, more than other kinds of reasoning, is intertwined with the same processes constituting chance occurrences. Of course, the nature of "chance" is that it deals, not with inevitabilities, but with unrealized yet conceivable probabilities. When the human subject engages nature with an eye to realizing what may lie beyond the stasis of its existential givens, they are banking on something that is a more or less daring exercise in a game of chance, one based in hope rather than certainty. The existential structure of the probable is in uncertainty, which itself is related to its lack of definite, predictable forms, its status as a "may-be". To intuit a "may-be" from a forthrightly given "is" involves an initial act of introducing flux into Being, a sudden and arbitrary dis-ordering of its familiar rhythms. The results of doing so may easily outrun attempts at control: betting on probables interrupts the habit-taking, perpetually recurring character of purely natural phenomena, sending these into degrees of disarray that, as Jung believes, are the birth pangs accompanying all new forms of development, including the psychic development he calls individuation. Hence, as in Peirce, Jung forwards a theory of possibilities becoming actualities through an evolutionary trajectory starting in vagueness and disorder, and moving across time into defined, orderly, and finally "habitual" forms. If we assume that minds are localized, self-contained phenomena that are the site of correct or incorrect interpretations of phenomena, then Jung's misreading of Kant is simply wrong and that is that. However, if we understand the principles of scientific discovery correctly, as I think Peirce did, namely, as a communal endeavor in which new realizations are achieved through a harmonious cooperation of minds, then Jung's error may be viewed as part of a transsubjective process of discovery. Furthermore, it is sometimes the case that what appears at first blush to be error can contain hidden nuggets of publicly verifiable truth not plainly spelled out in the object of investigation, but "hidden in plain sight", truth that other investigators may identify.

In Jung, the teleology of all intellectual discovery unfolds in unison with the events of daily life. For this reason, he describes the archetypes as becoming constellated in the particularity of a given life, the nature of which is a constantly developing and indeterminate process. As with many other matters, Jung is not as clear about this as we might wish. However, his aim to sketch out an ontological unity of the transcendent and the immanent through the notion of archetypes as made manifest, or actual, in "real time" is not hard to detect. As only one example, he conceives of treatment as a dialogue between two minds, which he analogizes to a uniquely transformative "chemical reaction" of mutual influence, a distinctive, irreducible event entirely without precedent (Jung, 1933/2009, p. 41). Related to this, further evidence for Jung's concept of the transcendent dimensions of mind as evolving in engagement with a real world is found in the recognition among some Jungians that his theory resonates with those of empirical neuroscience. This has led to a plethora of attempts to elucidate the nature and action of archetypes through neuroscientific findings about human attachment and the effects of environmental influences upon brain activity. Specifically, this trend of research cites the value of these natural science models for demonstrating the way in which inherited neurocognitive structures compel us to attach, instinctively, to other human objects, thus activating and over time "filling in" the archetypal predispositions by provoking their innate potentialities to unfold in object relationships, relational patterns that progressively take on more individual specificity and definiteness (Knox, 2003). A product of this appeal to brain research and attachment theory is, I believe, a "naturalized" transcendence, along the lines described by Pihlstrom. It further serves to establish Jung's theory of archetypes as a scientific metaphysics, also as defined by

Pihlstrom.

Describing Jung's archetypal theory as a scientific metaphysics also seems warranted by the fact that he was perpetually, as one of his biographers, Frank McLynn, states, "tacking between philosophy and biology" (McLynn, 1996, p. 306). Jung himself says as much. For example, in *On the Nature of the Psyche* he writes, as if by way of explanation, that this syncretic approach was demanded by the emergent complexity of the subject matter of his investigations. Arguably, this is the genesis in Jung's approach of what Pihlstrom calls a scientific metaphysics, one that expands the domain of natural science by the addition of metaphysical speculation. Says Jung:

I fancied I was working along the best scientific lines, establishing facts, observing, classifying, describing causal and functional relations, only to discover in the end that I had involved myself in a net of reflections which extend far beyond natural science and ramify into the fields of philosophy, theology, comparative religion and the humane sciences in general.

(Jung, 1947/1954, para. 421)

What Jung describes as the unforeseen need for an admixture of diverse disciplines may help us to understand what is sometimes described by Jung scholars, often in exasperation, as his waffling between vastly different definitions of archetypes. As Knox observes, these definitions may be variously classified as, "abstract organizing structures, sometimes as eternal realities, then again as core meanings; on other occasions, he adopted a very sophisticated ethological viewpoint, in which he identified archetypes as manifestations of instinct ..." (2003, p. 26). I suggest that Pihlstrom's concept of a scientific metaphysics, which he applies to Peirce's work, may also allow us to organize the hodgepodge of Jung's theorizing. Valentin Balanovskiy (2017) has much the same view of the empirical status of Jung's thought. He asserts that Jung attempts to form a scientific psychology related to but essentially different from strictly naturalistic science. This he terms a "science of individuation", one derived, in part, from what I earlier characterized as Jung's playfully "musing" if somewhat reckless appropriation of Kant's categories of experience, which led him to eventually expand the Kantian notion of time to include the spatial (hence tangible) dimension of experience. Balanovskiy proposes that Jung broadened Kantian thought in this way by appealing to modern physics theories which posit the unity of energy and mass. Jung credits the theories of Russian philosopher Nikolaus Grot regarding psychic energy as providing him with the concept of mind as energic process, and at a later date supplemented and broadened Grot's theory to include physicality, using a quantum view of the unity of mind and matter. This, in turn, becomes key to his controversial theory that thoughts, intense moods, and other immaterial dimensions of mind may manifest themselves temporally, a phenomenon he called "synchronicity". And synchronicity, while a concept that is mystical in tone, is a genuinely scientific proposition because its credibility rests, in part, on the evidence of observable, time-and-space-bound phenomena. Balanovskiy argues that in this domain of study Jung creatively expands on Kant's notion of space, by showing that in certain circumstances immaterial psychic dynamisms become materially, publicly observable:

(Jungian) psychology is the way of revealing that psyche has one purpose – individuation, and in the process of achieving this purpose we
gain enough data for comprehension. So, in this respect analytical psychology can be represented as the practical science of individuation, in
which comprehension replaces the characteristic features of knowledge
produced by natural sciences ... (Further), Jung, much like Kant, thought
that the future of psychology as a 'proper' precise science would be
closely connected with finding the way to make psychic processes and
contents intuitive and presentable *a priori* in space, despite the fact that,
according to Kant, they exist only in time. The point here is that Jung
was influenced by representatives of the energy theory, most of all by
Grot. The energy theory takes an important place among Jung's ideas ...
(This is) revealed in (Jung's) article *On Psychic Energy* (1912), and then
in *On the Nature of the Psyche*.

(1947, republished in 1954) (p. 393)

Here again we find Jung arriving at a new, truth-disclosive concept by playing fast and loose with a received set of ideas and expanding on these from
what might be preemptively dismissed as a "mistake" based in a dubious
mysticism. In sum, here is another facet of Jung's development of a holistic
mind-world metaphysics, one founded on a naturalized transcendentalism
in a Kantian vein.

Framing Jung's general theory as a scientific metaphysics offers us an
intellectual framework that is warranted by the objective content of his
work, and also stays close to Jung's subjective understanding of his forays into widely diverse fields of study. Further, the concept of a scientific
metaphysics, as it derives from the neo-pragmatist philosophical tradition, employs the pragmatic idea that we should strive to render verdicts
about the nature or "is-ness" of the world, including the relative truth or
falsity of our perceptions of it, *retrospectively*. This manner of assigning
definitions *a posteriori* (which we will recall is the main characteristic of
abductive reason) reflects the pragmatist attention to the often-confusing
datum of lived experience as the first order of business, a move informed
by the conviction that, as Jung states, "In all chaos there is a cosmos, in all
disorder a secret order" (1968/1990, p. 32). In any case, here we should
also note that pragmatism is not a monolithic set of *a priori* principles
about the nature of reality but a *method* of thinking. Different pragmatist

thinkers hold widely diverse opinions about all manner of things, about which they constantly argue; but the methodology of abductive, *a posteriori* analysis is asserted by all in this eclectic lineage to be the preferred stance for understanding phenomena truthfully. This is not to say that pragmatism rejects imposing *a priori* assumptions on reality: thought cannot arise in a void. For example, like Kant, pragmatist thinking takes experience as a given, one whose facticity must be assumed for thinking to begin at all.

However, pragmatist thinkers assert that the *a priori* should not be unduly idealized and given license to run roughshod over thought's processional flow. Further, the fact that different pragmatists come to vastly different conclusions about the same issues speaks, not to some deficit in their method, but to the observation that the world resists attempts to circumscribe its nature in foregone formulae and, for some pragmatists, that thinking contributes to the literal emergence of new facts. Some in this lineage, such as Richard Rorty, see this as evidence of Being's baffling multiplicity and deny both the possibility and usefulness of asserting a holistic vision of its nature, while others, like Peirce, find a final, penultimate unity in this diversity, one that is discoverable in principle. However, in the end, thinkers of both dispositions return to experience, and the degree to which its unfolding is made instrumentally fruitful or not by adhering to its particular trajectory and set of conclusions.

Musement, Play, and the Aesthetic Basis of Morality

While a rather stoical and "uptight" personality, throughout his adult life Jung was also intensely devoted to indulging a childlike desire to play. Over many years he created an impressive array of technically sophisticated artworks, using a diversity of media such as painting, stone-carving, metaphysically soaring medieval-esque prose, calligraphy, and ambitious architectural projects. These were personal therapeutic experiments and formed the basis for his development of the clinical technique of active imagination, in which patients are encouraged to employ some form of artistic creativity through which to evoke and take up a conscious, dialogical position toward the contents of the unconscious. This exercise provides a venue for engaging the teleological nature of the psyche, that is, of discovering as-yet-unthought directions in life and a fuller consciousness of personal destiny.

As Donald Winnicott (1971) believes, playfulness is an essential element in the creation of a free and flexibly generative subjectivity, which he thinks is why it is the most important way that children begin to find conceptual paths through the vicissitudes of experience. Like Winnicott, Peirce argues that play is the indispensable ground of all creative thinking throughout the life span. As described earlier, this is embodied in his elevation of "musement", a function of the retrospective logic of abductive inference, to the status of the sole method from which all genuinely innovative action in the world originates. Both Jung and Peirce echo Winnicott's belief that playful creativity, as an exercise in symbol-formation, is not merely an individual developmental process, but a life-affirming bridge between personal subjectivity and the larger domain of society and culture. Jung's hypothesis of the collective bedrock of all psychic activity is well known. And this same notion is implied in Peirce's belief that the experimental methods of modern science are essentially a collective form of revelatory musement. Understood in this way, science's methodological requirements of public replicability and falsifiability are adult refinements of the mutuality of children's play; or, put conversely, children's play is an early, undeveloped form of scientific experimentation.

Drawing upon the general vision of play as a cultural activity, we may legitimately understand a cultivated capacity for musement as figuring prominently in what is arguably *the* main historical mission of modernity, namely, the liberation of the individual from the depersonalizing, hence crippling hegemony of both intrapsychic and collective social forces. In principle, this need not be a prescription for an isolated hyper-individualism, but an attempt to establish a proper relation of the subject to the social and cultural landscape. This is critically important, given that the demise of credible, mostly religious symbols of group cohesion in modernity has led to the rise of ethically vacuous neo-fascisms, authoritarian populisms, and corporate capitalist narratives that exert power through seductive indoctrination rather than brute force. These systems exploit the modern problem of the "lonely subject" by incorporating subjectivity into the *participation mystique* of unconscious identity with group norms and aims. Nietzsche (1878/1986) put this rather bluntly when he wrote, "Today as always, men fall into two groups: slaves and free men. Whoever does not have two-thirds of his day for himself, is a slave, whatever he may be: a statesman, a businessman, an official, or a scholar" (Aphorism # 283).

In contrast, Nietzsche's free man is the *Ubermensch*, one who thinks and acts *uber* ("beyond" or "above") both personal psychological timidity and passive resentment, and the de-individualizing forces of the larger human herd that quietly enforces this construction of self (Nietzsche, 1883/2005). His prophetic dictum of the necessity of establishing and defending an originative Winnicottian intrapsychic and social "space" or Heideggerian "clearing" for oneself relates directly to his insistence upon the perpetually self-transcending playfulness of the free-spirited individual, that is, the person with a refined, even noble ability to creatively frolic. Because playfulness is a skill, it needs to be "worked at" with deliberateness, and this means jealously protecting time to do so. But "time" is precisely what Nietzsche's slave lacks. The slave mentality "has" no time, which undermines the development of a meaningful sense of possibility. Rather, it is a mentality hypnotized and thus "had" by larger collective forces. These disrupt innovative agency by extracting it from the forward-going ontological processes constituting the very structure of temporality itself, including its susceptibility to novel alterations by chance, as Peirce notes.

This leads to a pathological enmeshment in what Heidegger (1954/1968) calls the stasis of "enframing", a triumphalist use of thinking rendering the natural processes of life static through the aggressive imposition of linear reason. As such, enframing is an attack on the teleology of Being. In Peircean terms, such an assault subverts the abductive processes informing "becoming", which are at the core of the experience of the abductively-inferred "may-be" evoked by musement, through an enframing of time in an immovable stasis of "was-and-always-shall be". Among other things, this impedes the emergence of chance events into the flow of experience, which Peirce notes is important to the emergence of novel phenomena. We may observe this as a dimension of corporatized capitalist discourses, which enforce uniformity of thought in the workplace and exhibit a near-phobic dread of the unplanned and unforeseen.

While Jung is critical of much of Nietzsche's stance, which he feels evinces a certain hyper-individual alienation from the meliorative rhythms of the unconscious, he is also compelled by the implications of the Nietzschean *telos* for his own metaphysical position about the peril and promise of modernity. Hence, while Nietzsche discounts notions of a metaphysical domain as having any continued relevance to modernity, and even as opposing its liberatory agendas, Jung passionately believes that a genuinely and inventively individual existence is not possible minus an experiential concordance of the personal with the suprapersonal ground of Being, within the embrace of which it is relativized and hence, paradoxically, more fully realized. The "death of God", he believes, is no necessary sign of the insufficiency of metaphysics, but of our own failure to bravely rethink and revisualize if and how the Absolute itself has evolved over time. We might call this a collective failure of moral and intellectual nerve, one evident among both religious believers and agnostic or atheist moderns. For a large portion of latter group, this has culminated in a rush, particularly among the intellectual classes, to the fantasied security of a narrowly if not exclusively material-efficient construction of experience, a domain whose "truths" are now imagined as existing solely in the taken-for-granted veridicality of linear cause-and-effect, as conveyed to sense experience. Arguably, this is as much a thoughtless herd-phenomenon as anything we imagine typifies the behavior of those acting from so-called "archaic" and/ or "primitive" visions of the world.

The Winnicottian concept of "play" contains elements of a mature metaphysic of the kind found in Jung and Peirce, while staying more conservatively within the modernist confines of the interpersonal and cultural. As is well known, Donald Winnicott's notion of "mind" is heavily relational. Mindedness evolves from an indeterminately "musing" interaction of self and other, what Bion (1962/1984) calls "reverie", that yields an imagined, integrative third dimension of being, one that is affirmative of personal identity while also being ego-transcending. This experience inheres in a paradoxical "intermediate" realm in which the individual emerges into being as a defined subject through the productive fecundity of a dialectical intercourse with a desired object, one that is simultaneously "within" and "outside" of experience. And the reality of the experienced object – one which is simultaneously within, between, and yet not actually situated as either within or between the subjectivities of those engaged in the interaction, – is not to be interrogated or questioned, writes Winnicott, rather cryptically. That is, one does not challenge the reality of the imaginary, because the imagined is the genesis of the real as emergent within the subjectively vibrant structures of lived experience, and, to add a Peircean concept to this, the spontaneous alterations wrought by chance.

While Winnicott's notion of play contains an implied metaphysics of ego-transcendence, he does not develop this, but sticks more conservatively to the function of the imaginal in its function as a purely psychological and psycho-social phenomenon. Peirce and Jung go much farther, of course, adducing that the imaginative (for Jung, mytho-poeic) nature of consciousness extends beyond the personal and interpersonal, in its function as the singularly human point of entry into the truth-disclosive quiddity of Being. In different ways, and with varying degrees of willingness to extrapolate from immediate (personal and cultural) experience, all three thinkers suggest that to subvert the organic evolutionary process of a playful construction of experience is, ironically, to produce distortions in an individual's ability to accurately interpret the world at all. All of this and more is either directly stated or implied in Peirce's notion that our ability to clearly cognize and agentically improvise upon reality is ultimately grounded in, and expressive of, the core of what neo-pragmatist F.S.C. Northrop (1964) calls the "aesthetic continuum of Being". This is to say that to live productively "in touch" with reality is to view it artfully, as one who resourcefully "toys with" the givenness of its structures, playfully considering, manipulating, deconstructing, and innovatively reconstructing these into novel forms. Implied herein is the idea that we live more gracefully, ethically, and optimistically as we develop *savior faire* at playfully refashioning, revising, and/or translating those of the structures of Being that impress us as aesthetically appealing. The instinctive aesthetic appeal of these elements derives from their ability to expand and refine consciousness; more precisely, "playing" with spontaneously emerging thoughts reveals possibilities for broadening their applicability to other dimensions of experience, forming sometimes unprecedented associative "bridges" that broaden and lend accuracy to our perceptions, and hence enjoyment, of being-in-the-world. This casts light on why we enjoy the act of "knowing" far beyond its obvious utilitarian function in supporting survival. Rather, there is something intrinsically and deeply satisfying, even ecstatic, about the state of knowing itself. The progressive broadening of experience enabled by the interpretive act is somehow intrinsically worthy, which I think qualifies it as both fundamentally playful and aesthetic.

Despite his rather formal and patriarchal character, Jung also cites playfulness as essential to becoming aligned with the individuating *telos* of psychic reality. He writes of this in ways that essentially agree with Peirce's concept of musement:

Out of a playful movement of elements whose interrelations are not immediately apparent, patterns arise which an observant and critical intellect can only evaluate afterwards. The creation of something new is not accomplished by the intellect but by the play instinct acting from inner necessity. The creative mind plays with the objects it loves.

(Jung, 1921/1990, p. 123)

In this quote we see Jung's *de facto* pragmatist confidence in the "playfulness" of abductive inference to produce novel realizations, this through his belief in the creative action of *a posteriori* reasoning about an emergent inner process that autonomously announces itself to consciousness. Further, like Peirce, Jung asserts that herein we find the unfolding of what, over time, evolves into the epistemologically cohering properties of symbolic consciousness. This is the artful basis of our moral sensibilities, according to Peirce. Unfortunately, Peirce does not offer us a developed moral theory. However, his occasional comments are evocative, and suggest connections with his holistic vision of a continuity between knower and known. As alluded to earlier in this chapter, he understands principled moral concernfulness and its expression in the here-and-now, context-dependent domain of ethical behavior as grounded in the underlying aesthetic *qualia* of an evolving cosmos. In daily life, this means that to respond with moral care to another is to appreciate their being-in-the-world as an object of beauty.

Hence, Peircean moral realism, which is the conception of morality as an objective factor in the structure of Being, does not exist exclusively in the abstracted form of a Kantian categorical principle, but rather as an affirmation of Wordsworth's view that "truth is beauty and beauty truth". Hence, for example, we should treat each other kindly because kindness spontaneously generates moments of beauty rooted in a graceful (in Peircean terms, "symmetrical" and "rational") coherence of diverse interpersonal and circumstantial elements, one alluding to the Absolute source of all coherence itself.

Jung's conception of morality as an objective factor in the psyche, one emanating from the structure of a metaphysical Absolute itself, resembles Peircean moral realism in key respects. However, Jung opposes the Peircean notion that morality is grounded in what we may call an underlying "cosmic aesthetics". In the treatment situation, invariably concerned as it is with the gritty details of personal lives (the "ethical" realm in which universal morality is or fails to be realized) Jung's moral sensibilities prompted him to engage in quite down-to-earth confrontations with patients. For example, his sense of the forward-looking dimension of the unconscious sometimes impelled him to directly, if perhaps tactlessly, confront some of them with the ways in which their symptoms reflected their denial of the natural tele-ological property of the unconscious to impart ethical responsibilities to consciousness, which he viewed as an essential prerequisite for any move-ment beyond unconscious conflicts. Jung's uncompromising ethical stance in these interactions derives from his conviction that the course of indi-viduation, of becoming more fully oneself, has a transpersonal moral basis. This, of course, is as much as to assert the objective metaphysical reality of moral principles. For Jung, the Absolute, whatever we may conceive it be, "calls" to us, as Heidegger (1935/2000) puts it, and demands that we respond. This is a demand that, among other things, is moral. To fail to respond to the voice of conscience is to absolve ourselves of an existential duty imposed upon us by the *telo* of individuation, he insists, and for this we may pay dearly with uncanny and debilitating inner conflicts and/or fateful encounters in our dealings with the world.

However, as noted, absent from Jung's moral position is the notion that concerned responsiveness to others is grounded in an appreciation of beauty. For Peirce, on the other hand, to be morally critically self-reflexive is expressive of our spontaneous love of the world's beauty as an intrin-sically worthy end-in-itself. I suggest that Jung's denial of the aesthetic basis of morality and its expression in the here-and-now, context-dependent realm of ethics, also severs its connection to playfulness, a relationship that is implied in Peircean theory. This difference is due, once again, to their diverse uses of Kant. Jung's ethical theory is rooted in his acceptance of Kant's separation of aesthetic sensibilities from concerned moral respon-siveness to others. This is due to what Kant understands as the opposition of sensate pleasure to moral principles. Specifically, Kant interprets aes-thetic pleasure in objects, human and otherwise, as usury, in that the object is a means to the end of achieving pleasure, he thought, hence in some sense disposable – not worthy of concern except as a means to another end. Therefore, he reasoned, artful engagement with beings diverts us from adherence to the universal moral edict of treating each being as an end-in-itself, and therefore as intrinsically worthy of our devotion. It is this element in Kant's philosophy that Jung uses to justify his rejection of any suggestion that his own or patients' uses of active imagination are aesthetic exercises, a topic about which he is adamant to the point of seeming phobic. In a Kantian vein, he reasons that because the appeal of aesthetic engage-ment inheres in its pleasurable aspects, to participate in this therapeutic method as an exercise in art means to undermine its individuating potential. "Artful" enjoyment in such activity diverts us into the developmental dead-end of sensate pleasure, where we forget the moral imperative to expand consciousness, he insists (van den Berk, 2009, p. 75).

In contrast, Peirce, who overall is more consistently holistic in his thinking than Jung, adopts the Kantian notion of morality as a transcendent epistemic category of world-engagement, but not Kant's division between morality and the enrichment afforded by aesthetic playfulness via musement. Rather, he posits, in a Winnicottian vein, that our instrumental "use" of objects (including those providing aesthetic enjoyment) is continuous with genuinely appreciating their intrinsic worth as ends-in-themselves. While Peirce does not elaborate on this idea, I think it is possible to infer in this concept a unity of means and ends, which is consistent with his overall position of the continuity of mind and world. The concept of a means-ends continua is robustly developed in John Dewey's pragmatism. Specifically, his theory of aesthetic appreciation posits a Peircean line of continuity between the two, reflecting his overarching belief in the final ontological unity of Being (Dewey, 1934/1958). For Dewey, one does not engage an artwork with the view of progressing toward some temporally distant "destination" in which we achieve a consummated appreciation of the work waiting for us at the culmination of the stream of immediate experience. Rather, the "goal" or end of aesthetic appreciation is inseparable from the very process of consciously engaging in an act of aesthetic appreciation itself. Here, the distinction between "ends" and "means" becomes blurred: there is no way of extracting one from the other, except in the domain of abstract thought, given that they exist within the unbroken continuum of the stream of experience. So, in a sense, one is always already "there" in appreciating the singularly inherent worth of the aesthetically enjoyed object, according to Dewey.

Contemporary neo-pragmatist Scott Stroud (2011) integrates the Deweyan unity of means and ends with a theory of the aesthetic ground of moral concern, toward an argument for the aesthetically enjoyable nature of ethical action: we engage others with concern based upon an intuition of unity with the evocative beauty which shines forth from within their existence as a sensate attractive "other" in experience. This is the basis of concernful (moral) empathy, in a Winnicottian sense. As Winnicott (1969) proposes, the libidinal pleasure we find in "object-use" is potentially self-transcending, and in normal development culminates in the appreciation of the objectivity of the "other" as a quality worthy of, and even demanding, concerned ethical responsiveness. Hence, the full realization of the Kantian duty to engage the other as an ethical end-in-themselves is there within the forward-going *telos* of the interpretive act itself and cannot be extracted from this process except in acts of intellectual abstraction.

Like the child immersed in playful manipulation of objects, the adult who plays with the associations between scattered ideas finds this activity inherently, even physically, pleasurable. Connected to this is the observation of the function of sensate enjoyment in producing states of conviction. Obviously, we can be drawn into states of self-deception by the allure of sensate pleasure. But it is not apparent to me that this is inevitable, or that such an outcome says anything necessary about our desire for pleasure itself. In this regard, I might note the rather ordinary fact that it is difficult to ward off the uncontrollable emergence of the sense of sublime appreciation we feel in the presence of that which, in retrospect, we come to call "beautiful".

Beauty "strikes" us, unbidden, an immediate feeling that can only be diminished after the fact, by imposing a template of skeptical *post-hoc* interpretations on experience. In its originary, emergent form, the allure of the beautiful is an objective element of the psyche – "numinous" in the Jungian sense, a *quale* which I think underlies its capacity to convey a felt, enduring certainty about the *de facto* objective legitimacy of our experience of the beloved object. We may doubt everything, in principle, but still succumb to the conviction that the objects of our affection inherently warrant this depth of feeling. Such resoluteness is so thoroughgoing that it can, in certain cases, compel us to unambivalently endanger or even sacrifice our lives to preserve the survival of an object of experience, human and non-human, we perceive as beautiful. This is an experience of beauty so convincing that it leads to the ultimate moral act of willingly courting self-destruction. Interesting to note in this regard is the fact that many if not most people will instinctively risk their lives to save a stranger in peril, a fact that I think lends itself to explanations beyond the merely personal, such as submission to the imperious dictates of the superego, illusions of a Lacanian Other, or a blind biological impulse to preserve the species.

Of course, Jung's concept of the numinous is not uniformly allied with the beautiful *per se*. Rather, it refers more generally to the concept of the sublime, which also involves the experience of being overawed by the objective unfolding of an experience of raw, chthonic power beyond our ken. In contrast to Peirce, Jung does not see the cosmos as evolving toward the emergence of the beautiful alone. Rather, it is a telic process imparting an Absolute in which beauty is counterpoised against the awe-ful and magisterial sublimity of that which shocks and benumbs us, that in relation to which we realize our finitude and frailty. This may feature in both the natural and human realms. Hence, the destructive force of an earthquake or the detonation of a nuclear weapon contain their own sublime, rapturous coherence, albeit one different from that we feel when considering the delicate veins of a leaf or a noble act of forgiveness. Herein we see the Nietzschean and Schopenhauerian elements in Jung. For him, Being is not "moral" on any human scale, but an expression of sheer transpersonal becoming that is beyond good and evil. It is not within my purposes to analyze this difference between Jung and Peirce here, and I leave it to others to tease out the implications of these competing emphases. I will, however, suggest that a reading of Jung's oeuvre strongly suggests that, on balance, he thinks that the Absolute is to be trusted, despite its capacity to evoke terror. When all is said and done, he seems to propose that while we may be baffled, overawed, and sometimes frightened by the sublimity of experience, the ineffable Source of our being ultimately seeks our wholeness. Although this state of unity, the ideal endpoint of individuation, is not necessarily recognizably "moral", it is one that nevertheless fruitfully aligns us with the rhythms of Being. (As Jung once noted, wholeness is different from perfection.) In this context, we might also look to Jung's position on the absolute necessity of taking a moral account of oneself as part of the treatment process. It is hard to imagine that he would hold such a stance minus a belief that the values of concern, care, and ethical responsibility toward the world (including other human beings) are mere social constructions, without any relation to the ultimate nature of the cosmos. For example, in *Answer to Job* (1958/2011) he posits that moral consciousness is inherently present in the Absolute, albeit in latent and undifferentiated form. It exists as a potentiality, one maturing in a long historical process of evolution. Hence, *contra* modernist moral relativism, Jung forwards a soft metaphysical moral realism bearing comparison with that of Peirce. Thus construed, in Jung, morality is an overflow of an organic impulse to compassionately embrace and engage reality dialogically, and, considered as an archetypal *potentia*, it is as much an innate, metaphysically real *quale* of the Absolute as its darker, destructive elements. Jung argues that it is our obligation to assist the evolving cosmos, in part by helping to facilitate the emergence of moral consciousness within the Absolute. This development in the mental economy of the Absolute proceeds through our assertion of the legitimacy of the uniquely differentiated, "humanizing" quality of our belief in equity, proportion, and compassion. This is also an element in Peirce's notion of the Absolute, one reflected in his holism: humanity is intimately involved in the evolution of the cosmos, which means we are partly responsible for contributing to the ongoing development of the Creator-deity's personality. In this we see that both Jung and Peirce posit a relation between humanity and the divine that is inherently and intensely dialogical. As such, they are both squarely within the Western tradition of theism, with Jung coming down more on the Hebraic/Jewish end of the Judeo-Christian continuum than Peirce, as evident in his eye for the magisterial, sometimes threatening "otherness" of the Absolute.

From the foregoing we may also conclude that Jung's vision of the Absolute seems to tacitly agree with Peirce's concept of the loving or "agapic" nature of cosmic evolution, a metaphysic expressing his belief in a beneficent deity. Jung's overriding concept of human flourishing is that it is ultimately dependent upon aligning oneself with the aims of this metaphysical Other. This seems to imply that he advocates a vision of the Absolute as essentially trustworthy, and as warranting the surrender of oneself to its larger, albeit often mysterious ends. While this is not to explicitly assert that "God is love", it would seem foolish for Jung to propose that human fulfillment requires becoming attuned to the Call of an Absolute which, while an ambiguous admixture of all possible emotional and moral orientations, is not ultimately more motivated by a profoundly positive regard, if not love, for humanity than anything else. (Were this not the case, he might well have advised that we foster something akin to the ancient Grecian stance of stalwart, heroic defiance in relation to the Absolute. However, Jung constantly asserts that such an attitude ultimately undermines our proper relation to our own humanity.) I think this puts him in relative agreement with Peircean agapism. For both, the Absolute seeks to evolve so as to support its creation – it desires to become more conscious, as Jung says, which seems to imply a striving toward the Good, that is, the expansive creativity and appreciation of beauty associated with an evolved consciousness. More exactly, like Peirce, Jung believes that the capacity for moral concern exists as a latent potentiality within the supramundane Source of Being, and that humans can dialogically provoke and nurture the *telos* of its unfolding. For Jung, this is a metaphysical Other that has, and will always have, its menacing dark side.

Such darkness is also a fact of human developmental processes, though not typically one that we cite to deny our capacity to grow in loving concern; we understand that our innate capacity for narcissism and destructiveness may be tempered and humanized. Implied in Jung's metaphysics is that on this score we should judge the Absolute with the same equanimity that we strive to apply to ourselves and others. Specifically, this means that on balance, God, like human beings, "leans" or is mostly predisposed toward acting according to a vision of what is life-affirming and may be influenced to favor this orientation over others. For Jung, this is the meaning of the Christ-event, namely, that God became man for the purpose of interacting with humans and thus becoming conscious of a moral duty to respect and learn from their "otherness".

Concluding Thoughts: God, Imagination, and Orders of Being

In this chapter I have presented a philosophical analysis of the phenomenology of conviction. Using Peirce and Jung's theories of experience, I have maintained that the passage from uncertainty to reasonable resoluteness is a mental state emergent from a metaphysical Absolute. Further, I have argued that faith in the originary and creative function of an Absolute is logically credible, as much so as any of the logic used to dismiss such an idea.

Now, it may be objected that an advantage of an agnostic or atheistic stance, one that looks solely upon "this worldly" causation to form interpretations about meaning and purpose, is that dispensing with thoughts about an ineffable metaphysical intelligence beyond immediate experience greatly simplifies life. Arguably, doing so is even beneficial in that it refocuses us on solving tangible problems in the here-and-now rather than awaiting reward in, say, an afterlife, the consolations of oceanic consciousness, or other dubious states of being. To reiterate my comments at the start of this chapter, my answer is that these are perfectly legitimate objections: there is no necessity to adding the God-hypothesis to lived experience. People can and do live satisfying as well as admirably ethical lives minus any belief in a suprasensible Absolute. Metaphysical convictions are logically coherent but nonetheless unnecessary wagers, an aesthetic supplement to our interpretations of the world. They are not demanded by experience.

So, what's the use of religious faith or a spiritual orientation to life in this world? I think one answer may be found in the intimate relation of spiritual sensibilities to imagination. In acts of imagination, we actively and largely unconsciously project ourselves into different orders of being, which may be regulated by entirely different rules than the ones we normally live by. It is the constant experience of imaginative persons that in this visionary domain, they discover entirely new, innovative ways of conceiving reality that benefit them and others instrumentally. Stated philosophically, this is a view of imaginal life as possessing a cognitive function, and, in terms of this chapter's thesis, as potentially revelatory of new and often novel truths. Central here is the relationship of imaginative activity to possibility, to what it is that can be thought as a potential form of experience that beneficially reorders our relationship to its structure. In terms of imaginal, mytho-poeic and religious orientations to life, these fresh forms are of use in disclosing certain, possibly unprecedented, possibilities of life in the world as beautiful, compelling, and/or sublime. Herein lies their similarity to aesthetic renderings of Being, which also give new depth and meaning to experience, not by producing faithful reproductions of things as they are, but by implying more than the forms in which they are given.

It is the intervention of mind in the habit-taking fixity of the "given" that produces these fresh possibilities, or, more accurately, that call forth something novel from our experience of reality that would otherwise never have come to be. This is a view suggesting that we understand imagined worlds as, at their inception, "real" although only potentially "actual". The real nature of an imagined world can, and often does, become actual, if it is engaged thoughtfully and patiently over time, toward "working out" the manner in which its ontological topography may metamorphose into the live option of a Peircean "may-be" within daily life.

Here I will apply a greatly simplified version of the epistemological theory of contemporary neo-pragmatist Justus Buchler (1951), as elaborated by John Ryder (2013), to flesh out this idea. Buchler dwells on the nature of the truths disclosed in our imaginative constructions of the world, which he sees as expressed in naturalized "orders". There are vast numbers of such orders, each defined by their specific limits upon what can and cannot be considered relevant and/or possible within their specific domains. There are orders of nature, society, economics, sexuality, biology, religion, justice, race, art, and aesthetics, and so on, possibly interminably. While each order is knowable on the basis of its own rule-defined structures, elements of which do not admit of violation, none are "airtight"; they have different degrees of permeability and susceptibility to integration with other orders, according to the flexibility and potential generalizability of their internal rules of logic as we attempt to integrate these with other orders. Within its own purview, each order is fully real.

Here, the term "real" refers to the fact that an imagined world exists in a certain order of existence, one that is different from, but ontologically co-equal with all other orders. This ontic co-equality means that anything in experience exists in some order of being, be it imaginal, material, and so on, and hence is as entirely real as anything else. The category of the actual is different from that of the real. Here, actuality is defined as an originally real order that has found concrete expression in the facticity of one's navigation of the world, where it yields tangible, publicly verifiable effects. Hence, for example, the ontological order of economics admits of reevaluation and reinterpretation by that of justice, as when we take a different perspective on employee wages upon investigation of why measurably equally competent workers are paid at different rates. When we do so, we may find ourselves incorporating still other orders and their rules into our purview, such as sex, race, social class, and so forth. In this example, these orders attach themselves to the broader order of justice, where they act as interpretive "sub-orders" (we may also call them interpretive sub-categories). A sub-order serves to more narrowly define and enhance the focus and applicability of the larger order to which it is attached. Further, a real manner of envisioning the world may serve as either a dominant organizing order or a supplementary, discriminating sub-order, depending on what it is we wish to know. Thus, for example, the order of economics may act as a sub-order when we wish to cite certain factors toward the larger goal of writing the biography of a novelist who perhaps struggled financially. (For example, did their financial status influence the themes in their prose?)

In our example of the different wages earned by equally skilled workers, as we progress further down the particular path of query dictated by our end-in-view, adding or subtracting different sub-orders according to their ability to add depth, dimension, and nuance to our interpretation, we may emerge with a transformed vision of the nature of an economic order than the one we started with. It is one that is broader, more disclosively inclusive of different domains of Being, hence more responsive to the ontological structure of what seemed, on first blush, to allow for only certain, more limited interpretations. This being so, our ability to critique and realize certain possibilities within the structure of an economic order gains in sensitivity and nuance. Such a broadened existential horizon enhances our confidence to meaningfully engage experience, this is because our imaginative manipulation of diverse real orders provides us with more effective means to instrumentally effect change in the world. New integrations of logically compatible orders can create entirely novel orders, which may then become part of public consciousness. As only one example, the recently emergent field of "Queer Economics" is a hybrid of the orders of sexuality, gender, law, justice, and social policy, among others, all of which act as conceptually refining sub-orders to the governing order of interest, economics.

Each order has a definite logical structure. While these structures are more or less permeable, they do not allow for unlimited and/or arbitrary assimilation with other orders. Therefore, we are within our rights to judge syntheses of the logically incompatible aspects of diverse orders as dubious or even delusional: I may dream of leaping from the top of my apartment building and alighting from the Earth on a journey to Mars, but if I try to actualize this dream-image I will fail miserably and am perhaps likely to find myself first in an emergency room and later in a psychiatric ward, assuming I survive. The conviction driving my act would be a confusion of the order of dreams with the actuality of the material world, which forbids such a violation of its ontic structure. The order of dreams may become *fruitfully* actual when conjoined with other, more logically compatible orders, such as, say, the domain of metaphor that is a focus of psychoanalytic interpretations: in this order, a dream of flying may reveal unconscious ambition, denial of limitations or hardships, erotic desire, and so forth. The truthfulness of other integrations of orders may not be so dramatically contradictory, but simply dubious, that is, of questionable relevance and revelatory potential. This usually happens when an order is either too limited or too broad in scope to be usefully connected to other orders. The result of this is that the evolutionary *telos* of the order, in which its revelatory potential exists, is greatly constrained, and no practically useful expansion of consciousness results. That is, such an order may become actual but doesn't "go" anywhere instrumentally (actually) useful to human thriving. Orders with questionable actual applicability often figure as sub-orders in the greater order of humor. For example, a 1970 sketch from the British comedy troupe Monty Python's Flying Circus depicts a group of self-important men at a meeting of The Royal Society for Putting Things on Top of Other Things. The gathering begins officiously and with a sense of purpose, but, predictably, the members quickly run out of topics to discuss.

Beset by a dim but increasing awareness of their lack of relevance, the assembly abruptly and comically moves to dissolve the society. Although a real order according to our definition, the realization in actuality of this fictive assembly's mission is of no meaningful instrumental use; specifically, their object of knowledge (discerning what things are on top of other things) has the unusual distinction of being *both* simultaneously too limited and too broad to be practically integrated with other orders of being. We are left chuckling and thinking, "So … what?".

Because the effects wrought by the unifying assimilation of various logically compatible orders are actual, they are also publicly verifiable. The instrumental product evolving within the evolutionary process from potentiality to actuality is a Peircean Third, a unifying unifier or semiotic symbol that is a unique product of certain imaginal orders become actual. That is, a "working" symbol has become a "realized" potentiality, even an entirely unprecedented ordinal category of Being, enhancing our power to better our condition and/or the world in some way.

Now, relevant to this chapter is that, of all real and actual orders, the ordinal category of God is utterly unique in that it does not admit of limitation or any final specificity. God is All-in-All, implicated in every expression of Being, thus infinitely broad in its capacity to be integrated into all other orders. It is different from the order of religion, which serves as a specifying sub-order defining the parochial, pragmatic meaning of God in individual and/or group experience. In Peircean mathematical terms, God may be understood as the penultimate Set of all Sets, the all-encompassing Absolute order embracing all others. For this reason, it is necessarily conceptually ill-defined and opaque. It is an imaginal order that allows for an infinite number of interpretations, so many that it may be difficult to believe that those of different faith persuasions are actually talking about the same thing.

Ryder points out the virtues of the broad applicability of this neo-pragmatist definition of God, though he says that it has one limitation. Specifically, we recall that all orders are ontologically co-equal. This equality includes the order of God, which is not objectively or necessarily superior to, or in any other way dominant over other orders. It may be chosen by individuals and groups to serve as *the* cardinal order in their lives, with all other orders acting as subordinate sub-orders, although this elevation is not inherent in the nature of the order of God itself. This means that the order of God cannot accommodate concepts of a Creator-deity as existing antecedent to, "beyond", or "above" the created world itself. Ryder (2013, p. 126) argues that this poses difficulties for those theisms that posit a division between God and the natural world, with the deity conceived as standing apart from nature, either as existing prior to its creation or in some other way as a self-subsistent "wholly other": in this view, there is no creation *ex nihilo*. Intellectually inventive religious theists may find some way to reconcile Ryder's paradigm with their faith commitments. As only one example, Mikel Burley (2016) suggests a reinterpretation of the Christian doctrine of life after death as a paradoxically eternally present possession, a concept made credible by, as he writes, "supplementing the claims of religious thinkers with notions of four-dimensionalism and eternalism from theoretical physics and the philosophy of time" (p. 145). One wonders if this unusual and challenging model can be applied to situating the order of God in an eternally co-existing natural world, in which the deity and materiality are conjoined, although to pursue this here would lead us far afield.

Despite its baffling non-specificity, God has actual power to effect palpable change in individual and social life. When individuals and groups work to spell out the instrumental implications of their understanding of God, actual, verifiable results occur in their engagement with the world.

These effects are typically fundamental and sweeping in scope, due to the limitlessness of the order of God: for the deeply religiously convicted person, all other orders are or can be incorporated into its domain. As such, God is and always shall be a generative well-spring of resolve for vast numbers of people. This conviction is based in their experience that the imaginal order of God is entirely real, because aligning themselves intellectually, emotionally, morally, and behaviorally with its interpretive structures yields practical results in the form of enhanced hope, determination, and ethical/moral courage. (Of course, this says nothing about how we judge the actualized outcomes of a given religious order, ethically: the 9/11 attacks by fundamentalist Muslims were fueled by spiritual resolve as much as the social activism of nineteenth-century Massachusetts Protestant abolitionists.) We may endlessly debate whether or not the order of God is relevant, logical, or refers to the "really real". But I argue that doing so beyond a certain point is simply fruitless partisan drumbeating in the service of preferred, *a priori* ontological commitments, many of which are no more than dispositional biases. In contrast, the pragmatist approach suggests a more humble and democratically inclusive stance toward defining the truthfulness of this and other orders, one summarized in Peirce's famous pragmatic maxim, "Consider what effects, that might conceivably have practical bearings, we conceive the object of our conception to have. Then, our conception of these effects is the whole of our conception of the object" (Peirce, 1878, p. 293). I suggest that any theory, however subtle and well argued, that disposes of this most elementary, *a posteriori* test of its truth-claims is deservedly fated to become irrelevant.

The upshot of all this is that it is not only futile to argue with someone's metaphysical claims about experience, but also misguided when done minus inspection of the actual *effects* of their vision of the world upon their lived experience. Hence, for example, someone engaged in a Jungian analysis may come to understand their experience as helpfully informed and guided by a transpersonal *mythos*; perhaps they imagine themselves as on an archetypal "hero's journey", or as struggling nobly toward the realization of what the unconscious "intends" for them. Is this merely magical thinking? Jung's stance toward this matter is utterly pragmatic:

> No one can know what the ultimate things are. Therefore, we must take them as we experience them. And if such experience helps to make life healthier, more beautiful, more complete, and more satisfactory to yourself and to those you love, you may safely say, "This was the grace of God". No transcendental truth is thereby demonstrated, and we must confess in all humility that religious experience is *extra ecclesium*, subjective, and liable to boundless error.
>
> (Jung, 1938/1966, p. 114)

As Jung states, we may interpret in error. But interpret we must or fail to navigate the world in any way whatsoever. And as he also notes, metaphysical positions are like all others, in that they can best be judged *a posteriori*, by their actual effects upon experience.

As I have tried to demonstrate in this chapter, cognizing the world as evolving according to final causation whose dynamisms are emanations of a metaphysical Absolute, toward ends that preexist and loosely predetermine the unfolding of experience and even the cosmos itself, is as reasonable (or not) as the now-dominant bias that material-efficient causation explains everything. The final validation of the order of God lies not in the exercise of logical argumentation, though reasoned debate is vitally important so as to clarify and refine what we understand this order to mean in particular cases, but because it endures as an originary and effective positive force in lived experience. To paraphrase James, God is real because it is an order of being with actual effects. And the potential, teleological significance of these effects can only be fairly interpreted from a position of wonderment at the perpetual unbidden coming-into-being of our thoughts, which originate … well, who can say from "where"?

Notes

1 The term "pragmatism" was first coined by Peirce's close friend William James, as part of his efforts to promote Peirce's seminal ideas. However, Peirce, ever the iconoclast, objected to this moniker. Instead, he preferred to use a term of his own invention, "pragmaticism", for his philosophy (Peirce, 1884a/1934) on the premise that the difficulty of pronouncing the word would deter merely casual inquirers from investigating and possibly misinterpreting his thinking. Peirce's concerns notwithstanding, for the sake of simplicity in this chapter I use James' more widely recognized (and easier to pronounce) term.
2 What constitutes the "intelligence" of the Absolute is not defined consistently or in much detail by Peirce and Jung. Generally speaking, it is interpreted by both as a teleological cosmic creative process beginning in chaos (in Jung, a psychically unintegrated state of unconsciousness) and moving toward differentiation and clarity.
3 Related to this is the fact that Peirce does not equate experience solely with what psychoanalysis calls consciousness, largely because he rejects the notion of a clearly demarcated or "boundaried" personal subject. Rather, what he calls experience is a processional phenomenon expanding beyond a strictly individual subjectivity, including its conscious dimensions. Here, "experience" is defined (appropriately vaguely, given that it cannot be localized as an "internal" psychic event) as continuous with a trans-egoic phenomenal stream, suggesting a type of panpsychism.
4 Peirce uncritically accepted Lamarck's theory. This may be taken as a rare instance of undisciplined thinking on his part, as the Lamarckian notion of inborn primordial ideas, existing as fully formed psychic images, clashes with his neo-Kantian commitment to these phenomena as without content. I get the impression that Peirce simply did not read Lamarck carefully, if at all, which may happen among even famed scholars more often than we would care to know.

References

Almeder, R. (1973). Peirce's pragmatism and scotistic realism. *Transactions of the Charles S. Peirce Society, 9*(1), 3–23.

Balanovskiy, V. (2017). Kant and C. G. Jung on the prospects of scientific psychology. *Estudos Kantianos, 5*(1), 383–398.

Bergson, H. (1911). *Creative evolution* (A. Mitchell, Trans.). Henry Holt and Company.

Bion, W. (1962/1984). *Learning from experience*. Karnac.

Bishop, P. (1999). *Jung in contexts*. Routledge.

Brady, J. (2018). Kant and the idealists' reality problem. *Epoche Philosophical Monthly, 14*. https://epochemagazine.org/14/kant-and-the-idealists-reality-problem/

Buchler, J. (1951). *Toward a general theory of human judgement*. Columbia University Press.

Burley, M. (2016). Eternal life as an exclusively present possession: Perspectives from theology and the philosophy of time. *Sophia: International Journal of Philosophy and Traditions*, *55*(2), 145–161.

deVoogd, S. (1984). Fantasy versus fiction: Jung's Kantianism appraised. In R. Papadopolous & G. Saymaan (Eds.), *Jung in modern perspective* (pp. 204–228). Wildwood House.

Dewey, J. (1934/1958). *Art as experience*. Capricorn.

Dewey, J. (1938). *Logic: The theory of inquiry*. Henry Holt & Company.

Eagle, M. (1984). *Recent developments in psychoanalysis: A critical evaluation*. McGraw-Hill.

Einstein, A. (1931/2009). *Cosmic religion: With other opinions and aphorisms*. Dover.

Haack, S. (1992). Extreme scholastic realism: Its relevance to philosophy of science today. *Transactions of the Charles S. Peirce Society*, *28*(1), 19–50.

Hausman, C. (1993). *Charles S. Peirce's evolutionary philosophy*. Cambridge University Press.

Hayman, R. (1999). *A life of Jung*. Bloomsbury.

Heidegger, M. (1927/1962). *Being and time*. Harper and Row.

Heidegger, M. (1935/2000). *Introduction to metaphysics* (G. Fried & R. Polt, Trans.). Yale University Press.

Heidegger, M. (1954/1968). *What is called thinking?* Harper & Row.

Husserl, E. (1913/1973). *The idea of phenomenology* (W. Alston & G. Nakhnikian, Trans.). Kluwer Academic Publishers.

Husserl, E. (1936/1970). *The crisis of European sciences and transcendental phenomenology*. Northwestern University Press.

Jacobi, M. (1959). *Complex/archetype/symbol in the psychology of C. G. Jung*. Pantheon.

James, W. (1890). *The principles of psychology*. Macmillan and Company.

James, W. (1897/1956). *The will to believe*. Dover.

Jung, C. G. (1912/2003). *The psychology of the unconscious*. Dover.

Jung, C. G. (1916/1957). The transcendent function. In R. F. C. Hull (Trans.) and M. Fordham & G. Adler (Eds.), *The collected works of C. G. Jung, 20 Vols. [hereafter CW]: CW, 8. The structure and dynamics of the psyche* (pp. 67–91). Princeton University Press.

Jung, C. G. (1921/1990). *Psychological types: CW* (Vol. 6). Princeton University Press.

Jung, C. G. (1933/2009). *Modern man in search of a soul*. Psychology Press.

Jung, C. G. (1938/1966). *Psychology and religion*. Yale University Press.

Jung, C. G. (1947/1954). *On the nature of the psyche: CW* (Vol. 8, pp. 159–234). Princeton University Press.

Jung, C. G. (1958/2011). *Answer to job: Fiftieth anniversary edition* (R. F. C. Hull, Trans.). Princeton University Press.

Jung, C. G. (1961/1989). *Memories, dreams, reflections* (A. Jaffe, Ed. and R. Winston, Trans.). Vintage Books.

Jung, C. G. (1968/1990). *The archetypes and the collective unconscious: CW* (2nd ed., Vol. 9, Part I). Princeton University Press.

Jung, C. G. (2000). *The essential Jung: Selected writings* (A. Storr, Ed.). Princeton University Press.

Kant, I. (1781/2000). *Critique of pure reason* (P. Guyer & A. Wood, Transl. and Eds.). Cambridge University Press.

Kearney, R. (2001). *The god who may be: A hermeneutics of religion*. Indiana University Press.

Knox, J. (2003). *Archetype, attachment, analysis: Jungian psychology and the emergent mind*. Routledge.

Maddalena, G. (2015). *The philosophy of gesture: Completing pragmatists' incomplete revolution*. McGill-Queen's University Press.

Mayo, D. (2005). Peircean induction and the error-correcting thesis. *Transactions of the Charles S. Peirce Society, 41*(2), 299–319.

McLynn, F. (1996). *Carl Gustav Jung*. Bantam.

Nietzsche, F. (1878/1986). *Human, all too human* (M. Faber & S. Lehmann, Trans.). Penguin.

Nietzsche, F. (1883/2005). *Thus spoke Zarathustra* (G. Parkes, Trans.). Oxford University Press.

Niiniluoto, I. (1999). *Critical scientific realism*. Oxford University Press.

Northrop, F. S. C. (1964). The undifferentiated aesthetic continuum. *Philosophy East and West, 14*(1), 67–71.

Orange, D. (1984). *Peirce's conception of god: A developmental study*. Institute for Studies in Pragmaticism.

Paton, H. J. (1936). *Kant's metaphysic of experience*. George Allen and Unwin.

Peirce, C. S. (1878). How to make our ideas clear. *Popular Science Monthly, 12*, 286–302.

Peirce, C. S. (1884a/1934). Pragmatism and pragmaticism. In C. Hartshorne & P. Weiss (Eds.), *The collected papers of Charles Sanders Peirce, 8 Vols. [hereafter CSP]: CSP 5.582, Pragmatism and Pragmaticism* (Vols. 7–8, pp. 1–6). Harvard University Press.

Peirce, C. S. (1884b/1934). *The logic of the universe* (p. 6.192). CSP.

Peirce, C. S. (1891). The architecture of theories. *The Monist, 1*(2), 161–176.

Peirce, C. S. (1892). The doctrine of necessity examined. *The Monist, 2*(3), 321–337.

Peirce, C. S. (1903). *Nomenclature and division of triadic relations, As Far as they are determined (syllabus)* (p. 2.233). CSP. (Also digitized in *Harvard University Archives*.)

Peirce, C. S. (1903/1934). *Three types of reasoning* (p. 5.171). CSP.

Peirce, C. S. (1908/2020). *A neglected argument for the reality of god*. Good Press.

Pihlstrom, S. (2003). *Naturalizing the transcendental: A pragmatic view*. Humanity Books.

Ransdell, J. (1978). A misunderstanding of Peirce's phenomenology. *Philosophy and Phenomenological Research, 38*(4), 550–553.

Raposa, M. (1989). *Peirce's philosophy of religion*. Indiana University Press.

Ricoeur, P. (1965/2014). *De l'interprtation. Essai sur Freud*. Media Diffusion.

Ryder, J. (2013). *The things in heaven and earth: An essay in pragmatic naturalism*. Fordham University Press.

Smith, J. (1987). The reconception of experience in Peirce, James and Dewey. In S. Corrington, C. Hausman, & T. M. Seebohm (Eds.), *Pragmatism considers phenomenology* (pp. 73–91). University Press of America.

Stang, N. (2016). *Kant's transcendental idealism*. Stanford Encyclopedia of Philosophy. https://plato.stanford.edu/entries/kant-transcendental-idealism/

Stroud, S. (2011). *John Dewey and the artful life: Pragmatism, aesthetics, and morality*. Pennsylvania State University Press.

van den Berk, T. (2009). *Jung on art: The autonomy of the creative drive*. Routledge.

Whitehead, A. N. (1929/1978). Process and reality. *Corrected edition*. Free Press.

Winnicott, D. W. (1969). The use of an object. *The International Journal of Psychoanalysis, 50*(4), 711–716.

Winnicott, D. W. (1971). *Playing and reality*. Basic Books.

Chapter 3

Jung's Call to Eros
A Personal Journey

Tosia H. Zraikat

Had I dared to show my heart without disguise
without the camouflage of laughter
let it burst as it yearned into flame
would I really have drowned in tenderness –
lost that little tight thing I called myself –
fallen like a featherless sparrow too soon too far?
Would I really have burned to ashes? ...

(From *Book of Ashes*, a poem by Chapter Author)

Introduction

I came to psychotherapy because of Eros, late in life, and was surprised to encounter that god on the many paths that therapy has taken me. Although I had read much of Jung, I had not realized until I experienced it for myself the degree to which his psychology is infused with love and Eros connectedness, and directed towards the awakening, harmonizing, and manifestation of Eros in the life of the individual, and through her, in the world. My introduction to the power of Eros came seemingly out of the blue in a wild storm of emotions that I could not control and that did not abate. My first analyst told me shortly before our sessions ceased that I needed to come to terms with Eros, so when a few years later, feelings started gushing all over the place like a great flood from a broken dam, coursing through every part of my body, I was fairly certain that it was wild Eros knocking me around. Something was clamoring to get out, a desire for connection expressed at first as a new curiosity about the world beyond my own small one, and increased attentiveness to the changing content and movements of my inner world. I had no idea what to do about it, yet I also felt an underlying rightness to it, an unknown soul-purpose. So, though my rational mind screamed

DOI: 10.4324/9781003412823-4

alarm, I did not resist. Jung writes, "if I know that the god is a powerful impulse of my soul, at once I must concern myself with him, for he can become important, even unpleasantly so" (Jung, 1962, p. 129). Also, as von Franz writes, "The unconscious seems to tend toward disharmony in order that the Self may again be brought up into consciousness".[1] Sometimes, "the unconscious wants to burst apart the relatively harmonious setup in order that a higher level of may be reached" (von Franz, 1990, p. 38).

My life had become too ordered, too serene, and if Eros was shaking my foundations, it was, I knew, to shake up my soul, languishing from years of neglect. After a few weeks of this, I began analysis with a local Jungian therapist. "I could stop this if I tried", I told him, "but I know it is necessary for my soul. If I go back, it will feel to my soul like death". In this chapter I posit that Eros is much more than a repeating motif in Jung's psychology; it is central to his teleological orientation, and his therapeutic approach of individuation, a prime element of his life's work of helping others to achieve wholeness of personality and to function as authentic, moral, caring beings in the world. Individuation is not, as some have claimed, "an asocial, egocentric exercise"; on the contrary, when a person's intrinsic social being "is rescued from unconsciousness and related to consciousness he becomes for socially fit and better related to his fellow men" (von Franz, 1998a, p. 75, ff77).

Though consciousness can only be observed in the individual, it is of more than individual concern. As Jung states in his famous interview with Dr. Richard Evans of Penn State University, "the fate of the world hangs on a thin thread, and that is the psyche of man" (Evans, 1957). The state of human consciousness determines the consciousness of the world, and we see all around us that the world is at a time of crisis. "I'm absolutely of the … conviction that there is a *telos* in each community", Jung declares in a letter, "that this *telos* is a summation of the individual *telos*. Each man has his *telos* and inasmuch as he tries to fulfil it he is a real citizen" (Jung, 1992, p. 464). The aim of Jung's teleology was therefore both the individual and society, for he well understood, explains Jungian analyst and writer, Edward Edinger, that "The most effective way to redeem or transform the world is first of all to transform that little piece of it that is oneself" (Edinger, 1994, p. 30). I begin this essay considering the *telos* of Eros as a prime motif in Jung's psychology; the second part is mostly focused on the participation of Eros in my work with images and active imaginations, and I close with a few thoughts on the relevance of Eros to the wider society.

Jung and Eros

Jung's closest colleague, Marie-Louise von Franz writes of "his life-long commitment to the inner creative spirit … the source of an unusually large capacity for love that both enlivened and burdened his existence" expressed in the depth of his "participation, of sympathy and human warmth for his family, his friends, his patients and, in the end, for all of mankind" (von Franz, 1998a, p. 24). He had, she says, a "quality of intensive Eros" found in those "who turned toward their suffering fellow man in an attitude of love and who found their vocation through this attitude rather than in political or academic power struggles" (von Franz, 1998a, p. 25). It is, I believe, in his intense difficult mid-life encounters with love and his soul, recorded in his journals, later transcribed into his *Liber Novus*, that Jung truly comprehends the primacy of Eros in human life.

The philosopher from ancient Elea, Parmenides, is told of the goddess:

First of all the gods she contrived Eros" (Parmenides, C5th B.C.E./1919.). In Hesiod, Eros comes into being only after the earth and its depths: "In the beginning there was only Chaos, the Abyss, … then Gaia, the Earth … And Tartaros, … And Eros, loveliest of all the Immortals

(Hesiod, C8th B.C.E./1914).

He is the "primordial god (*protogenos*) of procreation … the driving force behind the generation of new life in the cosmos" ('Eros', theoi.com). "Eros is a *kosmogonos,* a creator and father-mother of all higher consciousness", writes Jung. "We are in the deepest sense the victims and instruments of cosmogonic 'love'", he claimed, interpreting love "as something superior to the individual, a unified and undivided whole" (Jung, 1965, pp. 353–354). "Eros is a questionable fellow and will always remain so," he writes.

He belongs on one side to man's primordial animal nature which will endure as long as man has an animal body. On the other side he is related to the highest forms of the spirit. But he thrives only when spirit and instinct are in right harmony

(Jung, 1977, p. 28).

There is, however, an opposite drive that can have the appearance of love and be confused for Eros. It derives from the "instinct of self-preservation", explains Jung, "the will to power" (Jung, 1977, p. 32) which expresses not

Eros but "the power of the ego" (1977, p. 34). It is not uncommon and can be recognized. "In reality human nature bears the burden of a terrible and unending conflict between the principle of ego and the principle of instinct: the ego, all barriers and restraint, instinct limitless, and both principles of equal might" (Jung, 1977, p. 34). "The will to power is surely just as mighty a *daemon* as Eros, and just as old and original" (1977, p, 34). Learning to recognize the difference between them and their different effects, one comes to understand what love is not, which can be invaluable. Though it is often used as such, love is not a means to gain power or some other conscious or unconscious personal goal, nor is it "emotionality and sentimentality", writes von Franz, which history has shown can be "a counterpart of brutality"[2] (2008, p. 18). What Jung calls love is specifically "differentiated love". It includes, she explains, "a certain distance based on differentiation: an understanding and a not-understanding, the latter consisting of a silent respect of the mystery of the other's individuality", which is much harder to achieve (2008, p. 18).

At the start of his *Liber Novus* journey, Jung is aware that Christianity lost its original philosophy of "all-embracing love" when "the power principle, the arch-enemy of all forms of love", became dominant (von Franz, 2008, p. 16). He also grasps that collectively, and for him personally, the civilizing "subjugation of the animal in man" is at odds with the "part of the animal nature that thirsts for freedom" (Jung, 1977, p. 258). The disharmony of Jung's spirit and instinct needed Eros to balance his overweening Logos not only in his love life but to move him further towards authenticity as a whole person, that is, towards his own individuation. He writes that that inner journey inspired the formulation of his therapeutic approach and individuation, giving him "the *prima materia* for a lifetime's work" (Jung, 1989, p. 199), much of which, as evidenced by his later major works, The *Psychology of the Transference, Aion* and the *Mysterium Coniuctionis*, concerned the exploration, elucidation and consummate expression of Eros. Jung had come face to face with one of the great mysteries of being. "What occurs between the lover and the beloved is the entire fullness of the Godhead. Both are unfathomable riddles to each other. For who understands the Godhead?" (Jung, 2020, vol. 7. p. 201).

Eros and Soul

"Soul is living being" asserts Jung,

the living thing in man, that which lives of itself and causes life ... But to have soul is the whole venture of life, for soul is a life-giving *daemon* ... Man cannot make it; on the contrary, it is always the *a priori* element in his moods, reactions, impulses, and whatever else is spontaneous in psychic life. It is something that lives of itself, that makes us live; it is a life behind consciousness that cannot be completely integrated with it, but from which, on the contrary, consciousness arises

(Jung, 1980, p. 42).

In 1912, Jung asked himself, "In what myth does man live nowadays?" and concluded that he and the Christian world, at least, "no longer have any myth" to live by (Jung, 1965, p. 171); we have lost soul.

The development of Western philosophy during the last two centuries has succeeded in isolating the mind in its own sphere and in severing it from its primordial oneness with the universe. Man himself has ceased to be the microcosm and *eidolon* of the cosmos, and his 'anima' is no longer the consubstantial scintilla, spark of the *Anima Mundi*, World Soul.

(Jung, 1958, pg. 476).

"The great malady of the twentieth century, implicated in all of our troubles and affecting us individually and socially, is 'loss of soul'", writes Jungian therapist Thomas Moore (1992, p. ix) and the depletion of the collective soul diminishes the world soul. "What's wrong with our society", says von Franz, "is that the whole collective consciousness doesn't valuate Eros anymore and Eros is personal. It is from one being to another being in a unique and personal way, and that is not evaluated" (von Franz in Whitney, 2004). This devaluing of Eros connectedness has led to the radical diminishment of personal soul and the world soul of which it is part, so that neither human nor the world can be whole. "Too much soul is reserved for God, too little for man. But God himself cannot flourish if man's soul is starved ... it is the function of Eros to unite what Logos has sundered" (Jung, 1982, p. 85).

In the *Gospel of the Beloved Companion*, claimed by its contemporary author, Jehanne de Quillian, to have been written by Mary Magdalen and passed down through generations in the Languedoc region of France, Mary is shown a vision of a "great tree ... [of which] the first great bough bears the fruit of love and compassion, the foundation of all things". To eat the fruit and be able to move towards higher levels of spirit (or consciousness), "you must be free of all judgement and wrath" (de Quillian, 2010, p. 117). This implies that love is teleological, not the apex of Christian teachings or self-realization as commonly taught, but the beginning of the journey, and also the force that carries one forward. Line 25 of *The Gospel of Thomas*[3] also articulates the *telos* of love as a generative force. The invocation, "Love your brother ... like your soul, guard him like the pupil of your eye" (Robinson & Smith, Eds., 1988, p. 129), assumes that one has the capacity to love another because he already loves his soul, which Jung knows is not the case in our times, nor for him personally.

Shortly after the realization of his mythlessness, Jung undertakes the inner journey of soul recovery recorded in the *Liber Novus*, which he later describes as "a voyage of discovery to the other pole of the world" (Owens, 2015, p. 5), a voyage on which he discovers his unbalanced attitude to love, feeling, and his soul. "I still labored misguidedly under the spirit of this time", he confesses,

> and thought differently about the human soul. I thought and spoke much of the soul. I knew many learned words for her, I had judged her and turned her into a scientific object. I did not consider that my soul cannot be the object of my judgment and knowledge; much more are my judgment and knowledge the objects of my soul. Therefore, the spirit of the depths forced me to speak to my soul, to call upon her as a living and self-existing being. I had to become aware that I had lost my soul ... I had to accept that what I had previously called my soul was not at all my soul, but a dead system.
>
> (Jung, 2009, pp. 128–129).

After meeting with the inner images of the prophet Elijah and his daughter, Salome, Jung writes

> "I had rejected my feeling, but I had rejected part of life. Then my feeling became a poisonous plant, and when it awakened, it was sensuality instead of pleasure, the lowest and commonest form of pleasure". Salome is the image of this pleasure, that suffers pain since it was shut out for too long. It then became apparent that Salome, "my pleasure was my soul"
>
> (Jung, 2009, p. 250, n197).

Ironically, even as Jung acknowledges his desire which is so encompassing that he calls it "my soul", he devalues it, associating it with poison, and the image of his soul is blind Salome, murderess of John the Baptist. In her erudite discussion of Jung's love life at that time, Brazilian psychologist, Maria Guerra, sees in this a reflection of Jung's overall attitude. "In projecting blindness on his representation of Eros, he was blind to his own capacity for love" (Guerra, 2014, p. 60). Jung admits as much. "Logos undoubtedly has the upper hand in this, my case … Logos has blinded and subjugated Eros" (Jung, 2009, Appendix B, p. 366).

> Logos means understanding, insight, foresight, legislation, and wisdom … Eros is desire, longing, force, exuberance, pleasure, suffering. Where Logos is ordering and insistence, Eros is dissolution and movement. They are two fundamental psychic powers that form a pair of opposites, each one requiring the other
>
> (Jung, 2009, Appendix B, p. 365).

Jung knew, writes von Franz, "that love needs to join with a compensatory Logos, as a light which shines in its darkness" (von Franz, 2008, p. 18). "In the psyche's future-orientation towards a synthesis of these forces", Edinger avers, Jung saw a revivifying "new goal and purpose for human existence" (Edinger, 1984, p. 59). *Coniunctios* (unions or marriages) of good and evil, light and dark, of Eros and Logos with their respective dissolving and ordering movements through which aspects of the personality could die and be born, and other opposites, are at the heart of Jung's new vision, its teleology, and reflected in every aspect of his therapeutic approach.

Guerra also observes that Jung "deprives … [Salome] of plentitude, making her less worthy than Elijah. This shows more differentiated thinking than feeling, the spirit of this time devaluing the spirit of the depths" (Guerra, 2014, p. 60). Jung is profoundly mistrustful of his soul, Salome, and accuses her of stealing something precious from humankind. Not surprisingly, her confession mirrors Jung's own denied and unexpressed desire: "Alas, that I can neither keep it nor conceal it! It is love, warm human love, blood, warm red blood, the holy source of life, the unification of everything separated and longed for" (Jung, 2009, p. 502). "Jung was caught between two worlds", observes Lance Owens. "The unifying and healing act mandated that he descend into earthy facts of flesh" (Owens,

2015, pp. 14–15), not only for love, Jung declares, but to be true to his instinctual nature, which is also within the purview of Eros. Logos might protest, but instinct would no longer be denied its expression.

> The acceptance of the undeveloped is therefore like a sin, like a false step, a degeneration, a descent to a deeper level; in actual fact, however, it is a greater deed than remaining in an ordered condition at the expense of the other side of our being, which is thus at the mercy of decay
>
> (Jung quoted in Owens, 2015, pp. 14–15).

Only after Jung admits his desire and values the urges of Eros can he bring himself into the more balanced attitude required for self-realization, though it costs him much. Jung writes,

> Loving reaches up to Heaven and resisting reaches just as high. They are entwined and will not let go of each other, since the excessive tension seems to indicate the ultimate and highest possibility of feeling … those two that rose up to heaven entwined are also good and evil
>
> (Jung, 2020, p. 237).

Here I am reminded of Alighieri Dante's vision in *The Inferno* of the tragic real-life lovers, Paolo Malatesta and Francesca da Polenta, killed by her brother, who soar in the air, clinging together, unrepentant of their passion even in hell to which they have been condemned for "lustfulness" (Dante, 1308–1320/1867). Later Jung rhapsodizes,

> The highest and the lowest became one. The opposites embrace each other, see eye to eye, and intermingle. They recognise their oneness in agonizing pleasure. My heart is filled with wild battle, but not with the battle of being torn apart, but from the struggle to survive together. The waves and bright rivers rush together, one crashing over the other
>
> (Jung, 2020, p. 237)

In learning to hold together within himself the powerful forces of Eros and Logos and all they represented, Jung experiences perhaps for the first time the phenomenon that would preoccupy him for the rest of his life, the *coniunctio* – "the archetype of the union of opposites" (Jung, 1989, p. 3f). Concomitant with reconciling the opposing forces of love, Jung realizes that he is also "differentiating and conjoining fragments of himself, powers that had been seen before only in projection, inner facts cast outward into women, men and things" that now "implored integration within him" (Owens, 2015, p. 57). The reverberations of this work are, for Jung, enormous. It "was the *prima materia* for a lifetime's work", he later wrote (Jung, 1989, p. 199), from which he created a therapeutic approach to help those willing to take their own inner journeys in search of self-realization and wholeness – the process of individuation, the aim of which is "nothing less than to divest the self of the false wrappings of the persona on the one hand and of the suggestive power of primordial images on the other", that is, to surrender the social masks one presents to the world, and the influence of the collective unconscious with its norms, shared values, and expectations (Jung, 1977, p. 174). "Individuation", Jung explains, is a "process by which a man becomes the definite, unique being he in fact is" (1977, p. 174).

Eros and Consciousness

"It is a common misconception that Jung's over-riding concern was the unconscious in man", writes Jung's close friend, Laurens Van der Post. Rather, Jung's work on the unconscious

> was a result of his over-riding concern for consciousness in man … Metaphorically, he was concerned with making fire for greater light out of the darkness of the mind; and to determine among other things what it was in man that so often arose to extinguish such little light as he possessed
>
> (Van der Post, 1988, p. 62).

Jung articulates this in his late life reflections:

> I understood that within the soul from its primal beginnings there has been a desire for light and an irrepressible urge to rise out of the primal darkness … It is a maternal mystery, this primordial darkness. The longing for light is the longing for consciousness
>
> (Jung, 1965, p. 269)

Light is contained in darkness and emerges from darkness, and through the entropy, eclipse or death of things, light falls back into the dark to be reborn anew. The raising of the inner light from the primal womb is a fundamental drive of the human soul.

"The purpose of human life is the creation of consciousness" (Edinger, 1984, p. 57). Driving it is Eros, the force that binds together and disperses; that causes heaven to long for earth, and earth for heaven, that draws things together, and also urges things toward their own expression and fulfillment. Jung holds that, "the concept of Eros could be expressed in modern terms as psychic relatedness" (Jung, 1982, p. 65), hence, it is connected with consciousness in all its forms. Like nature, consciousness is a living being with a meaning and telic purpose in itself. "Man's task is to become conscious of the contents that push up from the unconscious" (Edinger, 1984, p. 16). That is also the task of psychoanalysis, to help a person experience and participate in this striving of consciousness and its teleological movement through encounters with the content that arises from the unconscious. That is what I experienced in my personal treatment; the analyst made me aware of the autonomy of psyche and the dreams and images that pushed into my awareness whether I wanted them or not, so that I sometimes sensed an intelligence greater than mine working in its own way in service of an expanded consciousness and the goal of wholeness. In other words, I became aware that there were three of us in every session – myself, the analyst, and in one form or another, the autonomous psyche with its own intentions. At times, it felt as though God were there, at other times, the Devil – the many-faced, sometimes dark, sometimes radiant-light God I had experienced as a child.

Here I am reminded of the tremendous insight that Jung experiences in Africa, that "man is indispensable for the completion of creation; that, in fact, he himself is the second creator of the world" without whom creation "would have gone on in the profoundest night of non-being … Human consciousness created objective existence and meaning, and man founds his indispensable place in the great process of being" (Jung, 1965, p. 256). Writes Jungian analyst, Robert Johnson, "Through the human race the huge unconscious psyche of Nature has slowly made a part of itself conscious … it is the role of human beings to carry that evolution forward" (Johnson, 1989, p. 6). He continues, "The purpose of learning to work with the unconscious is not just to resolve our conflicts or deal with our neuroses … We cooperate with the process whereby we bring the total self together; we learn to tap that rich load of energy and intelligence that waits within" (1989, p. 9). "The essential new idea", writes Edinger, "is that the purpose of human life is the creation of consciousness" (1984, p. 17).

The unconscious brings things to consciousness, and if we engage with those contents, consciousness is expanded. It grows towards ends that are inscribed in the *telos* of the psyche. And consciousness in turn affects the unconscious, an effect that I have observed for myself in the development or transformation of certain ideas and images. Influences can move 'down' from ego consciousness to the unconscious.

Every concept in our conscious mind ... has its own psychic associations [that] are capable of changing the 'normal' character of that concept. It may even become something different as it drifts below the level of consciousness (Jung, 1964, p. 29). These "subliminal aspects" of conscious experience may not seem to affect us, "but in dream analysis they are very relevant for they are the almost invisible roots of our conscious thoughts" (ibid). Jung also found, as he puts it, that "Just as conscious contents can vanish into the unconscious, new contents, which have never yet been conscious can arise from it. The unconscious can be a source of "images and ideas ... that cannot possibly be explained in terms of memory" (Jung, 1964, p. 26). "Completely new thoughts and creative ideas can also present themselves to the unconscious ... They grow up from the dark depths of the mind like a lotus and form an important part of the subliminal psyche" (Jung, 1964, p. 25).

I had considered myself a fairly loving person, but as our sessions progressed, it became obvious that my attitude had hitherto been dominated by Logos-thinking with Eros largely repressed. Placed at a very young age in an orphanage by a government unsympathetic to unmarried mothers, I had learned to hide my feelings because they got me into trouble and made me a target for teasing. Though some things were hard to bear, I learned not react to the little cruelties that children sometimes inflict on other children, or the criticism or harshness of adults, and to appear confident and cheerful. Inwardly, though, I became full of resentment, anger, and a dreadful loneliness. By the time my mother and stepfather (who I believed was my real father) took me home, my head was full of fairytales (the old dark kind that are regrettably no longer considered suitable for children) and dark thoughts, and my inner world was a perilous labyrinth where I wandered, thoroughly confused about myself and the world, increasingly associating love and desire of any kind with fear, abandonment, and shame. If anything, I felt even lonelier at home than before, and oscillated between filial love for my mother and coldness, as I couldn't warm to her.

In one session, I recalled Hans Christian Andersen's tale of *The Snow Queen* who takes Hans, a cynical, unfeeling boy who is enchanted by her beauty and irresistible candy, to her castle, telling him she loves him. Once there, she leaves him, and he becomes so cold that his tears turn to ice, and his heart is almost frozen. He is rescued by his loving friend, Gerda, who has endured much to find him, including capture by a robber girl whose affection is immature and rough. When Gerda embraces the almost-frozen Hans, his heart melts and he at last recognizes the love and beauty that had surrounded him at home. That tale always intrigued and frightened me, I told my analyst. I had read it many times, trying to understand the strange relationship in it between love and cruelty, and in some roundabout way, I associated it with the story my mother told me years later of my biological father throwing me as an infant into the snow where I lay until she rescued me. The analyst wondered if the image of a wild river that often occurred to me might symbolize the melting of *my* frozen tears. I *had* unconsciously continued through most of my life an antithetical pattern of relating to my mother – wanting and rejecting, closeness and aloofness, caring and coldness, loving and hating, fire and ice – inwardly, like Hans, becoming more and more frozen while outwardly, trying to appear, even to myself, warm. It was not that I did not want to care and be sincerely loving, but I dared not. Relationship was strictly contained under the watchful, critical, suspicious eye of Logos, and not allowed to interfere with my self-sufficient persona or my avoidant, seemingly tranquil, safe, little life.

The participation of Eros in the psyche is obvious in the relational nature of all levels of the psyche and its telic impulse towards personal growth, but Eros is not just participatory, insists Edinger, it is intrinsic to consciousness. Without Eros connectedness, without "withness" consciousness is incomplete (Edinger, 1984, p. 36). We do not become more conscious alone. Jung wrote that the psyche has an "urge to a higher and more comprehensive consciousness" ... [and] to fulfill its purpose, needs all parts of the whole, including those that are projected into a 'You'" (Jung, 1989, p. 101).

The unrelated human being lacks wholeness, for he can achieve whole-ness only through the soul, and the soul cannot exist without its other side, which is always found in a 'You'. Wholeness is a combination of I and You, and these show themselves to be parts of a transcendent unity whose nature can only be grasped symbolically ... Hence wholeness is the product of an intrapsychic process which depends essentially on the relation of one individual to another

(Jung, 1998, pp. 82–83).

That is, consciousness requires Eros. "Where 'knowing' is a function of Logos, 'withness' is a function of Eros ... consciousness, is in its root mean-ing, a conjunction, a union of Logos and Eros" (Edinger, 1984, pp. 52–53).

Von Franz affirms to this double aspect of consciousness when she writes, "According to the scholastic theory of knowledge you can only get knowledge through love, which means that you only acquire knowledge by loving your subject, by being fascinated by it" (von Franz, 1980a, p. 116). This feeling for something is an aspect of Eros. It is libido, it is energy, it is dynamic, the generative spark.

On the one hand emotion is the alchemical fire whose warmth brings everything into existence and whose heat burns all superfluities to ashes ... But on the other hand emotion is the moment when steel meets flint and a spark is struck forth, for emotion is the chief source of conscious-ness. There is no change from darkness to light or from inertia to move-ment without emotion

(Jung, 1982, p. 27).

Edinger clarifies further: To know something is not consciousness in the full sense of "knowing with". To achieve consciousness, the ego must not only be the knower, it "must also go through the experience of being the object of knowledge", that is, to both know subjectively and to be known objectively by an 'other' (Edinger, 1984, p. 41). Jung explains it thus:

Individuation has two principal aspects: in the first place it is an internal and subjective process of integration, and in the second it is an equally indis-pensable process of objective relationship. Neither can exist without the other, although sometimes the one and sometimes the other predominates

(Jung, 1989, p. 72).

This 'other' can be another person with whom one has a relationship, or the Self, the "inner guiding factor" or "regulating centre that brings about a constant extension and maturing of time personality" (von Franz, 1964, p. 163). It is not sufficient for the ego to be conscious for it is in a reciprocal relationship with the Self. "The ego has a responsibility to the Self to be its knowing subject as well as its known object" (Edinger, 1984, p. 53). While in psychotherapy, an individual may project this "knowing other" onto the therapist, who can temporarily become for her "a substitute for the inner 'knowing one', i.e. the Self" (1984, p. 41).

For the telos of individuation to be activated, the active participation of the individual is essential. The person is not allowed to be passive in the therapeutic process. "Therapy aims at strengthening the conscious mind", says Jung, adding that wherever possible, he tried to "rouse the patient to mental activity" to subdue and get above their confusion, for "the unconscious can be integrated only if the ego holds its ground". It is the therapist's task to help the individual "in freeing the ego con-sciousness from contamination with the unconscious" (Jung, 1989, pp. 108–109). The role of the therapist as the "knowing other" is, therefore, no small matter, as I discovered for myself. As the observing other, my therapist continually encouraged me to attend closely to what was aris-ing from the unconscious and my inner impressions of it, even when it was difficult to do so and I might seek to create a distraction. His persis-tence helped to keep me focused though my mind wanted to wander to something easier. Some might be able to do that work on their own, but I don't know that I could have, without the analyst, remained grounded in myself. Sometimes, the therapist says, "I have no idea", and regards me silently. I can feel uncomfortable or nervous at such times, or annoyed, but then, Jung says, something may happen, perhaps a memory or a sudden image "that points the way ahead" (Gerster, 2008, p. 410), not usually in a direction one expects. It's as though the psyche decides to speak up with its own direction.

Eros in Jung's Psychology

For Jung, the concepts of connectedness and relationship, as embodied by Eros, were essential parts of therapy from the very beginning. Regarding his early work in the asylum at Burghölzli, he confides in Laurens van der Post, "I learned there that only the physician who feels himself deeply affected by his patients could heal" (van der post, p. 128). "The analysand can be transformed only to the extent that the doctor has been himself transformed" (von Franz, 1998a, p. 64). Not long before Jung's death, Van der Post praises his "gift of propinquity and respect for what I called the essential 'otherness' of all persons and things" (1988, p. 60). "We can get in touch with another person by an attitude of unprejudiced objectivity", Jung writes, "not a purely intellectual and detached attitude of mind but ... a human quality – a kind of respect for the secret life of such a human life ... It is a moral achievement on the part of the doctor" (Jung, 1955, p. 234). While a degree of objectivity and distance are necessary in the therapeutic relationship, it is, Jung believes, the genuine care of the therapist and his desire for the person's development, that is, his alignment with the relationship energy of Eros, that helps the person to look inside herself to find what is true for her, no matter how unacceptable, and to bring it forth, to be seen for the person she really is. That is where therapy starts, said Jung in a 1957 interview with Dr Richard Evans: "In therapy you treat the patient as he is in the present moment, irrespective of causes and such things" (Quoted in Evans, 1957, p. 50). "I was compelled always in the beginning to respect my patients' own truth and idiom and never treated two patients alike," he tells van der Post, who recalls from their long conversations together that Jung "used the word patient with great reluctance because he felt that people in trouble with themselves gave him precious insights that he could never have obtained any other way and preferred to talk of ... persons working with him" (van der Post, 1988, p. 60).

Jung's "respect for ... the essential 'otherness' of all persons and things" (van der Post, 1988, p. 60) sometimes resulted in a healing that Jung himself could not explain, attributing it to "the grace of God" (van der Post p. 375). God, yes, working through the instrument of Jung's care and his authenticity. Von Franz was very critical of

the false kindness and all-bearing friendliness, which certain analysts show to their patients, following the model of the general practitioner's persona style ... It is an escape that serves to avoid finding out and adequately expressing one's true feelings, which are not always kind and all-bearing, and an escape from ongoing frictions and collisions of feeling

(von Franz, 2008, p. 11).

"The physician … must meet the patient with his whole personality and open himself to the irrational forces from both the patient's and his own unconscious" (von Franz, 1998a, p. 64). If this is not Eros connectedness, I don't know what is, and it is a crucial element of Jung's psychology and therapeutic approach. The generous, courageous openness of the analyst can foster in a person the will and courage to respond in kind, and eventually to love herself enough to engage fully and deeply in the work.

"Love is of fundamental importance to the human, and, as careful inquiry consistently shows, is of far greater significance than the individual suspects", suggests Jung (1977, p.18). Love not only enriches, deepens, and drives, it also contains and moderates. Without the mediation of love, man would be at the mercy of unmodified instinct. "Inter-human Eros", Jung knows, is "the preconscious ground of all communication and community, as well as being that psychic element which, through its power to compensate and limit, stands opposed to the boundless or one-sided drive to live out any single instinct" (von Franz, 1998a, p. 125). "That is why", adds von Franz in a footnote, "Jung constantly stressed the fact that we should be less concerned with perfection … than with completeness or wholeness, not excluding any essential human disposition … in our psyche" (1998a, p. 131f). Until a person has sincerely engaged with love, struggled with it, if need be, she is not yet an initiate of the soul's quest to know itself, a quest that Jung showed is, at the very least, as profound as the quest for the Holy Grail. In his 'Late Thoughts', he mused, "I sometimes feel that Paul's words – 'Though I speak with the tongues of men and of angels but have not love' – might well be the first condition of all cognition and the quintessence of divinity itself" (1965, p. 353). Love is the first step into the mystery of the Self. Though many, perhaps most, stop at love's enchantments and go no further. Without love, without the drive of Eros to connection, to relationship, or wholeness, there is no drive to know one's soul, to know oneself and others for who they are rather than who we want or expect them to be, no yearning for connectedness, no motivation to strive for authentic being, or individuation. Without the energy of Eros, the psyche does not open the doors to its secrets and may appear to block our efforts even as it throws up hints and urgings.

Wrestling with Eros

When Eros burst into my awareness, it was like being pushed about by a great force without direction, but soon after beginning work with my therapist, it felt like being shot with fire – the flaming arrows of Eros

– and they truly did hurt. I was aghast. If this was love, I could not stop it … nor did I want to, if truth be told. "Eros does not tend toward … the side of consciousness, conscious will and conscious choice", writes Jung in the *Red Book*, "but toward the side of the heart, which is less subject to our conscious will" (*Liber Novus*, p. 366). I was Eros-possessed. "There are", writes Jung, "forms of instinctive concupiscent that come … from hunger, from wanting to possess" (Jung, 1989, p. 9). In a case study, Jung describes something very similar to what I experienced. He writes of a patient's

> "violent, sentimental demand for love, so impassioned that she feels herself overwhelmed. This demand has the character of an overpowering infantile craving, which, as we know, is blind. So we are dealing with an undisciplined, undifferentiated, and not yet humanized part of the libido[4] which still possesses the compulsive character of an instinct, a part still untamed by domestication. For such a part some kind of animal is an entirely appropriate symbol"
>
> (Jung, 1977, p. 86)

It felt animal-like to me, and animal images did indeed arise in conjunction with it, first a great bear then a lean wolf that I discuss further on. Whatever this feeling was, it clearly cared not a whit for reason or will; it was relentless and felt like madness, like the Dionysian frenzy that I had always read about with dread. Thinking of this mythologically, I had been captured by the god Eros, but if I had offended some god, it was the insane-making Dionysus, god of *ekstasis*, and he would have his retribution.

In fear of what I might do, more than anything, anxious and deeply embarrassed, I told the analyst. This is where the rubber meets the road, I thought. To my immense relief, he took it in stride and went on as before, delving deeper and deeper into my psyche. But I was struggling. Whatever it was, it was consuming, painful, and exquisitely real. Jung speaks of the "central significance of the transference in psychotherapy on the one hand and in the field of normal human relationships" (1989, p. 159). "Where you have no projection, you have no relationship … Attention … is created either by the concentration of consciousness, or by love, and behind both is projection (von Franz, 1980a, p. 118). "Unless we are possessed of an unusual degree of self-awareness, we shall never see through our projections", writes von Franz, "but must always succumb to them" (1998b, p. 7).

But projection cannot be trusted. "The effect of projection is to isolate the subject from his environment, since instead of a real relation to it there is now only an illusory one", says Jung in *Aion*. "The more projections are thrust in between the subject and the environment, the harder it is for the ego to see through its illusions" (Jung, 1970a, pp. 9–10).

I do not intend to label my feelings here, rather, to emphasize how independent of my will they were, and how hard I tried to make sense of them, but I was blowing against a storm. Von Franz writes that

> the word 'transference' should only be used in an intentional way to address some illusory projections on the side of the patient or the doctor. It should never be used for the feeling relationship which builds up in the course of the encounter in therapy
>
> (2008, p. 11).

And, quotes Jung: "The so-called dissolution of the transference often consists in ceasing to describe the nature of one's relationship as 'transference'. This designation degrades the relationship as a mere projection, which it is not" (Quoted in von Franz, 2008, p. 11). When I asked the analyst about transference, he wisely said nothing, and continued looking into the symbols and images that erupted from the unconscious in dreams, spontaneous art, and active imagination. This quickly became the major part of our work together.

A World of Images

One of Jung's greatest contributions is his confirmation that the contents of the psyche are real. "There is nothing for it but to recognize the irrational as a necessary, because ever-present, psychological function, and to take its contents not as concrete realities ... but as psychic realities, real because they work" (Jung, 1977, p. 95). "When the individual has eventually learned to 'let things happen'", to acknowledge and somehow engage with what arises as valid psychic content, "a new attitude is created, an attitude which accepts the non-rational and the incomprehensible simply because it is what is happening" (Jung, 1962, p. 95). Engagement with these elements is essential. It is not enough to just look at inner images. "One has to enter into the process with one's own personal reactions" (von Franz, 1998b, p. 104).

After a fantasy has been fixed in some specific form, it must be examined both intellectually and ethically, with an evaluating feeling reaction. And it is essential to regard it as being absolutely real; there must be no lurking doubt that this is 'only a fantasy'. If this is practiced with devotion over a long period, the process of individuation ... can unfold in its true form

(von Franz, 1964, pp. 195–196).

Jung also emphasizes the ethical aspect of working with images. "It is ... a great mistake to think that it is enough to gain some understanding of the images and that knowledge can here make a halt. Insight into them must be converted into an ethical obligation" (1965, pp. 192–193).

Regarding images and symbols, I had always tended to 'let things happen' simply because they did. I had childhood dreams and 'visions' so vivid and real that I often could not distinguish inner from outer experience and responded to them as real. At that age, knowing nothing about the psyche, I took these images as symbolic messages from my soul, which I experienced as an autonomous entity within and around me, or from God, and left it at that. I was especially puzzled by images of people, sometimes religious figures who were not at all as they were presented in religious teachings and could be frightening. Once in my teens, as I dug furiously in the garden, which I often did when forbidden to express anger, the Virgin Mary came before me, standing just above the ground. "What do you want?" I asked rather snappishly because I didn't believe in her. "Continue digging", she said with a little smile, and my anger dissipated. The symbolic life and visions are not generally acceptable topics of conversation, and people can react harshly. Maybe they just do not know. "In our normal state of consciousness we are seldom aware of the fact that the unconscious psyche makes a substantial contribution to our perception of reality and that we never perceive reality as such", explains von Franz. "Hence we are scarcely aware that even this normal state relates to the outer world we are moving in a field of images that deviates considerably from the 'reality' that has been demonstrated by physics" (von Franz, 1998b, p. 195).

Over time, even after becoming acquainted with Jung's ideas about the psyche, I tended to downplay the symbolic aspects of my life other than dreams. By the time I entered into psychoanalysis, armed with at least a basic knowledge of Jung and his ideas on the psyche and its images, and determined to know and become fully myself, I was quite prepared to engage with my unconscious and its contents, but after a lifetime of having my images and 'fantasies' (as Jung calls them) dismissed, ridiculed, or even forbidden, I was initially cautious, looking for the smallest signs of doubt or skepticism from the analyst. There was nothing of the kind. Instead, he taught me by his example to trust my psyche and its contents, to accept that they were meaningful, and to use them as windows into myself. Our discussions added to my self-knowing, which sometimes brought something new into the equation, adding to consciousness. This pertains to the therapist as well, says Jung.

> "He is not just working for this particular patient, who may be quite insignificant, but for himself as well and his own soul, and in so doing, he is perhaps laying an infinitesimal grain in the scales of humanity's soul. Small and invisible as this contribution may be, it is yet an *opus magnum*"
>
> (Jung quoted in Edinger, 1984, pp. 22–23)

Bear Image

"Libido can never be apprehended except in a definite form; that is to say, it is identical with fantasy images", Jung explains. "That is why … we give the unconscious a chance to bring its fantasies to the surface" (1977, p. 215). Working with images in analysis proved enormously fruitful and was the heart of our work together. One powerful dream symbol that arose early in our sessions was a bear called Urso (I did not choose the name. It was given). I dreamed I was confronted by a great brown bear standing tall on its hind legs among boulders on a mountain that reminded me of Yosemite National Park in California, a favorite place of mine. Behind his head shone a bright stylized sun with rays. He said he wanted to eat me. My first reaction was to get away, but it occurred to me that if I were inside the bear, I would be inviolable, so I agreed. That was the dream. When I intuitively sketched it, the bear was behind me, holding me, and I appeared at ease. There was also a strong erotic element to the drawing that I pretended not to notice. Like the bear in the Brothers Grimm tale, *Rose White and Rose Red*,[5] Urso proved to be a protector, beloved and loving. If an animal appears in fairytales or dreams "without any wrong admixture", writes von Franz, "wolf as a wolf, and a bear as a bear … then it simply represents one instinctive drive in its positive and negative form" (1990, pp. 101–102). Bear-Urso was that, but a lot more.

The therapist observed that the goddess Artemis, who demanded that her followers remain virgins, and generally disliked men, was associated with a bear. I had in my early adulthood identified with Artemis. "The name Artemis means water, – that which reflects reality back to the onlooker" (Mascetti, 1994, p. 71). Therapy was for me that mirror. Previously, I had considered myself truthful, discovering only through therapy that I had hidden from myself so much of my inner reality, my emotions, and beliefs. Like Artemis, however, I would become enraged if I felt my privacy infringed upon, especially by male persons, rage that I did not yet realize I had borne since childhood. Instead of turning the offending male into a deer and setting my hounds on him, as Artemis did to Acteon when he spied her bathing (Mascetti, 1994, p. 71), I coldly shut that person out of my life. Though I did not see that severity in my sketch of Urso, the analyst did, and commented on it. Urso was clearly of some relevance to my psyche and its urging towards greater consciousness. In *Aion*, Jung portrays the bear as an image of the self.

The self can appear in all shapes from the highest to the lowest, inasmuch as these transcend the scope of the ego personality in the manner of a daimonion. It goes without saying that the self also has its theriomorphic[6] symbolism. The commonest of these images in modern dreams are, in my experience, the elephant, horse, bull, bear

(1970a, p. 226).

Intuitively, however, I most strongly linked bear-Urso to my analyst and our therapeutic environment. "From analytic experience", says Jung,

one knows that the early dreams which patients bring for analysis are nonetheless of special interest, because of the fact that they bring out criticisms and valuations of the physician's personality, which previously would have been asked for directly in vain. They enrich the conscious impression which the patient had of his physician, and very often concerning important points.

Also, "they are naturally erotic observations" (Jung, 2016, p. 29). While the bear felt wild to me, and dangerous – reflected in claw marks drawn on my body – it gave me a feeling of being protected and cared for. It 'had my back', an especially meaningful concept for me. Although the analyst asked if there was a sexual element to the dream image, I could not at that time admit it.

Another therapist might have blithely described my association of the analyst with the bear image as a projection. My therapist wisely did not. He knew from my drawing and our discussion of it that Urso represented to me what I most wanted, and that I perceived in him those qualities – care, protection, reassurance, and imperturbability. Instead, he matter-of-factly accepted the relationship of Urso with my feelings for him, suggesting that they could be useful to me, which they were, for they drew me into a deep exploration of my beliefs about love: its untrustworthiness; the manipulations of the will to power that I either mistook for, or pretended to be, love; the desire for love, on one hand, and resistance to it, on the other. "Symbols are natural attempts to reconcile and unite the opposites of the psyche", writes Jung (1964, p. 96). I recognized this opposition in me: wanting to stand firm on my own values and priorities, to ask for and take what I wanted and needed, yet fearing to offend and be rejected, feeling responsible for others, relinquishing for the sake of peace. Bear-Urso represented to me both the steadiness and acceptance of my therapist, even when I told him ugly things, and also unpredictability, potential savagery, and the need to be cautious and careful around it. My mother, who had loved me, had that wildness in her, and I came to see that so did I, that I too had wounded those I cared about. Urso also represented powerful instincts and urges of my youth, including the instinct for self-preservation and the urge for self-gratification, to take what I needed or wanted, and the intense guilt associated with that. For since childhood, I had been taught and had acquired from fairytales a strict morality of sacrifice and self-abnegation that, while I did not come even close to living its ideals, influenced me greatly and caused me much moral distress.

Urso also represented ignored or repressed physical instincts, "physiological urges" that "often reveal their presence only by symbolic images" (Jung, 1964, p. 58). I had resisted my animal-instinctive self with its troublesome, shameful impulses and longings, and repressed it, nurturing instead an image of myself as free of desire, spiritually inclined, serene in my intellectual equanimity. Urso had come to help bring me down from mind into my instinctual animal body. A year or so before bear-Urso, I had dreamed I was an animal in a ferny underbrush, being fed soup from a rough wooden bowl with a wooden spoon by a bear-like grandmother animal. I had interpreted that dream as concerning my relationship to the environment, to nature. Exploring the Urso image helped me to see that the earlier dream had also urged me towards my 'natural' self, my shunned animal-instinctive nature. Urso also held for me a persistent childhood fear of being harmed and abandoned that I explored in depth with my therapist, and also, a conflicted desire to be both taken in and to take in.

More importantly for me, with the analyst's participation, Urso helped me to counteract a very negative animus. My mother, fairytales, and some very unpleasant experiences with the masculine were not the only factors affecting my attitude to love and trust, especially to men who I considered overall, with some exceptions, undependable and dangerous. Another very influential factor was an inner voice of warning, cynicism, or derision that had spoken to me for so many years that I took it for the voice of my inner self or soul. As a child, I thought it might be the voice of fearsome giant faces that often peered at me from the clouds, the 'watchers' ... or God, whose eyes I always felt on me. "Until one clears the negative relationship to the animus", Jung told psychotherapist Esther Harding,

> the voice of the animus is as the voice of God within us; in any case, we respond to it as if it were. ... When we are not aware of the negative aspect of the animus, we are still animal, still connected to nature, therefore unconscious and less than human
>
> (Harding, 2008, p. 47).

In one dream, three black parrots said to me, "stupid, stupid, stupid", the same words that I often heard my head. The animus was especially vociferous regarding being loved or loveable, even cared about, which, it would insist, I definitely was not. And I believed it. Had life not proved it true? Others might be loved, but not me. Others might be loveable, desirable, worthy of love, but not me. Something in me was flawed and made me fundamentally unappealing and unworthy, even, though I wanted to believe otherwise, to God. Such is the negative power of the *animus*, the archetype of the masculine in woman.

Jung's comment that "the animus often appears as a painter or has some kind of projection apparatus or is a cinema-operator or owner of a picture-gallery" helped me to recognize him. "All this refers to the animus as the function mediating between conscious and unconscious", Jung writes, "the unconscious contains pictures which are transmitted, that is, made manifest, by the animus, either as fantasies or, unconsciously, in the patient's own life and actions" (1980, p. 189). In one dream, I handed over a large golden box full of precious things to a painter to whom I had already given much. As I did so, I wept as though my heart was breaking, wept in sorrow for all that I could have done, but had given over to him, unbidden. The painter remained in the deep shadows in that dream, oblivious to me, surrounded by beautiful works that I knew should have been mine. Until reading Jung's comment, above, the dream had puzzled me greatly. Now its meaning was clear, and to the analyst I mourned all that I had not done, the abilities not used, the ideas not followed through because my negative animus had convinced me that I was incompetent, talentless, and unworthy of achievement.

"The *anima* [the archetype of the feminine in man] contains all of a man's experiences of and reactions to women, beginning with his mother", Jung explains. "Similarly, the *animus* contains all of a woman's experiences of and reactions to men, beginning with her father" (Jung, 1977, pp. 258–259). My experiences with men, especially in my younger years, were sometimes threatening, emotionally debilitating, and in a few instances, physically harmful, and I had no positive male figures, so it was inevitable that I developed a strong, insistently negative animus. In an interview with psychotherapist filmmaker Frans Boa, von Franz says,

> The negative animus tries to cut off women from any kind of relationship by belittling the relationship or calling it crazy or by some other means … it's … these kind of … self-destructive thoughts which put themselves between her and her femininity, and her possibility of relating to an outer man in a positive sense … When a woman has not recognised and integrated the masculine power within her, it can literally possess her, rendering her unable to .draw on the strengths, even her own femininity, or to have genuine mutually supportive relationships with men
>
> (von Franz quoted in Boa, 1985).

Nor could I draw on feminine images for balance, not on my desperately unhappy mother or my stoic, dutiful grandmother, or the girls in the fairytales I loved who tended to be submissive, all-enduring, brave but self-effacing and self-sacrificing like the Handless Maiden, who obligingly sacrifices her hands to pay her father's debt to the devil.

Often, when in the early stages of analysis, I expressed persistent doubts about my worth or capabilities, or criticized myself, the analyst would ask,

"Who is saying that?", prompting me to distinguish my voice from that other, the voice of the negative animus, and to see it as a psychic entity with its own will that could be opposed. "The essential thing is to differentiate oneself from these unconscious contents by personifying them and at the same time to bring them into relationship with consciousness. That is the technique for stripping them of their power" (Jung, 1965, p. 187). At the same time, the analyst was showing me, through his own example, a very different kind of masculinity than I had experienced for most of my life, one that could be supportive of me and my sovereignty. And because I had strongly associated the therapist with Urso, the bear became an integral factor in the positive masculine complex that was slowly forming an affirming *animus*. I had, not so long ago, a series of dreams of friendly young men coming to the seashore in small boats to invite me to go with them. Each time, I timidly declined, the last time, ruefully. Maybe they were positive animus in my psyche that just got tired of waiting. Two more recent dreams suggested that they might still be there. In one, I was with an anxious boy in his late teens whom I could not reassure; in the next, I was being helped by a friendly young man who I thought might be the boy, now more mature and confident. Perhaps, the analyst and I speculated, another animus is growing in my psyche, as the power over me of the old negative one is dismantled.

Concurrently, and without my knowing, the therapist (and in some ways, the bear-Urso image) came to represent for me the supportive, protective, trustable father I had never known. A therapist "may serve to 'reparent' a person who has not experienced 'these gifts'", writes James Hollis, providing the "affirmation, the modeling, the encouragement and challenging we need from the father archetype … [to] help compensate for what was missing in the actual biography of the patient". It is "no small gift … and potentially healing to the patient" (Hollis, 2004, p. 46). When I recognized the father image in my therapist, his solicitousness, and the reassurance I gained from his sometimes stern articulation of boundaries and personal responsibility, I understood for the very first time what a positive father image can mean to a girl or a woman, whatever her age, and how disempowered she can be (as I had been) by the lack of it.

Wolf Image

A very different image that arose soon after the bear, and that was from then on concomitant with the bear, was a wolf. It was becoming easier for me to talk about sexual urges without much embarrassment, but von Franz posits that an erotic stimulus is not always what it seems. It could be "a disguised unconscious impulse, which really implies knowledge or a progress of consciousness, which appears first in this form" (von Franz, 1980a, p. 57).

> Something wants to come up from the unconscious, but there is a short circuit, and it appears as a sexual urge, because there is some sort of difficulty in getting on further … The advice is in such cases is to wait and first ask the thing that rushes in for all its secrets

(1980a, p. 59).

What came in, though quietly, was a powerful image called Lobo who appeared in a brief dream as a shadowy wolf. In an active imagination on that image, wolf was in a forest on a moonlit night, indicating that I should follow him. He was lean, hungry looking, with fierce eyes and ragged fur, not part of a pack but solitary. He led me to a small clearing among tall straight trees, and lay down before a low, broken stone wall, curling his tail around him. I sat away from him, not frightened but nervous, for now and then, he growled at me, revealing shiny red gums and large strong teeth to remind me what he was. A small fire flickered close to the stone wall, the apex of our triangular arrangement. I was deeply affected, and at home, in a highly emotional state, I drew it.

Wolf-Lobo reminded me of my grandmother's memories of being afraid of wolf howls in mid-winter Russia, and my mother's stories of children eaten by wolves. It reminded me of terrible, recurring childhood nightmares of a man dismembering babies in an industrial kitchen that was full of body parts hung on meat hooks. I could see him though glass doors, and turning to get away, I would be faced with more glass doors behind which raged a pack of wolves. Each time I opened the doors, they would lunge at me, biting savagely and I would beat them off with the animals whose teeth had locked into my bleeding arms. Wolf-Lobo was not savage, though I knew he could be, but he was menacing, hungry, lonely, and lean, evoking sharp memories of a hungry, lonely childhood and a myriad of unseen things that pushed at me like anxious ghosts. Though I knew myself with a family, a history, a reality that made sense, and felt cared for by the therapist-bear synergy, the Lobo image brought back to me a long-forgotten childhood sense of feeling alone, lost, and terrorized in a world full of demons.

Something in me identified strongly with the wolf's gauntness. The analyst had previously drawn attention to many experiences connected with my belly, the pelvic area, that had arisen in our conversations – blood, surgical resections, infection, sexual violence, pain, a vivid childhood dream of my mother eviscerating herself as she whirled about laughing, emptiness, loss, and physical hunger. All this was implicit in the wolf-Lobo image, and reinforced for me by von Franz's powerful description of a "growling wolf within, the iron grim". I quote her at some length:

> The wolf … often represents a capacity which is very closely connected with people who have a wolf problem, namely, a general, all-devouring greed … the wolf is always the victim of his hungry stomach. When that gets the better of him, he loses all intelligence … In his paper on the transference … [Jung] says that very often such a terrific greed awakes in people that they want to eat everybody and everything – for example, to eat their analyst completely. It is not even on the level of a sexual transference, but on an even more primitive level, for it is to 'have' the other: to have everything … This great desire to eat everything is very often the result of great frustration in childhood, which had built up a kind of bitter resentment on one side, combined with the greedy desire to have and eat everything. The 'grim' then is a kind of sulky resentment because one can't have the thing. … They get caught in a kind of vicious circle of cold resentment and greed, which is often fittingly symbolised by the wolf
>
> (von Franz, 1990, pp. 202–203).

From the beginning, I had experienced the Urso-bear image as mostly positive. True, it had brought me into confrontation with an unconscious negative mother complex that conflicted greatly with the conscious image I had held of my mother as loving and loved by me; it had shown me that I was dominated by a negative animus, but my personal imago was not too much threatened, and I felt rather pleased with my progress in becoming self-aware. Wolf-Lobo proved to be another thing entirely. He did not come to protect me, I discovered. When, at the analyst's suggestion, I dropped into that childhood nightmare of wolves and asked why they fell upon me, I was told, "To wake you up to fight back". No, in big matters, I had never fought back, just switched off and endured. I was proud of my ability to endure. That is why Lobo emerged, to stir up my spirit, and also, like the helpful wolf in the Russian tale, "Tsarevich Ivan and the Grey Wolf", to take me where I must go. "Since I have eaten your horse", he tells the Tsarevich, "I shall be your true and faithful servant", and keeps his word even though three times, the Tsarevich fails to follow his wise instructions (Tsarevich Ivan, 1966, pp. 20–32). Wolf-Lobo also served me well, taking me deeper into unknown regions of my psyche, into the dark and dirty shadows, and back into the light.

In alchemy, "the wolf is the animal of Mars. Astrologically, Mars characterizes the instinctual and affective nature of man. The subjugation and transformation of this nature seems to be the theme of the alchemical opus", writes Jung (1970b, pp. 39). Jung notes that wolf is also an "initiating animal; he has this significance in Canto I of Dante's *Inferno*" (Jung,1970b, pp. 39). In his mid-life and a "dark night of the soul", Dante finds himself in a dark forest looking for "the straightforward pathway" and thinks to take a mountain path that seemed to lead up to the light. But "almost where the ascent began", he finds his way blocked by a panther, then a lion, then "a she-wolf, that with all her hungerings Seemed to be laden in her meagreness … brought upon me so much heaviness … Which, coming on me by degrees Thrust me thither where the sun is silent". The shade of the poet Virgil appears, full of harsh words about the wolf that blocks the way upward and offers to guide Dante along another road down through hell (Dante, 1308–1320/1867). Only by going into the dark place of the unconscious where he will encounter the shadow side of humanity and himself can Dante climb to the light. Virgil reviles the she-wolf that blocked the mountain path, but she is a helper, forcing Dante to the path on which he has to go, as Lobo pushed me to where I would rather not go.

"At first we cannot see beyond the path that leads downward to dark and hateful things", writes Jung "but no light or beauty will ever come from the man who cannot bear this sight" (Jung, 1955, p. 215). So must we all who want to redeem our lost souls go into the dark shadow, not voluntarily but pushed onto that road by fear or heaviness of spirit or desperation. Through wolf-Lobo, I was made to recognize distasteful and difficult aspects of myself. Where bear-Urso made me feel safe and protected, wolf-Lobo aroused painful childhood memories of hunger, emptiness, desperately wanting to be loved and touched, and powerful longings, eventually taking me deeper into inexpressible rage. When a Chinese acupuncturist told me years ago that certain features of my body were manifestations of intense, protracted childhood anger, I scoffed because I remembered myself as a generally affable child. In therapy, it was wolf's lean hungry belly that I first identified with, the wanting, the terrible longing, and angry resentment so overwhelming that it felt like swimming in mud. In childhood, I had felt so weak and ashamed of my longing that I strove to want nothing, to desire nothing, to elevate myself above the world of people and feelings like the saints, martyrs, and ascetics I sometimes read about; I would become coolly detached and superior. Over time, though, the anger, the pain, the hurt, and the unexpressed seem to have sunk into the depths where they were forgotten. What remained, if I cared to see it, was outrage, rage that exploded when I encountered gross injustice, rage against false accusations, rage at seeing another child mistreated, rage over mistreatment of the environment or indigenous people, a kind of "holy rage" sometimes associated with the wolf in mythology which, says von Franz, "is why the wolf is not only destructive. It all depends on how it is dealt with, and what the situation is when it comes up" (1990, p. 199).

As Lobo woke up, so too did dark memories and feelings, and I was often in tears of self-pity. My belly literally ached. In one active imagination, I 'dropped' into my belly which was a brass bowl, full of blood but paradoxically empty, empty, empty ... and full of tears, the melting tears of Hans in the *Snow Queen*, tears of loneliness, frustration, and longing. Like wolf-Lobo, I was hungry. It had been literal hunger back then in the orphanage as well as emotional hunger, but now, it was suggested, the child in me needed to be nourished, to be held, loved, touched, cared for, to be mothered, and the instinctual self needed to be allowed its expression. I needed to draw on the loving, connecting, relationship energies of Eros, which is difficult, improbable, Jung suggests, if one has not accepted oneself.

So much of the analyst's work with me, I now appreciate, was trying to foster self-acceptance and self-love in me. "Self-forgetting virtue is an unnatural alienation from one's own essence, which is thus deprived of redemption", writes Jung in his *Black Book* journals as he sought to reconcile with his soul and his authentic self.

It is a sin to deliberately alienate the other from his self by means of one's own virtuousness. This sin rebounds on us. It is submission enough, amply enough, if we subjugate ourselves to our self. The work of redemption is always first to be done on ourselves. This work cannot be done without love for ourselves. Selfless love is a sin because it is not true. We can never abandon ourselves, or else we will abandon our work of redemption. But we should also not use the other for our own alleged redemption. The other is no ladder for our feet

(Jung, 2020, vol. v, p. 239).

Reconciling with Eros

Eros is considered an unruly energy but as the psychoanalytic process evolved, it became more and more obvious to me that, in one way or another, Eros was present, a dynamic participant that sometimes seemed to purposely push our work with images and symbols in unexpected directions. A symbol always "implies something vague, unknown, or hidden from us" (Jung, 1964, p. 3). "It has a wider 'unconscious' aspect that is never precisely defined or fully explained. Nor can one hope to explain it. As the mind explores the symbol, it is led to ideas that lie beyond the grasp of reason" (Jung, 1964, p. 4). Elsewhere, Jung states,

> In making the shadow conscious, analytic treatment causes a cleavage and a tension of opposites which in their turn seek compensations in unity. The adjustment is achieved through symbols. If all goes well, the solution, seemingly of its own accord, appears out of nature. Then and then only is it convincing. It is felt as a grace
>
> (Jung, 1965, p. 335).

After months with Urso, I was reading beneath a wide tree at a coffee shop when I suddenly felt wholly embraced by the Urso image: it now totally surrounded me. There was a transcendent quality to it, as though a pool of sunlight had fallen around me and through me, making me clean. I felt totally emotionally free. And in that radiance, I could 'see' that Urso held for me the super-charged Eros-libido feeling for the therapist that had so troubled me. I had thought that I must have subliminally channeled that wild libidinal energy into the Urso image, where it was contained, creating just enough emotional distance to allow me a little much-needed objectivity, but the psyche had worked its own magic without me. How often does the ego mind take credit for the work of the autonomous psyche?

I understood that had some of my passion and desire *not* been held for me by the Urso image, I might not have been able to depotentiate it, and would probably have dumped it onto the therapist. That great wave of feeling might have awoken dangerous archetypal energies that might have drowned me, and if I did not go mad (which had felt like a real possibility at the time), it might have ruined our therapeutic relationship. Now, I told the analyst, my feelings had calmed enough for me to see him more objectively, not as savior or rescuer, but ... what? Carer, he offered. Yes. Certainly that. At the same time, I saw that part of the Urso image (not all of it) had somehow reformed itself into a comforting trinity of male bear, female bear, and libido (Eros), transmuting part of that erotic energy into mother love – I was infused with it – in the process, reconciling my negative mother image with the positive mother-bear. According to Professor of European Archaeology, Marija Gimbutas, the Mother Bear associated with the adamantly virginal goddess Artemis, who was ironically also goddess of childbirth. "She is young, she is beautiful, she is goddess of childbirth she has the power to stimulate growth and she is the bear mother nursing the divine child" (Gimbutas, 2001, p. 183).

In an active imagination on another image entirely, I was led to the other libido image, Lobo, who transformed from ravenous wolf into the alchemical wolf that eats the dead king who will be reborn, then into a mother wolf. However, it was not the king that died but rather, an aspect of me that nourished a new child about two to three years old. Here was the wolf image associated in Norse mythology with the "death-winter goddess, Skaoi" whose sacred animal, the wolf, "eats the bodies of the dead" and the Germanic Holla, "goddess of death and regeneration" (Gimbutas, 2001, pp. 194–195). Lobo did not die, as the alchemical wolf does; instead it became in part a mother wolf licking blood from the new child's beaming face. The context is not relevant here; it is just enough to say that the Lobo image, as the Urso image had done, became two images, one male, one female, with two different qualities. Male Lobo was still the ravenous, hurt one that had befriended me and, now calmer, was often at my side, whereas she-wolf was tender to the new child, protective, representing a different kind of mother love in which I felt not sexuality, as I did with Urso, but ferocity, a kind of burning anger. I did notice a fire burning in the background of that scene, and thought it might mean that Lobo must burn, as the alchemical wolf is burned, but not so. Nevertheless, the analyst and I explored my anger toward my mother, my mother's anger, anger associated with sex, and anger towards men by whom I had been mistreated. I was digging, but not yet far enough.

Soon thereafter, I dreamed I was in a small, neat garden in front of a pretty house, looking on a hedge for a capsicum to put into a salad. They were few and blemished, but I picked several, then dropped a gold ring and knelt in the dirt to find it. Glancing up into the hedge, I saw a bird sitting just below the surface, well hidden from view. It was completely still and I knew it did not want to be seen, so for some moments, neither of us moved, each pretending to be unaware of the other. Then I noticed many perfect little green capsicums growing around it, unnoticed from the top. Not wanting to disturb the bird, I left them, thinking of coming back for some later. The analyst and I explored possible meanings – marked fruit and perfect fruit, things of greater value hidden in the shadows, the risk of disturbing something that should not be disturbed, patience, the bird as a messenger – and so on. Then he wondered whether having to kneel in the dirt to find the ring might represent the need to be humble, to look at things from below rather than above. That simple suggestion led to a radical shift of my attitude.

I had been trying, as was my habit, to think things through, to see things from a higher intellectual or moral perspective, when all the time throughout analysis, I had been given images of mud, rotting vegetation, wild animals, and dreams and images of myself as an animal so close to the ground that its aromas filled my nose, grubbing in the dirt to find a gold ring. All full of different meanings, but also, I could see, given to humble me, to make me recognize my unconscious conceit, my over-valuation of intellect and under-valuing of feeling, the body and its instincts, and a childish belief in my specialness. Get into the dirt, I was being told, into your feelings, the body, and its instincts. Look at things from there. I did, and it led me to rethink myself, my memories, and my relationships. Maybe that part of me frozen in childhood had been cold to my son, who had unexpectedly become so hostile to me, when I had thought I was loving. Maybe he had sensed the unexpressed anger towards men from my childhood and in my marriage, and thought it was directed at him. Maybe he was not so much hostile as hungry for love and nurturing, like Lobo, like the child me, and filled with angry resentment that it did not come. The therapist mentioned the mythical minotaur, and I saw in that image my son trapped in a dark maze, confused, feeling unloved, and angry. Had I *not* been the loving, supportive mother I believed I was? Had I, believing myself to be open-minded and accepting, suffocated his spirit instead of nurturing it? Did I blame my mother for deserting me, for not protecting me when she herself was so vulnerable, so utterly broken, when she desperately needed the love that I did not give her, though I thought I did?

With this humbler attitude, I came to understand that in closing off my instinctual self and repressing and shaming my own sexuality, I had disrupted the natural flow of libido, denying myself energy that could support my wellbeing and growth, and preventing myself from loving. Jung writes this profoundly moving passage concerning the inability of some to love.

It is … difficult to imagine that this rich world has become too poor to offer an object for the love of human atoms; nor can the world and its objects be held accountable for this lack. It is rather *the incapacity to love which robs mankind of his possibilities.* This is empty to him alone who does not understand how to direct his libido towards objects, and to render them alive and beautiful for himself, for Beauty does not indeed lie in things, but in the feeling that we give to them. That which compels us to create a substitute for ourselves is not the lack of objects, but our incapacity to love a thing outside of ourselves … The resistance to loving produced the inability to love

(Jung, 2016, p. 107, emphasis his)

Thanks to my analyst, I no longer take responsibility for the harm done to me by others that made love so problematic for me, especially in my early childhood; but I do accept responsibility for choosing not to see possibilities for love and beauty when they were offered to me. I take responsibility for cowardice and fear and for holding on to the wolf's burning resentment.

In active imaginations, I saw my belly as a wide golden bowl filling with good things. It reminded me of the rough wooden bowl from which I was fed nourishing soup by the grandmotherly animal. Talking about how she agreed to complete the dying Emma Jung's book on the Grail, von Franz tells that in a dream, Emma Jung handed her a bowl of soup. "The soup bowl is one of the symbols for the grail associated with the mother. It means 'I hand now this soup bowl to your mother instinct'" (von Franz, 1979). The relationship of the grandmother animal's soup bowl dream with the filling golden bowl in my belly, and the new motherly images of Urso and Lobo, with their different kinds of mother love, indicate to me a pressing need to come to terms with my long-shunned femininity, and that its new image must allow whatever forms of psychic energy arise, including erotic energy and anger.

Looking at these images and fantasies mythologically, I saw that both Urso and Lobo are associated in different ways with rebirth, Urso as the mythological mother-bear whose winter hibernation and emergence in Spring with cubs represents a kind of death and rebirth, and Lobo through death and transformation. I also came to understand the relevance of the fires in the Lobo scenarios to my process of individuation. The small fire that formed the trinity of Lobo-fire-me in that first active imagination scene before the stone wall in the forest was the fire of my own unrecognized anger that Lobo was bringing to the fore; it was the fire of the primal instinctual animal self with which Lobo connected me, and the flame of Eros that inflames the heart, that was fueling the analytic journey. The fire in the distance when Lobo licked the bloody face of the child in the other scene, the fire that I had feared might burn him to ashes, was the alchemical fire of transformation, the flame of Eros that destroys what must be sacrificed. What was that fire destroying in me? Ego, vanity, fearfulness, romantic illusion, self-centredness, self-deception, anger that did not serve my growth … and pride. How could I not have realized before that some of that shame, that fear of being vulnerable, that resistance to instinct, including love, was pride? I deceived myself with semantics.

I still have far to go with this work and with these and other images that continue to be part of my inner life, and am constantly discovering new meanings in them. But having recognized the ubiquitousness of love in its many aspects in the processes of becoming myself, I follow this spiral pathway with a much deeper sense of purpose and hope and acceptance of my humanness. The fire in my fantasies is not incidental. It represents the flame of Eros – as emotion, desire, telos, as the expansion of consciousness, and also, I remind myself, the transformative, generating alchemical fire that incinerates what must be destroyed so that the new can be born.

Final Thoughts

Jung, who had seen for himself the damage wrought by immature consciousness and consciousness swamped by the collective, writes, "The more we become conscious of ourselves through self-knowledge, and act accordingly", the more

> there arises a consciousness that is no longer imprisoned in the petty, oversensitive personal world of the ego … Widened consciousness … [brings] the individual into absolute, binding, and indissoluble communion with the world at large. … the unconscious produced contents which are valid not only for the person concerned but for others as well, in fact for a great many people and possibly for all
>
> (Jung, 1977, p. 178).

Jung "showed that individuation is not possible without the differentiation of Eros", writes von Franz (2008, p. 19), and the teleological thrust of his therapy necessarily includes the conscious integration of Eros in the developing personality. In her final lecture given in 1986, *C.G. Jung's Rehabilitation of the Feeling Function in Our Civilization*, von Franz describes differentiated Eros as "a new form of love a whole-making effect of a certain kind of Eros [relatedness], which is an emanation of the individuated personality" (2008, p. 17, her brackets.). On a personal level, it is "a form of love coupled with insight", Eros integrated with Logos, and, unlike emotional or driven love, "include[s] a certain distance" (2008, p. 18). "Every relationship has its optimal distance, which of course has to be found by trial and error", explains Jung (quoted in von Franz, 2008, p. 18), which can be very painful (ibid).

The social value of differentiated Eros cannot be over-estimated and is undeniably implicit in the telos of Jung's therapy. He writes, "The object of psychoanalysis is to free the libido from its fixations". Thus "set free", the libido "serves for the building up of a personality matured and adapted to reality, who does willingly and without complaint everything required by necessity" (Jung, 2016, p. 265). Much of the destructiveness of our society towards other societies arises "from a basic lack of respect for the other human being and his different system of values – in plain words, a lack of true differentiated feeling", writes von Franz (2008, p. 12). Through "whole-making, healing Eros", she continues, "even the opposites of the collective versus the individual may be reconciled" (p. 19), a matter of concern as pressing (if not more so) in our time of increasing corporate and state domination and the ominous rises of fascism as it has ever been.

I see psychotherapy as I have received it – with graciousness, authenticity, insightfulness and love in the way of earnestly desiring my wellbeing and growth while valuing who I am now – as the ideal path to wholeness. Perhaps its greatest gift to me has been an appreciation of all aspects of Eros, including sexuality, in my reality and the world, and the difficult, sometime agonizing development of a more differentiated Eros. While most of us can appreciate the value of the connecting, relationship aspect of Eros that prompts us to connect with others, to care about things, and seek genuine relationships with people, nature and things, we can be quite oblivious to the equal importance of the instincts, including sexuality, which demand their own expression through us. It took therapy to help me understand that. Sexuality is "of the greatest importance as the expression of the chthonic spirit", says Jung, of that aspect of spirit that is grounded in matter, in the earth, in our bodies (1965, p. 168). The same may be said of sensuality, the appreciation and desiring of the senses that is also a manifestation of Eros that adds richness and depth to our experiences of the world and our senses. "Stop and smell the roses" may sound trite, but think of all that it implies: being in the moment, mindfulness, slowing down, tasting the world we are in, and appreciating that we are alive in a world full of little beauties. It means something that the sense of smell is the sense most directly connected to the brain.

The distortion and repression of Eros, on the other hand, is of enormous consequence with potentially devastating personal and social consequences. Most of the issues that I worked on with my analyst were related to denied or inhibited Eros, in me or in others who harmed me. I am now able to see some of those others as themselves wounded by distortions of Eros energy, and can let go of some of that anger, hopefully more as I integrate more of the therapeutic insights. Psychotherapist and writer James Hollis attributes two of the main psychological maladies of our time, addictions and paraphilias[7], to a thwarted or corrupted relationship with Eros. What they have in common, he says, "is the desire for connection … In every case the existential longing is transferred to a surrogate and the symbol is reified into an obsession followed by a palliative behaviour or compulsion" (Hollis, 2004, p. 107). "The most dangerous person, as the daily news illustrates, is the person in denial of the erotic energy which courses through the soul", he writes (2004, p. 106). Most of us won't reach that level of dangerousness, or suffer the effects, but unless we learn to embrace Eros in ourselves, neither will we ever be whole or wholly alive. Part of us will always be stunted or dead, and, like a damaged leg, will continually throw us off balance until we can no longer function as we should or as we want to. It is so much better to attend to the instincts and let them manifest themselves in ways that increase our wellbeing, make life a little more interesting, and help us to express the fullness of our unique, authentic selves.

Jung speaks of the numinous in sexuality, its capacity to take us beyond pleasure and satisfying of instinct to a connection with the heart and thence to spirit. Medieval female mystics sometimes took this so far that their whole being became an expression of Eros. As Jacques Lacan suggests, at a time when "male theologians had asserted that in order to experience God, body and sensuality must be absolutely overcome", and "woman/ femininity [was] comparable to matter, the darkest, basest depths of the body", religious ardor became for some women "an immediate experience of a love relationship. So outrageous and so personal, so intimate and so emotionally intense and erotic was the relationship that this experience of love overflowed into raptures" (Lacan quoted in Calza, 2016, pp. 9, 10). Much less extreme, but also expressing the perfectly natural effect Eros can have on the senses, is the erotic stimulus one might receive while listening to music, or viewing a piece of art, or surveying a scene in nature. Eros is god of far more than just sex and can also be embraced in all kinds of non-sexual, non-invasive or threatening ways.

One way to tune into Eros energy, and become more psychologically and physiologically balanced, is to reconnect deeply, sensually, and frequently with nature, whether it be a local ecosystem, a river, a tiny field mouse, edible wild plants, or a woods on a moonlight night. Recognize it or not, in our very essence and on all levels, we are intrinsically connected to nature, and she to us. Our relationship with nature also affects our inner nature. "Man is estranged from his soul, therefore from his own inner nature, by being lost in the outer world. Excessive interference with *outer* nature creates of necessity disorder of the *inner* nature, for the two are intimately connected", writes depth psychologist, C.A. Meier (1983, p. 2).

> In order to keep in harmony with the concept of Wilderness … apart from analysis I know of nothing better than to keep the outer Wilderness alive and to not let it be ruined. … For, as long as you don't interfere with it too badly, it functions beautifully
>
> (Meier, 1983, p. 12).

The Hermetic principle, 'as above, so below' also applies to horizontal relationships. As we are in ourselves, so we are to the world, including nature. One affects the other. "Whenever we touch nature we get clean", observes Jung. "People who have got dirty through too much civilization take a walk in the wood or a bath in the sea … Entering the unconscious, entering yourself through dreams is touching nature from the inside" (quoted in McGuire, 1984, p. 142).

Nature has been a part of my psychotherapy. I drive to our sessions at the end of a green valley, passing through trees, past rock pools, and as we speak about inner things, outside the analyst's window I see a hillside of dense forest. Nature is restorative, reassuring, and offers so much opportunity for us to love and to find beauty. Love and close connection with

nature can help us open up to and revitalize the flagging and often atro-
phied energy of Eros in ourselves and our society. Movements such as 'forest bathing', 'earthing', the largely youth-led climate action movements,
and the emergence of ecopsychology and deep ecology indicate increasing
awareness of the importance of close connection with nature. According to
Jungian analyst and ecopsychologist Dennis Merrit,

> Jungian ecopsychology offers one of the best frameworks for analys-
> ing our dysfunctional relationship with the environment – and with each
> other – through an archetypal analysis of the layers of the collective
> unconscious … Ecology begins in our relationship with 'the little peo-
> ple' in our dreams and dreams can be used to help us connect deeply to
> the land
>
> (Merrit, 2021, audio).

Though not mentioning Jung, environmental activist and philosopher Arne
Naess, the impetus behind the Deep Ecology movement, points to a crucial
relationship between Jung's individuation and the concept of "ecological
self".

> We may be in and of nature from the very beginning of ourselves. Society
> and human relationships are important, but our own self is much richer
> in its constitutive relationships. These relationships are not only those we
> have with other humans and the human community … but also those we
> have with other living beings. Our lives are enhanced through increased
> self-realization, which implies a broadening and deepening of the self …
> Our self-love will assist in the self-realization of others … Then we can
> act beautifully
>
> (Naess, 2008, p. 82).

Movements and attitudes such as these, which are a few of the many emerging across the world, suggest that we are in the process of creating a new
mythology, and no new mythology can meet the soul and spiritual needs of
our society if it does not revitalize and renew our primal connection with
the earth and other living beings. Nor will it serve us well if the connecting,
relating, unifying, consciousness-generating, and transformative energies
of Eros are not at its heart. It is up to us, individually, to ensure that it is,
and we can do that by entering an attitude of intimate conscious connection

and relationship with our inner and outer realities. Do whatever inner work we need to connect with and accept the myriad of things that we are – our feelings, instincts, dreams and visions, our values, and our whole personality, its dark and its light. Determine to relate to others and the world authentically, to free ourselves as far as we are able from preconceptions about ourselves and others, especially from our often immature, sentimental, self-serving conceptions of love. Undertaking the task of increasing consciousness is, I believe, an act of love. While psychotherapy is the ideal path, there are others.

Environmental and social activism, if undertaken with a balance of Eros and Logos, love, and reason, can become deeply consciousness-expanding and transformative. One's attitude to love, however, is critical, explains Emerick in his paper "Love, Activism, and Social Justice". Some approaches to love, "while understandable and attractive, are seriously problematic, as they tend either to obscure important differences in the ways that various groups are socially situated or to enable inaction by trusting that justice is inevitable" (Emerick, 2020, p. 2). "Real kindness", he writes, "involves caring about others as complete people, including as moral agents … holding them to account for what they have done and expecting them to be better than their past selves" (2020, p. 10). "It's vital, then, … to retain a clear understanding … of what they mean when employing the language of love" (p. 13). In Jung's *telos* of Love, Eros is differentiated, emanating from an "individuated personality", the alchemical *"Homo putissimus* 'most pure' or 'true man'" who is "'no other than just what he is'"[8] (von Franz, 2008, p. 18). When we work towards individuation and wholeness, we open up to the energy of Eros, and learn to use it in ways that are personally meaningful and also serve the greater good.

> .....*Or might I – despite dire warnings from the inner crowd –*
> *might I-- in the powerful surges of life unchecked*
> *love freely given everywhere –*
> *have been protected in the conflagration?*
> *And might that hard little nut of I*
> *have emerged from the ashes*
> *burned into something free something Radiant?*
>
> *(by Chapter author)*

Notes

1 "Jung defines consciousness as "the function or activity which maintains the relation of psychic contents to the ego" [CW 6, P700]. "Everything of which I know, but of which I am not at the moment thinking; everything of which I was once conscious but have now forgotten; everything perceived by my senses, but not noted by my conscious mind; and everything which, involuntarily and without paying attention to it, I feel, think, remember, want, and do; all the future things that are taking shape in me and will sometime come to consciousness: all this is the content of the unconscious" [CW 8, P382].

2 History has revealed the presence of a sometimes dark, destructive underside of sentimentality and emotionality (von Franz, 2008, pp. 17–18), which is also evident in our times.

3 The Gospel of Thomas, an extracanonical collection of traditional sayings of Jesus, is one of the Nag Hammadi Coptic texts discovered in 1945 in Egypt. It is attributed to Didymos Judas Thomas, believed by some to be the brother of Jesus and one of his apostles.

4 Jung conceived of libido as "cosmic energy or urge manifested in the human being .... Sexuality and its various manifestations, Jung sees as most important channels occupied by libido, but not the exclusive ones through which libido flows." (Beatrice M Hinkle, 2016, p.xvii)

5 The story is available at https://etc.usf.edu/lit2go/175/grimms-fairy-tales/3182/snow-white-and-rose-red/

6 in animal form

7 Sexual disorders related to atypical objects, situations or non-consenting others (Wikipedia).

8 I respectfully defer to the use of 'man' where it is indicated in the texts, though I choose to take it as referring to a human of any gender or mixed.

References

Andersen, H. C. 'The snow queen' (Translated by J. Hersholt). https://andersen.sdu.dk/vaerk/hersholt/TheSnowQueen_e.html

Boa, F. (1985). The way of the dream: Marie-Louise von Franz in conversation with Fraser Boa. Windrose Films. Marie-Louise von Franz. https://www.youtube.com/watch?v=yXQTDTcup04

Calzà, M. G. (2016). 'The Thinking Heart'. Jung Journal: Culture & Psyche. 10.4, 3–14, DOI: 10.1080/19342039.2016.1225244

Dante, Alighieri. Dante's inferno D. Lamb, Editor. https://www.fulltextarchive.com

De Quillian, J. (2010). The Gospel of the Beloved Companion: The Complete Gospel of Mary Magdalene. Createspace Independent Publishing Platform.

Edinger, E. (1984). The creation of consciousness: Jung's myth for modern man. Inner City Books.

Edinger, E. (1994). The mystery of the coniunctio: Alchemical images of individuation (Originally presented in lectures at the C. G. Institute of San Francisco October 19–20, 1984) Inner City Books.

Emerick, B. (2020). 'Love, Justice and Social Justice.' Draft copy prior to publication. In Love, justice, and autonomy: Philosophical perspectives. R. Fedock, M. Kühler, & T. Raja Rosenhagen editors. Routledge. https://philpapers.org/archive/EMELAA.pdf

Evans, R. (1957). *Interview with psychologist Dr. Carl Jung by Dr. Richard Evans of the University of Houston. Audio.* Originally released by Penn State University. https://www.youtube.com/watch?v=IUWpr0gR81A

Eros. Accessed at https://www.theoi.com/Protogenos/Eros.html

Gerster, G. (2008). An eighty-fifth birthday interview for Switzerland. *C.G. Jung speaking: Interviews and encounters.* in M. William & R. F. C. Hull Editors. Princeton University Press.

Gimbutas, J. (2001). *The living goddesses* (M. R. Dexter, Editor. University of California Press.

Grimm Brothers. *Snow-white and rose-red.* https://www.worldoftales.com/fairy_tales/Brothers_Grimm/Grimm_fairy_stories/Snow-White_And_Rose-Red.html#gsc.tab=0

Guerra, M. H. M. (2014). *The love drama of C. G. Jung: As revealed in his life and in his red book.* Inner City Books.

Harding, E. (2008). *C.G. Jung speaking: Interviews and encounters.* in M. William & R. F. C. Hull Editors. Princeton University Press.

Hollis, J. (2004). *Mythologems: Incarnations of the invisible world.* Inner City Books.

Johnson, R. (1989). *Inner Work: Using Dreams and Active Imagination for Personal Growth.* Harper Collins.

Jung, C. G. (1955). *Modern man in search of a soul.* Harcourt Inc.

Jung, C. G. (1958). *The collected works of C. G. Jung, vol. 11, psychology and religion: East and West* (Translated by R. F. C. Hull H. Read, M. Fordham, & G. Adler, Editors). Bollingen Series XX. Pantheon Books.

Jung, C. G. (1962). Commentary by Jung. *The secret of the golden flower: A Chinese book of life.* (Translated by R. Wilhelm). Brace, Joovanovich.

Jung, C. G. (1964). *Man and his symbols* (C. G. Jung & M. L. von Franz, Editors). Picador.

Jung, C. G. (1965). Memories, dreams, reflections (Translated by A. Jaffé, Ed. & R. Winston). Vintage Books, Random House.

Jung, C. G. (1970a). *The collected works of C. G. Jung, vol. 9, part ii, Aion: Researches into the phenomenology of the self* 2nd ed. (Translated by R. F. C. Hull). Bollingen Series xx. Princeton University Press.

Jung, C. G. (1970b). *The collected works of C. G. Jung, vol. 13, Alchemical studies* (Translated by R. F. C. Hull). (Bollingen Series xx). Princeton University Press.

Jung, C. G. (1977). *The collected works of C. G. Jung, vol. 7, two essays on analytical psychology.* 2nd ed. (Translated by R. F. C. Hull) Princeton University Press.

Jung, C. G. (1980) *The collected works of C. G. Jung, vol. 9, part i,* Archetypes and the collective unconscious. 2nd ed. (Translated by. R. F. C. Hull). Bollingen series. Princeton University Press.

Jung, C. G. (1982). *Aspects of the feminine.* Princeton University Press.

Jung, C. G. (1998). *The psychology of the transference.* Routledge.

Jung, C. G. (2009). *Liber Novus (The red book)* S. Shamdasani, Editor (Translated by M. Kyburz & J. Peck). Philemon Series. WW Norton & Co.

Jung, C. G. (2016). *The psychology of the unconscious: A study of the transformation and symbolisms of the Libido* (Translated by B. M. Hinkle). Kegan, Paul, Trench, Trubner & Co. Ltd.

Jung, C. G. (2020). *The Black Books. 1913–1932: Notebooks of transformation Vols. 1–7.* S. Shamdasani, Editor (Translated by L. Martin, M. J. Peck, & S. Shamdasani). Philemon Series. 1–7). WW Norton & Co.

Jung, C. G., Adler, G., & Jaffé, A. (1992). *C. G. Jung Letters vol 1*. (Translated by R. F. C. Hull). C. G. Jung, G. Adler, & A. Jaffé, Editors. Princeton University Press. https://doi.org/10.1515/9780691234632

Mascetti, M. D. (1994). *The song of eve*. Arum Press Ltd.

Meier, C. A. (1983). Wilderness and the search for the soul of modern man. In *A testament to the wilderness: ten essays on an address by C A Meier*. Third World Congress in Inverness.

Merrit, D. (2021, October 21). *Jung and the environment. Audio*. C. G. Jung Institute of Chicago. https://jungchicago.org/blog/from-the-archives-jung-the-environment-with-dennis-merritt/

Moore, R. (1992). *Care of the soul: A guide for cultivating depth and sacredness in everyday life*. Harper Collins.

Naess, Arne. (2008). *The Ecology of wisdom: Writings by Naess Arne.*. A. Drengson, & B. Devall, Editors. Berkeley: Penguin/Random House.

Owens, L. (2015). *Jung in Love: The Mysterium in liber Novus* (Monograph edition. Originally published as a chapter in: Das Rote Buch – C. G. Jungs Reise Zum Anderen Pol der Welt). Gnosis Archive Books.

Parmenidens. *Poem of Parmenides: On nature*. (Translated by John Burnet, 1919). Accessed at: HYPERLINK "http://philoctetes.free.fr/parmenides.pdf" philoctetes.free.fr/parmenides.pdf. (Originally published 5th c. B.C.E.).

Robinson, J.M. & Smith, R. Editors. (1988). 'The gospel of Thomas' (II *2*). *The Nag Hammadi library in English* (3rd ed.). Harper One.

Hesiod. (1914). The Theogeny (Translated by H.G. Evelyn-White, 1914). Accessed at: https://www.theoi.com/Text/HesiodTheogony.html. (Originally published in 8th c. B.C.E.).

Tsarevich Ivan (1966). *In Valilisia the beautiful: Russian fairy tales*. Progress Publishers.

Van Der Post, L. (1988). *Jung and the story of our time*. Penguin.

von Franz, M. L. (1964). Individuation. in *Man and his symbols*. C. G. Jung & M. L. von Franz (Eds.).

Von Franz, M. L. (1979). *Interview Bollingen 1979*. https://www.youtube.com/watch?v=ItDEC3zwftc

von Franz, M. L. (1980). *Alchemy: An introduction to the symbolism and the psychology studies in Jungian psychology*. Inner City Books.

von Franz, M. L. (1982). *Interview Bollingen 1982*. https://www.youtube.com/watch?v=4mK-YambXQA

von Franz, M. L. (1998a). *Jung: His myth in our time*. Inner City Books.

von Franz, M. L. (1998b). *Projection and recollection in Jungian psychology: Reflections of the soul*. Open Court Publishing.

von Franz, M. L. (1990). *Individuation in fairytales*. Shambhala Publications.

von Franz, M. L. (2008, Spring). 'C. G. Jung's rehabilitation of the feeling function in our civilization.' Knusacht lecture. *Jung Journal, 2*, 2. 9–20, DOI: 10.1525/jung.2008.2.2.9

Whitney, M. (2004, July). *Matter of heart: The extraordinary journey of C. G. Jung* (M. Whitney, Dirs.). Kino Lorber Films. https://www.youtube.com/watch?v=Ed3vPb9bmcw

Chapter 4

The Ravenous Hydra and the Great Tree of Peace

The Teleology of Indigenous and European Civilizations

Shane Eynon

Introduction

Where have we been? Where are we now? And where are we going? These are existential questions that occupy the minds of many. The question of where we are going in the future fills many with fear, dread, and paranoia. The question of where we have been, and our history as humans, has been a matter of contentious political and academic debate for the past 40 years. We now seem full of confusion and disorientation, not only for the people of the United States, but even for humanity after years of economic turmoil, wars, and pandemics. As to where we are going, this outlook is nothing short of paranoically dystopian. This anticipation of a dystopian future is tethered to our collective past and its vision of our future. However, this narrative of the past and its former utopian visions of a future are rooted within the dominating collective psyche of the Anglo-Settler mythology and worldview. At one time, this vision of the future and telos of the European collective mind became the dominant way of imagining the future. This imagining of the future told a story to itself of the spread of European civilization as a good and noble crusade bringing light and the betterment of humankind across a dark and vast expanse. Once this project was complete and all people were civilized to the European vision, once the whole of nature was under the dominion of this civilization, then a paradise would unfold. This is not how things turned out once all the frontiers of the European gaze were conquered and the Earth fell under the domination of European civilization over the past 150 years.

Now we find ourselves at the threshold of another liminal space as the dominant psychological forces of the European psyche have carried us all along its river to this point in time. There is no longer the sustaining myth of a Frontier to mark the line between the civilization of Anglo-Saxonism

DOI: 10.4324/9781003412823-5

and the dark Other (Gradin, 2019). Some visions and imaginings of the future contain an inevitable endpoint or aim that, once realized, creates a sense of disorientation and confusion. Once a vision is realized, there can either be a time of re-imaging and transformation or repetition and retrenchment. These may be the possible choices of the collective imagination under ordinary circumstances. However, we face Earth's sixth mass extinction event this time, which was caused by a form of European civilization. Termed the Anthropocene, this epoch-making shift can be traced back to the increasing power of capitalism and the ideology of market economies (Angus, 2016).

In American culture, based on the Enlightenment era Anglo-Saxon myths, the telos of the United States is compulsively repeating a pattern of continuous warfare, civil strife, and domination through capitalism and markets as a new religion. This new religion is based on beliefs, creeds, and ideologies that have gradually overtaken Christianity as Euro-American culture's prevailing organizing social principle. Just as Christianity dictated moral behavior, cosmology, and worldview, it also shaped the psycho-social fabric of people by creating a metaphysical cartography charting a teleology ending in eternal salvation or damnation. This endpoint was to be a great apocalypse in which God judges the right and wrong of people. As capitalism grew from the foundations of Christianity and the Enlightenment, it contained within itself the psychological and spiritual roots of these worldviews. As these worldviews grew further away from a basis in the natural world and became more artificially a product of the human mind ever more divorced from contact with the rest of nature, they took on the most destructive elements of the psyche. At this moment, the death drive prevails, and the apocalypse is a foregone conclusion.

Crafting a vision of what could be and imagining an alternate future can be achieved in numerous ways. There are many ways to envision and imagine what the future could hold. By comparing historical and social teleology, we can synthesize or transition into a new psychological vision instead of repeating the artificial death-rebirth cycle that started in Rome and Greece over two thousand years ago.

Teleology, Psychoanalysis, and Analytical Psychology

Over a century ago, European civilization began turning its gaze deeply inward through the new discipline of psychoanalysis. As Sigmund Freud began to explore the psychological suffering of individuals who sought help with their extreme distress and symptoms of mental illness, he found a dark side to the European psyche. He began by exploring the emotional lives of women in Vienna who needed help with uncontrollable and unexplainable symptoms without physical cause. He noticed a trend that these first patients suffered from the memory of traumatic experiences. From there, he extrapolated outward to the nature of problems within the collective European civilization. His central thesis in *Civilization and its Discontents* (1929) was that (European) civilization placed social demands on people that psychologically conflicted with their unconscious desires and instincts, resulting in personal and social illness. However, Freud primarily focused on reductive causality in his analytic method.

In his earliest correspondence with Freud, C.G. Jung discussed the possibility that the human psyche had a teleological drive or function (*Freud/ Jung Letters*, 1994). Freud was focused on examining a causal and reductive explanation for human suffering and psychological disorders, which he determined to be the social and religious forces of civilization that repressed the libido or drives of individuals. He dismissed Jung's teleological interests.

In Jung's work, shortly after breaking theoretically from Freud, he maintained an increasingly teleological view of the human mind, primarily within the unconscious (Papadopoulos, 2012). He could switch between a teleological analysis of the individual and a collective society in his writings. Jung gradually focused more on the collective psyche during World War 2 and the invention of atomic weapons. He became increasingly critical of the collective ideologies emerging over his lifetime as the source of human suffering.

Summarizing Jung's central ideas is challenging, as they are vast and cover many academic research fields. It could be argued that Jung's central idea is that the collective social system of European civilization created a profoundly deep alienation and dissociation for modern humans who became ensnared within its systems and that these collective social forces which demand adaptation also act in opposition to the unconscious teleology of the individual. In the conflict between conformity to the dominant collective ideology (European civilization) and the individual teleology, which Jung termed individuation, each person becomes unmoored, unwell, and suffers a loss of soul.

To better understand modern civilization's forces, Jung sought experiences with other cultures that had not entirely fallen under the dominion of the European collective worldview. He traveled and spent time observing and conversing with members of indigenous peoples within colonized Africa, India, and the United States. Perhaps one of the most profound interactions happened in his meeting with Ochwiay Biano (translated in English as Mountain Lake), who was an elder of the Taos Pueblo People.

In his book *Memories, Dreams, Reflections* (p. 248), he recalls a conversation he had with Biano in 1925, which is reported as follows:

Biano: "How cruel the whites are: their lips are thin, their noses sharp, their faces furrowed and distorted by holes. Their eyes have a staring expression. They are always seeking something. What are they seeking? The whites always want something; they are always uneasy and restless. We do not know what they want; we do not understand them; we think that they are mad". I asked him why he thought the whites were all mad. "They say they think with their heads", he replied.

"Why, of course. What do you think with?" I asked him in surprise.

"We think here", he said, indicating his heart.

Here we can see a glimmer of how the forces of European colonization across the globe are reflected toward the observer of those living under the domination of these systems and modes of life. At that point in 1925, some still lived within other lifeways on the frontier of the United States' 'Manifest Destiny' to gain dominion over all lands between the Atlantic and Pacific. Jung may not have fully understood the increasing pressure from the United States federal and state policies to assimilate Biano's people into a Euro-settler civilization. These included taking children away from tribes by force to attend Residential Schools or making the religious practices of indigenous people illegal.

In any case, Jung had a very moving vision that he reported and attributed to his interaction with Biano:

I fell into a long meditation. For the first time in my life, so it seemed to me, someone had drawn for me a picture of the real white man. It was as though until now I had seen nothing but sentimental, prettified color prints. This Indian had struck our vulnerable spot, unveiled a truth to which we are blind. I felt rising within me like a shapeless mist something unknown and yet deeply familiar. And out of this mist, image upon image detached itself: first Roman legions smashing into the cities of

Gaul, and the keenly incised features of Julius Caesar, Scipio Africanus, and Pompey. I saw the Roman Eagle on the North Sea and on the banks of the White Nile. Then I saw St. Augustine transmitting the Christian creed to the Britons on the tips of Roman lances, and Charlemagne's most glorious, forced conversions of the heathen, then the pillaging and murdering bands of the Crusading armies. With a secret stab I realized the hollowness of that old romanticism about the Crusades. Then followed Columbus, Cortes, and the other conquistadors who with fire, sword, torture, and Christianity came down upon even these remote pueblos dreaming peacefully in the Sun, their Father. I saw, too, the peoples of the Pacific islands decimated by firewater, syphilis, and scarlet fever carried in the clothes the missionaries forced on them. It was enough. What we from our point of view call colonization, missions to the heathen, spread of civilization, etc., has another face – the face of a bird of prey seeking with cruel intentness for distant quarry – a face worthy of a race of pirates and highwaymen. All the eagles and other predatory creatures that adorn our coats of arms seem to me apt psychological representatives of our true nature.

(Jung, 1989, p. 248)

The Ravenous Hydra

To better understand the forces of European Civilization, a symbol of its psychological function will help to shed light on understanding where these forces came from and where they are going. Hopefully, it will act as a method to grasp better what Jung called a "truth to which I was blind".

The Hydra was a mythological creature first cited in Greek mythology. In mythology, it was a multiheaded water snake-like dragon. There are various versions of a multiheaded water serpent dragon found across cultures. In modern popular culture, it was reintroduced to symbolize an offshoot of the Nazi party, as it was imagined to exist as a shadowy clandestine organization. Using technology, secrecy, manipulation, and terror, it had as an organizing mission world domination. And much like the original Greek myth of Hercules fighting the Hydra, its efforts are opposed by Captain America.

In the original myth, Hercules is typically interpreted as the force of masculine heroics, intellect, and cunning, defeating the undefeatable immortal monster of instinct (Nature's negative aspects symbolized). The Hydra was a symbol used many times across the Roman and Greek worlds. The Hydra lived in a lake near the underworld and was described as having multiple heads that could regrow when severed, with one being immortal. In the original myth, every aspect of the Hydra was venomous. Below we follow parts of Edinger's interpretation of the Hydra myth.

> Heracles' second labor was to overcome the hydra of Lerna, a monster with poisonous breath that would generate two heads any time one was cut off. This is an apt image of a certain aspect of the unconscious that cannot be dealt with by ordinary means. One sees it represented in dreams in which the dreamer, encountering some small creature, perhaps an insect or reptile, tries furiously to stamp it to death, only to watch it grow bigger. The hydra has something of that same nature: one head is cut off and two emerge. Some new method had to be devised to deal with the hydra, so Heracles persuaded his nephew Iolaus to assist him, and as soon as one head was cut off, Iolaus immediately cauterized it, which prevented it from regrowing. This seems to refer to the application of affect: not only is there a discriminating operation, signified by the clean cut of the blade, but there is also an application of affective intensity fire that produces the cauterizing effect.
>
> The problem of the hydra is probably related to repression, since another of its attributes was that one of its heads was immortal; even when it was cut off it remained invulnerable and it had to be buried under a big rock, a repressive operation. We can say that Heracles dealt with the hydra of Lerna by repressive measures, a stratagem that led in the long run to his undoing. After he had disposed of the hydra, he took its poison and used it thereafter to tip his arrows. As we shall see, the poison of the hydra finally destroyed Heracles himself.
>
> (Edinger, 1996, p. 997)

In America, the collective efforts to colonize its frontiers took on many aspects of a Hydra, which we will see later is cited in multiple indigenous prophecies. The Anglo-Saxon project of the United States was driven primarily by a multi-pronged conquest of all lands west of the original colonies along the Atlantic. These lands were seen as a source of never-ending enrichment and endless resources – a promised land igniting an insatiable and ravenous greed.

The idea of conquering the 'West' with its 'unused free land' inhabited by numerous and vast populations of 'savage' indigenous peoples became a theological delusion. Yet, it organized, focused, and united Anglo pioneers, settlers, the military, politicians, and capitalists into a rapacious force of conquest and domination almost immediately after the United States became independent from Britain. At the time, these Americans saw themselves as akin to heroic Hercules, civilizing and conquering the dark forces of nature.

However, just as the individual wears a mask to present the perfect version of how she or he wants to be seen, the collective also wears a mask. The Americans saw themselves as Hercules, but what was repressed and denied was the Hydra and its shadow duality. All the evil and barbarity the Americans attributed to everything (i.e., the natural world) outside its frontiers was a projection of America's shadow. This shadow was the disassociated and repressed drives, desires, and impulses that actuated and drove a frenzied and manic westward conquest over the Appalachian Mountains. In this way, we can see America as both Hercules and the Hydra conjoined as a singular psychological entity.

As the heads of the hydra (land speculation, settlers, farmers, soldiers, capitalists, slavers) snaked over the frontier, they either killed or removed the indigenous populations who held the sovereign right to their territories and, in the process, committed both genocide and ecocide on a scale scarcely paralleled in history. Rapid industrialization in the older eastern colonies and the promise of free land and fortune in the 'West' attracted an unprecedented wave of migration from Europe to the United States in the 1800s. The American expansion and conquest project became rationalized through Manifest Destiny's mythos, the teleological aim of which was a superior people divinely commissioned to conquer and dominate the vast Other (nature and non-Anglo peoples). This myth has not ended as an organizing force in America; it has only been slightly altered to rationalize the moment's needs. Even after the frontier was pushed to the furthest west and American dominion was complete on the Continent, it continued pushing the frontier of the Manifest Destiny mythology through ecological and human wars that have been endless and global.

Then, something happened in Vietnam. America lost and was denied the promise of the foundational mythology. The tide had turned. Then, it lost again – in Iraq and Afghanistan. In the 1970s through the early decades of

2000s, the 'American Dream' of endless economic prosperity and improving quality of life for all through the magical powers of capitalism and free markets started to sputter and collapse – wages and growth stagnated.

The United States had never considered this a possibility for over two centuries. The Hydra's poison was sickening Hercules. Psychologically, the American population started to undergo a profound shift. Diseases of hopelessness and desperation became more pervasive (declining health statistics, poverty, addiction, increased mortality, spasms of rage, and mass shootings). America had begun to lose faith in its institutions. Consumerism and entertainment could not be a safety valve to quell America's rage. A deep fear, uneasiness, and uncertainty set in, leading to more paranoia as those at the bottom of the American hierarchy started frantically seeking a scapegoat to blame. Community cohesion and solidary started the process of collapse. The spasm of unrest that began during the Vietnam era returned with ever greater force, but this time, the Earth's environment as we've known it, is on the verge of collapse. America's teleology turned from a Utopian delusion (Mohawk, 1999) to an increasingly Dystopian teleology.

Shapeshifting and Transformations

Humanity faces stark choices. We can collectivity continue to live in denial and desperately place false hope in our ingenuity and technology to save us. However, this would be a repetition of attempting to rely on what we have known and belligerently living in denial – or we can change. We have at our fingertips almost all the knowledge of humanity stored and accessible to us. We can easily see examples from the past of what has worked to live harmoniously, symbiotically, and sustainably on the Earth for the benefit of all life. The challenge before us is allowing the old myths to die and collectivity seeking a new way to live. But much would need to change very quickly. Resistance to change and accepting the need to transform ourselves globally are the almost insurmountable obstacles we face. We can either change ourselves or have change forced upon us by the laws of nature herself.

Changing globally as a species will require accepting errors and mistakes, clear and rational minds, and collective efforts. The human world built over the past five hundred years is ending rapidly. Fortunately, we have models of how people facing similar dire situations have successfully shapeshifted themselves collectively to live in peace and harmony with the

Earth. We will examine the Haudenosaunee and the Great Law of Peace as examples of people who were almost driven to collapse but found a way to change using their imaginations to alter their teleology. The mythology of 'shapeshifting', common to many cultures including those of Native American tribes, will be described as a means of altering our choices and their consequences.

The Great Tree of Peace

One of the central symbols of the Haudenosaunee People is the Great Tree of Peace. This symbol is centered on the Eastern Pine Tree. It is often the tallest tree in a forest when left to grow undisturbed. The tree's needles come in bundles of five (representing the original five nations unified under the Great Law). At the top of the tree is an Eagle representing the need to be vigilant and farsighted in protecting the peace. Under the tree are buried the implements of warfare. And growing out from the tree are the white roots of peace that could be followed by anyone who wished to shelter under the tree. This symbol was used as an organizing vision of the Great Law because it was evergreen and continuously growing taller (not out) as it was tended to and cared for. Every member of the community and each clan had a responsibility to maintain the Tree. Under the Tree, according to oral tradition, were soft pine needles that offered rest and tranquility. In front of the tree was a central council fire where all could meet to discuss the people's concerns, collectively search each other's minds for the best solutions to pressing matters, and find the solutions that would benefit those next seven generations yet to be born (Wallace, 1946).

One of the other primary myths of the Haudenosaunee is the creation myth. This mythos is older than the Great Law of Peace and is sometimes called the Sky Woman story. In this story about the world's creation, a woman (one of The Ancient Beings) who dwelt in the Sky World fell through a hole created by her husband, who had dreamed that the Great Celestial Tree should be uprooted. She looked down through the hole created by the uprooted tree and saw another world covered in water. She had become so curious that she leaned over too far and began to fall. As she fell, she grabbed some vegetation around the hole and parts of the Celestial Tree (Parker, 1989).

As Sky Woman fell toward the world below, all the animals saw her distress, had compassion for her, and held a council together. All the animal beings agreed to help her. First, the geese came in great numbers to break her fall and place her on the back of a great turtle that came up from the depths of the waters so that she would not drown, and it would be her resting place. Sky Woman revived on the back of the turtle, and the animals sought to help to make a world for her (Parker, 2020).

When Sky Woman had fallen, she had brought some of the seeds and plants from the celestial world in her hands. The animals all worked on diving to the bottom of the waters to find earth to place on the Turtle's back to help her. Many animals and fish attempted to bring the earth from under the waters, and many died. Only the muskrat was able to bring up just enough earth to place on the Turtle's back. This earth expanded, and the seeds and roots began to grow in the earth. In some versions of the story, the Celestial Tree grows again on this new land from which all the necessary food and medicines for humans grow. The story continues in detail about the continuation of life on Earth, or Turtle Island (what we now call North America) (Parker, 1989).

Psychologically, this creation story creates a very different relationship toward the Earth and all living things compared to the Biblical or Greco-Roman creation myths. The central message psychologically of the Biblical creation story is that of hierarchy (man comes before woman), human sin and its consequences for men and women (life is pain and punishment), and a God who punishes what He creates. The Biblical creation myth also explicitly sanctifies man's dominion over all life on Earth. As we see in the Sky Woman myth, the relationship between humans and the earth is flipped from the Biblical story. In the Sky Woman story, psychologically and realistically, humans are utterly dependent upon vegetation, animals, and the Earth itself for the survival of the human species. All the natural world agrees to act together to nurture humankind.

And conversely, Nature could agree not to do so, as subtly implied in the story. However, compassion for humanity comes from Nature without preconditions. This subtly infers that Nature is compassionate to all life as it is willing to make efforts and even sacrifice itself for humans. The relationship between Nature and Humans in the Sky Woman story is one of compassion, gratitude, and an acceptance of human dependence on the natural world. Here, the Earth can exist without humans and/or a Creator-God, as it is not dependent upon the human domain to continue. Humans exist on Earth as fallen visitors at the mercy and beneficence of the rest of Nature. The first human was a woman. In terms of the psychology of gender relations, the belief that the original human being was a woman has enormous psychological implications. In Haudenosaunee culture, the fact that a woman came first seemed only fitting and natural. Women are seen as the creators of life and the default mode of the human, with males being a complementary equal necessary for the continuation of life.

In both Haudenosaunee myths above, we can see the central motif of the Tree of Life. Jung spoke extensively about the symbolism of the Tree in the collective psychology of humanity (pp. 1432–1434, Jung, Zarathustra Seminar). The tree's growth and nurturance and the focus on the future generations' welfare was the principal use of The Great Tree of Peace as a symbol in Haudenosaunee culture. This central symbol emerged during a transformation and shapeshifting of the Haudenosaunee's mind after a prolonged civil war between the then-separate peoples. This was accomplished through a messenger from the Huron called Deganawidah, or the Peacemaker. According to the oral tradition, he believed he was destined to help end the bloodshed among all the Onkwehonwe (the original people of Turtle Island). He succeeded in his efforts. His overall message is too complex to be told in a short chapter, so a summary must suffice. The Peacemaker set out to reorganize society in such a way as to minimize conflict utilizing very practical methods. Peace (Sgeno/Sken:nen) was the organizing principle. However, the English word for Peace connotes an absence of strife and conflict. This is not precisely what Peace meant to the Haudenosaunee. Peace is more of a verb, an active state of mind that is cultivated through practices in all aspects of life. Peace is actively seeking out a state of being within oneself and with all of nature. It does not connote the absence of conflict alone. Peace is a way of being in the world with the final aim of maintaining a harmonious life for all by reflecting on the ways of nature. Therefore, warfare and conflict were seen as going against nature's example.

As the Peacemaker worked to establish the 'New Mind' or the 'Good Mind' across the five nations of the Haudenosaunee, he set down efficient principles for organizing people to minimize conflict. The people were organized into clans (extended families) that met and used three criteria in deliberations: 1. Peace (does this best preserve the peace?); 2. Rightness (is this morally correct in the same way the natural world is correct?); and 3. Power (does this decision help the next seven generations?). We can see how the conceptions of Peace, Righteousness, and Power differ significantly from Anglo-Settler conceptions of these words (2023). Therefore, the Great Law of Peace kept teleology forefront as a guiding principle for their culture and communities. An active psychological teleology is how a decision or policy today impacts seven generations into the future, keeping the future in mind for today's choices.

The Peacemaker worked to establish the Great Law many generations before European colonists came to Turtle Island. He foretold several great snakes that would create havoc, disrupt the peace, and destroy the ecology (Wallace, 1946). Many have interpreted this warning as the coming of the European colonists. This brings us back to the Ravenous Hydra and how its forces have sown death and confusion for once-thriving civilizations on Turtle Island. Today, the Haudenosaunee people are striving to reclaim their unique forms of being after years of colonization efforts (Mohawk Warrior Society, 2023). They are, as a people, in disharmony due to differences resulting from the influences of forced assimilation and genocide. Many different influences, from religion and capitalism to the adoption of Euro-settler ideologies, have resulted in disunity. The Haudenosaunee have a remarkable capacity for re-invention and adaptation. Some of these attempts at adapting have resulted in conflict today due to the infestation of their myth-based codes with European values. One example is the Code of Handsome Lake, which sought to help people at the most extreme point during colonization. The Code of Handsome Lake attempted to help people avoid alcoholism and survive Anglo-settler forces, but some critics found Christian missionary influences within the Code. Today, the Code, The Great Law, and the US-established tribal governments are all sources of friction between enrolled members of the small and scattered territories in New York State and Canada.

In summary, the Ravenous Hydra of America is at a critical point in its history. The teleology behind its found mythologies is failing, leading to a dystopian self-fulfilling prophecy. Yet it continues to destroy and consume ecologies at a world-annihilating pace. The concept of 'shapeshifting', as interpreted by Native American psychologist Eduardo Duran (2019), points a way out of this destructive course. Shapeshifting is a broadly transcultural concept embodied in the story-telling traditions of many cultures, including those of indigenous peoples and premodern Europe, where it is embodied in ancient tales of the abilities of spirit beings to metamorphose into various forms, animal and otherwise. Duran reinterprets this mythic theme in modern terms by integrating it with scientific theories. In his work, shapeshifting is the process in Natural Law where no part of the universe is ever static, but rather always in flux. The earth itself is in a constant state of change over different periods of time. Life is a continual series of developmental and evolutionary cycles. Humans are at first a single cell that unfolds and changes in shape and form continuously throughout a lifespan. The human mind is never static, but always shifting and changing in a flux of emotions, thoughts, and reactions on a moment-to-moment time scale. Therefore, shapeshifting refers to the natural process of constant change unfolding over time from shape or form. Time, energy, and matter together are always in a state of change seeking balance, harmony, and equilibrium. This is the only true constant of the universe and natural law.

Applied to the perilous course upon which America is heading, shapeshifting away from this mode of being requires a new psychological worldview and system of social organization. Our nation does not have the luxury or the ability to deny and repress its worse instincts any longer. It must face collectively what it has wrought and change course. As John Mohawk (1999) correctly pointed out in his book *Utopian Legacies: A History of Conquest and Oppression in the Western World,* from the time of the Greeks, the highest ideals of European thought have paradoxically resulted in the most destructive forces on the planet, such as genocide, ecocide, enslavement, economic plunder, and domination, to global war. Solutions can be found by stopping the search for unattainable and fantastic ideals, accepting our place in the world with humility, and seeking to coexist helpfully with each other and Nature. This is folly when people seek a higher ideal that sets them apart from others and Nature. They believe they have 'the answer' to problems and can make things perfect. As idealism grows higher, so does that which must be denied and repressed within grow more substantial. This form of hubris has led to repeated destruction and pain. We could choose to foster that which has been shown to create the best way for all life on earth, and that comes down to having healthy and strong relationships with each other and the rest of nature. We do not need an ideology or religion to achieve this as an aim for humanity and the Earth, our mother.

We will end with a series of dreams of an Onkwehonwe male in the US military during the Global War on Terror. Over a month in this series, this person had dreams in which he saw portions of the Earth torn open, rivers re-routed, and the deaths of many people and animals. He saw battlefields of the past as an Elder escorted him. In the final dream, this person was on patrol for the military and came upon an opening in the forest. In this clearing, over a dozen Onkwehonwe elders met him. Each male and female greeted him and handed him the fruit from the Great Tree. He was instructed to open it, taste the fruit, and spread the seeds. The fruit he saw was a miniature version of the Earth, and inside was a rainbow, and at the center was a ball of light. He tasted the fruit, and it tasted of all the best things. He was instructed to take the seeds from the fruit and plant it, but as he returned to his base, he was no longer recognized, for he had been transformed by tasting the fruit. And the seeds were then understood to lead to a shift in the mind and people's relationship to the Earth.

This is not the first time this type of dream has been recalled by Indigenous peoples. Multiple dreams have been recorded with similar themes and motifs. It had been customary among the Onkwehonwe to share their dreams and to re-enact them. They understood that dreams contain and impart a unique way of seeing the world that promotes insight into the individual or the community. Dreams were not considered a mystical or metaphysical phenomenon as sometimes characterized by modern Europeans but were seen as a natural process of being human (Graeber & Wengrow, 2021).

My heartfelt gratitude goes out to my teacher Dr. Eduardo Duran, my sister Dolores Jimerson, my brothers, Matt Hill and Robert Mele; and the many teachers and Elders from Seneca and Mohawk families who read and helped to shape this Chapter. SE

References

Angus, I. (2016). *Facing the Anthropocene: Fossil capitalism and the crisis of the earth system*. NYU Press.

Duran, E. (2019). *Healing the soul wound: Trauma-informed counseling for indigenous communities*. Teachers College Press.

Edinger, E. F., et al. (1996) *The New God-Image*. Chiron Publications.

Freud, S., & Jung, C.G. (1994). *The Freud-Jung letters: The correspondence between Sigmund Freud and C.G. Jung*. Princeton University Press.

Graeber, D., & Wengrow, D. (2021). *The dawn of everything: A new history of humanity*. Farrar, Straus and Giroux.

Grandin, G. (2019). *The end of the myth: From the frontier to the border wall in the mind of America*. Metropolitan Books.

Hall, L.K. (2023). *The Mohawk warrior society: A Handbook on sovereignty and survival*. PM Press.

Jung, C.G. (2011). *Memories, dreams, reflections*. Vintage.

Mohawk, J. (1999). *Utopian legacies: A history of conquest and oppression in the western world*. Clear Light Publishers.

Papadopoulos, R.K. (2012). *The Handbook of Jungian psychology: Theory, practice and applications*. Routledge.

Stephanson, A. (1996). *Manifest destiny: American expansion and the empire of right*. Hill and Wang.

Chapter 5

Archetype of the Machine

Jody Echegaray

Introduction – Whispers of the Machine

Whispers of machines are heard sparsely in Jung's original writings, the earliest from his cousin's transcribed utterances during séances witnessed in late 1899 for Jung's dissertation research into somnambulistic phenomena (Helene Preiswerk; as detailed in Shamdasani, 2005). These would later be published in the first volume of his collected works (Jung, 2014/1902). In what we today might label a dissociative state, Helene described visions of an advanced technological civilization on Mars which had given up scientific and philosophical pursuits. The last mention – excluding those appearing in endnotes and indices – is found in volume 18 (Jung, 2014/1954) in written correspondence to the Swiss weekly magazine *Weltwoche*. There Jung responds to a request to speculate on the then-current preoccupation (i.e., mid-1950s) with flying saucer phenomena, where he was asked what effects the knowledge of being observed by an advanced alien civilization might have on our own. Jung's response takes him beyond imagined observation and toward extrapolations of domination and colonization – largely owing to the advantages conferred on such a civilization not through their advanced connection to psyche, but rather their connection to advanced technology. These and other references within his writings hint at his understanding of the ambivalent relationship between the human and the machine. He seems to intuit an increasing conjunction of psyche, science and technology as well as the tantalizing presence of the machine manifesting as contemporary myths and symbols. It is this conjunction and this presence that seems to energize his musings on flying saucer phenomena – which stand as contemporaneous symbols of the Machine in the modern era. As he writes:

DOI: 10.4324/9781003412823-6

Naturally, the first thing to be consigned to the rubbish heap would be our science and technology. What the moral effects of such a catastrophe would be can be seen from the pitiful decay of primitive cultures taking place before our eyes. That the construction of such machines [flying saucers] would be evidence of a scientific technology immensely superior to ours admits of no two opinions. Just as the Pax Britannica put an end to tribal warfare in Africa, so our world could roll up its Iron Curtain and use it as so much scrap along with all the billions of tons of armaments, warships, and munitions. That wouldn't be such a bad thing, but we would have been 'discovered' and colonized – reason enough for universal panic!

(Jung, 2014/1954, § 1439)

Though volume 10 contains a later work on flying saucer phenomena and was published in 1958, it is notable that the first and last references in the collected works employing the signifier "machine" both invoke comparison to advanced civilizations. The machines themselves are imbued with a cosmic, objective capacity to qualify these civilizations as advanced. In the first mention, machines are fantastical creations accompanying an artistically and philosophically sterile society, intimating the machine's capacity for catalyzing inertia; in the last, as a symbol of overwhelming power, intimating its capacity for engendering subjugation. It is perhaps also a prescient description of our current, technologically mediated milieu – from computational systems to social media – and similar effects on our civilization.

Between these two textual appearances and intimations of capacities, the machine is referenced throughout his collected works in various ways: as a dismal process of automatism driving the thought disturbances and processes of psychosis – in opposition to the living flow of the human mind and psyche (Jung, 2014/1960); as a metric of cultural and technological development of a civilization and concretization of that civilization's achievement of "directed thinking" (Jung, 1956/1967, p. 16) characteristic of modern consciousness; as an object in contrast to the human psyche, which Jung differentiates from a machine as not reconfigurable or reprogrammable at will and embedded in history and historicity (Jung, 1956/1967); as the modern backdrop of our personal and collective lives (Jung, 1966/1977); as both a metaphorical and actual mechanism which transforms energies from one form to another – e.g., cultural, psychic, biological, and physical (Jung,

1969b/1981); as a primitive level of psychological functioning – pejoratively likened to animal consciousness in terms of its automaticity (Jung, 2014/1970); and as something we are deeply embedded in, dependent on, and suspended in dual roles as both user and servant (Jung, 2014/1961). Despite the ubiquity, power, horror, and transformative scope of the machine as described by Jung, the root word machine appears a mere 77 times in the collected works. Of those, 14 appear in the indices or notes, leaving a total of 63 within-text references. By contrast, the word anima appears 1284 times, psyche 2962 times, and unconscious 8890 times.

Although comparatively infrequent, his invocation of the machine seems to qualify it as any other Jungian symbol – an energized multiplicity bound within a telic and thematic psychic ecology of meaning, influence, and intentionality. This domain of the machine is delineated as distinct from a biological or "natural" one but as acting alongside, from within, or upon it. Like all symbols displaying this indeterminate, polysemic character, this symbol implies an associated archetype. And following Jung's suggestion on the nature of archetypes as evolutive where he writes "every archetype is capable of infinite development and differentiation" (Jung, 1968/1980, para 12), one that may reflect a mutation and recombination of archaic archetypes. Yet it is one that has arguably been relegated to an afterthought within analytical psychology. In the following sections, I will attempt to describe how the Machine has become our contemporary myth and an archetypal presence circulating within many domains, from contemporary popular culture to theory and philosophy to the consulting room. As such, it may represent not only a presence fully realized and threaded through the world and psyche, but also a part of the human story since antiquity, and a telic indicator of the direction of future discourses.

The decade following the period of the 1950s that found Jung (Jung, 2014/1959) speculating on flying saucer phenomena and their potential meaning also saw an increasing exploration of the scope and penetration of technology, often prompting examinations from the modern era looking backward. Sociologist Jacques Ellul (1964), historian and philosopher of technology Lewis Mumford (1967, 1970), and media theorist Marshall McLuhan (1996), for example, all sought to explore the ever-increasing creep of the technological into contemporary human existence. Looking toward prehistory and the ancient world, both Ellul and Mumford advanced hypotheses that the implementation of technical procedures – and the first "machines" in the sense of human military and labor collectives and techniques – emerged from a multiplicity of factors: psychological processes, the structuring capacities of ritual and religion, and increasingly complex social organization to name but a few. Both Mumford and Ellul opined that the kernel for the appearance of technics and their evolution into technologies had roots in the psychic depths. Mumford invoked the unconscious (1967) while Ellul hinted at the presence of an organizing principle channeling instinctual energies into a telos of creative and technical expression:

> One is left with an enigma, and there is some point in emphasizing that there is here the same mystery as the appearance of life itself. Each primitive operation of man implies the bridging of such an enormous gulf between instinct and the technical act that a mysterious aura hovers about all subsequent development. Our modern worship of techniques derives from man's ancestral worship of the mysterious and marvelous character of his own handiwork.
>
> (Ellul, 1964, pp. 23–24)

70 years following Ellul's observations, many humans find themselves inhabiting a thoroughly technologically saturated civilization amidst an increasing ubiquity of machines, with comparatively fewer discussions exploring this "mysterious aura" or psychic factors apart from the egoic concerns of efficiency and market dynamics. Contemporary energy and transportation grids; financial systems; music, television, and film entertainment production; biological and quantum computing research; artificial intelligence (AI); smart phones and homes; augmented and virtual reality (AR/VR) applications and spaces; robotics in manufacturing sectors; pharmaceutical research and drug manufacturing processes; synthetic biology; medical research, treatment, and tracking; cyberwarfare; and omnipresent streaming and social media. All inhere in and speak to this ubiquity in our current technological ecology – one offering an endless palette of selection, distraction, immersion, information, and threat. All speak to an orientation toward the machinic as a contemporary metaphor as well as material catalyst co-constructing our present civilization. One might conduct a casual survey of their living and working spaces to identify which objects or processes are not in some way powered, constructed, assembled, transported, or transacted via technological process – from cookware to computers, fashion to medication, personal entertainment to personal transportation.

Of the original three aspects of the Greek term *phármakon* – poison, scapegoat, and remedy – technology and the Machine tend to be viewed primarily belonging to the first two categories in critical and analytical circles, and the latter in utopian, scientific, and technological ones. Within contemporary theoretical and philosophical domains, the machine appears as a polyvalent ambiguity, and is often more central to cultural, political, economic, philosophical, and scientific discourses than in Jungian thought. As in Jung's original writings where the Machine is invoked symbolically, and from which we can posit an associated archetype, modern domains also tend to begin from a grounding assumption of oppositional dualities – i.e., between the synthetic/machinic/technological and the natural/psychic-subjective/biological. Yet this grounding assumption quickly gives way in the face of an increasing blurring of conceptual distinctions found in contemporary discourse and science. There, we do not find the machine invoked as a symbol in the Jungian sense. Rather it typically appears as metaphor or signifier, and often as a cornerstone or area of structural inquiry.

It is important to foreground that many contemporary and postmodern ontologies often present as distinct from, and antithetical to, those of traditional analytical psychology – beginning with their primary focus on what might broadly be termed "materialist" rather than the psychic. Materialist here refers not merely to matter or physical systems, but also abstract and nonphysical systems that – while entangled with or incorporating material/physical objects and processes – are not reducible to them. Such systems include economics, language, political governance, sociocultural formations and forces, history, and academic and scientific systems (e.g., philosophy, psychology, ethology, mathematics, physics, chemistry, etc.).

The purpose of examining these other contemporary disciplines and domains is not to reductively demonstrate how their discourse around technology and the machine might bear one-to-one correspondence with concepts or discursive frames in analytical psychology, but rather to affirm essential differences vis-à-vis their ontological premises – while simultaneously searching for points of contact. As Jungian analyst Christopher Hauke (2000) concluded (following Jung) – in the final analysis, all discourse occurs at the level of human subjectivity and thought, presupposing a boundedness within the psychological and embodied finitude of human horizons. While it might be tempting to reductively demonstrate how these discursive formations exist in nascent or occluded form within analytical psychology (or vice versa), it seems more advisable to instead examine intriguing points of contact while simultaneously affirming difference.

Holding this paradox lightly, we might ask: what might these other ways of thinking and working have to offer analytical psychology by way of their machinic discourses? What is extractable or able to be incorporated, by way of mechanics, concept, or analogy, into analytical thinking and practice? And, ultimately, why the Machine? What drives the adoption of this central metaphor and fixation? A recent example of this method can be found in Jungian analyst Mark Saban's (2020) examination of philosopher Gilbert Simondon's extensive treatment of individuation (2017, 2020). Simondon conceives of individuation occurring in multiplicities not confined to the human – e.g., natural, chemical, technological – where being is already plural and collective, and where individuation stretches across preindividual, individual, and transindividual registers of reality. This establishes a philosophically rigorous framework bridging human, natural, and technological domains, both plural/collective and singular/personal. As Saban notes, this allows individuation to "move beyond Jung who by identifying psyche with interiority gets trapped in an individualistic model whereby society is seen at best as an outer obstacle to the freedom of the subject to achieve the inner journey of individuation" (Saban, 2020, p. 96).

In terms of an analytical psychology lens, I posit that the increasing ubiquity of the machine as organizing principle/metaphor in these contemporary philosophical and scientific domains, as well as the larger culture, is indicative of the presence of a complex enveloping an archetypal core – a core that I refer to here as an emergent archetype of the Machine, inhering in objective psyche. It is one whose "emergence" may have been ongoing throughout much of our history, intensifying its distinction from older archetypal forms more rapidly in the modern era. At the same time, in the spirit of inquiry set out above, it is important to understand and illustrate the increasing references to, and incorporation of, the machine (or Machine, to connote this archetypal presence) within the discourse of these domains outside analytical psychology – that is, why have they chosen the machine as their metaphor and fundament, according to their own logic? In holding our paradox of allowing points of confluence as well as difference, the following represents a brief window to review these ontologies dispassionately rather than reflexively argue against them from the perspective of analytical psychology alone – something that, while potentially fruitful, merits a separate and more fulsome examination. One such example can be found in Hauke's (2000) investigation of postmodern philosophy/critical theory and analytical psychology, *Jung and the Postmodern: The Interpretation of Realities*, where he subjects Jung and a diverse spectrum of thinkers and systems – from Lacanian psychoanalysis to Kristevan critiques of gender and power dynamics to Deleuzian perspectives on Nietzsche – to conceptual comparison and collision. He concludes:

> postmodern fragmentation is no negative and destructive attack on modernity and its values but is the consequence of a psyche differentiating in these accelerating times and seeking an expression of and a revealing of itself to itself in ways that seem challenging to modernity. The creativity of the unconscious, it seems, has found the conditions to make itself known in cultural forms, not necessarily with any aim in view – or any goal in the modernist sense – but more as an activity entirely for itself, for its own celebration.
>
> (Hauke, 2000, p. 284)

The How of the Machine: In – and as – Contemporary Theory and Culture

We are inebriated with the technological. From Ellul, Mumford, and McLuhan and through much of twentieth-century continental philosophy, aspects of the technological and machinic weave through the writings of philosophers and critical theorists. There they are implicated in multiple ways: as stewards of a process of cultural consumption seen in the increased movement toward simulation-oriented forms of experience (e.g., media, video games, virtual and augmented reality; see Baudrillard, 1988/2020); as configuring and generating new forms of human knowledge (Lyotard, 1984); as co-determinative with all forms of individuation (Simondon, 2017, 2020); and as fundamentally entangled in the ongoing evolution and a force driving human history, social, and cultural formations – a process structuring both biology and mind (Stiegler, 1998, 2008). For philosopher Bernard Stiegler and Simondon, as with Mumford and Ellul, the machinic and technological are co-occurring catalysts of, and companions to, the entire span of humanity's development.

Philosopher Gilles Deleuze and psychoanalyst Felix Guattari place the concept of the machine at the center of their joint collaborations (1983, 1987). Here the machine is not merely a signifier for technological or mechanical devices, but both an actualized occurrence as well as a conceptual category for the fundamental parts of all systems – i.e., an entity imbued with innate capacities for connectivity and production. For Deleuze and Guattari, machines are an ontological fundament of their philosophy. They create the infinitely emerging variations that manifest as both material objects and immaterial flows of historical, philosophical, social, and political energies and events (i.e., becomings). Machines serve as regulators of energic, material, and informational flows. They facilitate the functioning and connective aspects of material objects, biological, and abstract systems (e.g., cultural and legal systems, financial markets, the mediasphere). As such, they constitute and facilitate the complex emergences of all systems, everywhere – from currency exchanges to cultures to particle accelerators to biological life itself. As they write in the opening pages of their first collaborative work, *Anti-Oedipus*:

> Everywhere it is machines – real ones, not figurative ones: machines driving other machines, with all the necessary couplings and connections. An organ-machine is plugged into an energy-source machine: the one produces milk, and the mouth a machine coupled to it. The mouth of the anorexic wavers between several functions: its possessor is uncertain as to whether it is an eating-machine, an anal machine, a talking-machine, or a breathing machine (asthma attacks). Hence we are all handymen: each with his little machines.
>
> (1983, p. 1)

Machines here are ubiquitous and impersonal. They function prior to and outside of human subjectivity and consciousness, and are composed of, and canalize, energy in the form of desire. Desire, in the Deleuzian-Guattarian usage, might loosely analogize to a presubjective/asubjective Jungian flow of libido. Jung qualifies libido as: "no more concretely conceivable than the energy known to the world of physics. Libido is … nothing but an abbreviated expression for the 'energic standpoint'" (Jung, 1969b/1981, p. 30). Deleuze and Guattari summarize their understanding of how this "energic standpoint" in the form of desire and "matter" (material aspects of the world) correspond and become entangled within machines:

> a direct link is perceived between the machine and desire, the machine passes to the heart of desire, the machine is desiring, and desire, machined.

> Desire is not in the [human] subject, but the machine in desire – with the residual [human] subject off to the side, alongside the machine, around the entire periphery, a parasite of machines, an accessory of vertebra-machinate desire.
>
> (1983, p. 285)

In Deleuze and Guattari's work, these desiring-machines are interconnected with and serve as the energic/libidinal catalyst for other types of machines: e.g., abstract machines (conceptual systems and frameworks such as physics, mathematics, philosophy, law, etc.), social machines (political, economic, and sociocultural formations and institutions, etc.), physical machines (physical objects, mechanical and computational systems, etc.), and perceptual machines (those by which we register and perceive our reality – e.g., sociocultural values and norms as well as biological cognitive and perceptual systems, etc.). These are linked together with and by desire-machines, forming networks of heterogenous machines called assemblages. These assemblages, in turn, exist on planes or spaces of possibility, where they function as larger, collective machines, with desiring-machines as the crucial "libido-canalizing" aspect of these machinic networks/assemblages. In this sense, assemblages are living, mutative process-structures, albeit impersonal and transcending human agency – with desire energizing them.

The emphasis on the machine, which for Deleuze and Guattari is not a metaphorical but rather an ontological fundament, seems far afield from Jungian conceptualizations of flows of libido animating natural systems and inhering in psyche. Yet Jung himself seemed to give consideration to a similar ontological thrust, stating "the human body as whole is a machine" (Jung, 1969b/1981, para 81) and broadening this to include natural, synthetic/cultural, and psychic phenomena:

> When the beaver fells trees and dams up a river, this is a performance conditioned by its differentiation. Its differentiation is a product of what one might call "natural culture", which functions as a transformer of energy, as a machine. Similarly human culture, as a natural product of differentiation, is a machine; first of all a technical one that utilizes natural conditions for the transformation of physical and chemical energy, but also a psychic machine that utilizes psychic conditions for the transformation of libido.
>
> (Jung, 1969b/1981, para 81)

Deleuze and Guattari's perspective should not be confused with a techno-animist or a panpsychist position where consciousness inheres in or animates machines (and assemblages) but rather where machines form connections from a material milieu and facilitate the emergence of human consciousness. This machine/assemblage-on-a-plane configuration can be said to represent an analogy-by-inversion to the bridging or connective aspect found in Jung's concept of the psychoid. An inversion that is defined by their denial of consciousness as foundational, which qualifies assemblages as apparently antithetical to Jung's psychoid. At the same time, the assemblage of machines suggests a similar notion of a connective fabric conducting and transforming energy across vastly heterogenous or oppositional facets of reality.

In attempting to delineate this psychoid archetype, something which Jung himself qualified as "irrepresentable" (Jung, 1969a/1981, para 417), Saban summarizes:

> The psychoid archetype possesses three different aspects. First, it is inaccessible to consciousness. Second, located in the meeting place between the psychological and the physiological, it combines or transcends both. It can show up therefore in the relationship between a person's psyche and their body. Its third and most significant aspect refers, in Roderick Main's words, 'to the relationship between a person's psyche and the physical world beyond that person's body'.
>
> (Main, as cited in Saban; Saban, 2011, para 2)

Where Jung describes the psychoid as "a bridge to matter in general" (Jung, 1969a/1981, para 420) between the putatively archetypal, the physiological/instinctual, and the material, Deleuze and Guattari describe the relationship of machines to assemblages: "The ... machine does not exist independently of the assemblage, any more than the assemblage functions independently of the machine" (Deleuze & Guattari, 1987, p. 121). The machines that constitute assemblages are described somewhat paradoxically as simultaneously enabling "continual ... flow" (Deleuze & Guattari, 1983, p. 36) and "defined as a system of interruptions of breaks (*coupures*)" Deleuze & Guattari, 1983, p. 36). They go on to describe:

> These breaks should in no way be considered as a separation from reality; rather, they operate along lines that vary according to whatever aspect of

them we are considering. Every machine is related to a continual material flow (*hylè*) that it cuts into. It functions like a ham-slicing machine,
removing portions from the associative flow; … the mouth that cuts off
not only the flow of milk, but also the flow of air and sound; the penis
that interrupts the not only the flow of urine, but also the flow of sperm.
Each associative flow must be seen as an ideal thing, an endless flux,
flowing from something not unlike the immense thigh of a pig. The term
hylè in fact designates the pure continuity that any one sort of matter
ideally possesses.

(1983, p. 36)

In both cases, assemblages and the psychoid both posit an impersonal
layer of reality through which information, energy, and intentionality
propagate and act within and upon the world, including their constitutive
role in human subjectivity, albeit in different order. In Jung's psychoid
this constitutive role is catalyzed by a continuous and conductive fabric
between the psychic and the material, whereas for Deleuze and Guattari
this constitutive role emerges from the discrete and disruptive connective
function of machines – that is, a continuous flow subjected to interruption
by means of the very machines that link together to facilitate this flow.
For Jung, the connective function of the psychoid presupposes and is in
the service to the presence of "consciousness", with the psychoid bridging the matter-psyche spectrum from atoms to archetype. For Deleuze
and Guattari, machines are tasked with the connective-but-disrupted flow
engendering existence of production itself, of which "consciousness"
emerges as but one product.

This fundamental difference of the primacy of psyche and "consciousness" (used here in the sense of sentience encompassing both conscious
and unconscious process) between the two highlights a point of ontological incompatibility; while the connective/bridging function between vastly
different aspects of reality suggests a point of consilience. Again, it is
important to highlight Deleuze and Guattari's usage of the term machine as
distinct from merely a physical or mechanical object but rather as an impersonal and fundamental ontological unit that can manifest in many forms,
with physical machines as but one.

Despite the problems with scope and the considerable differences in
their premises and focus, a number of theorists and scholars have sought
to find points of congruence and theoretical interpenetration between

Deleuzian thought and analytical psychology: beginning with Deleuze's own essay on masochism referencing Jung's rendering of the incest prohibition as set forth in *Symbols of Transformation* (2004), Hauke (2000), Deleuzian scholar Christian Kerslake (2007), critical theorist Barbara Jenkins (2018), edited volumes by Jungian scholar Roderick Main, professor of sociology Christian McMillan, and Jungian psychotherapist David Henderson (McMillan et al., 2020; Main et al., 2020), and philosopher Grant Maxwell (2022). Although a full rendering of Deleuze and Guattari's philosophy is beyond the scope of this chapter, the penetration of their thinking has been pervasive. Smith et al. (2022) write that the impact of Deleuze's thinking "reaches beyond philosophy; his work is approvingly cited by, and his concepts put to use by, researchers in architecture, urban studies, geography, film studies, musicology, anthropology, gender studies, literary studies and other fields" (Smith et al., 2022, para 2).

Unlike Jung's focus on psyche and human experience, contemporary strands of philosophical thought and critical theory – for example, object-oriented ontology (OOO) and posthumanism – mirror Deleuze and Guattari's effort to move away from an anthropocentric standpoint where human psyche, motivation, and activity is taken as the preferred epistemological perspective. The "objects" in OOO (as opposed to human subjects, subjectivity, and consciousness at the center of humanistic sciences and much of philosophy) are affirmed as events, forms, and non-human others in the universe that have ontological status as beings, independent of human interaction with or direct perception of them (e.g., protons, chemical bonds, insects, black holes); while in posthumanism, the areas of value, ethics, and focus are not relegated to the anthropocentric but, increasingly, the technological, non-human biological, and ecological (see Miah, 2008; Blanco-Wells, 2021). In both, there is a view from a cosmic perspective of entangled objects culminating in emergences and events rather than an anthropocentric aperture, a move affording "objects" their own "suchness" and being without being validated by or predication on the human. As stated, this stands in contrast to Jung's focus on the psyche and human as tending toward the primary focus. At the same time– as Saban suggests in his examination of Simondon's writings on individuation – this allows an expanded palette of consideration vis-à-vis potential occasions of contact with analytical psychology.

Specific variations of these strands, like philosopher Levi R. Bryant's machine-oriented ontology (MOO; Bryant, 2014) and feminist scholar Donna Haraway's posthumanism, are also heavily influenced by their orientation toward machines as the central metaphor. Bryant draws on Deleuze and Guattari's thinking, where the machine also serves as an ontological primitive and basis of his theory and philosophy. As with Deleuze, and again in contradistinction to Jungian thought, Bryant's ontology is conceptualized as "flat" There is no hierarchy of being, no metaphysical principles that are foundational and held as eternal, favoring neither human nor non-human domains, energy nor matter, but rather an orientation toward ongoing processes of difference and change – unfolding and interacting to produce new configurations of systems and machines. Machines are distinguished as either corporeal (e.g., bodies, oceans, anything constituted by matter) or incorporeal (e.g., literature, mathematical equations, music), and can interact to manifest in the world as a spatiotemporal event (e.g., a production of a particular play, usage of a particular set of equations to calculate engineering tolerances for a mechanical component, tuning a piano, etc.). Much as in Deleuze and Guattari, machines are connective, combinatoric, and serve to catalyze novel sets of differences and change in the world through the transformation and conveyance of energy, relationship, and interaction – a sea of becomings.

This notion of machine, enlarged beyond the merely mechanical and enfolded into the material matrix of the world, is intriguing and suggests a contemporary facet of the emergent archetype of the Machine; i.e., one that has not as its goal the production of physical, mechanical or computational objects alone but also systems, combinatorics, and syntheses of production itself. It is a creative and catalytic impulse, abstract but manifesting within and through psyche, human creativity, cultural activity, and the material world. This aspect, parsed in contemporary conceptual language, suggests a correspondence to archetypal forms and alchemical analogies found in the Jungian canon – e.g., the archetype of Mercurius (see, for example, Jung's chapter *The Spirit Mercurius* in CW13, 1967/1983) and the alchemical *caelum* (Jung, 1963/1989).

Haraway's (1985/2006) posthumanism evokes mythic qualities of the machine, albeit also in a non-Jungian sense, as a myth reflective of our current historical moment, encountered in contemporaneous storytelling. For Haraway, however, the machine serves as one possible telic map – not in service of personal individuation – but rather collective and political consciousness, movement, and adaptation. In her widely-read *A Cyborg Manifesto* (1985/2006), she argues in favor of the feminist liberatory potential of one specific type of machine (or rather, human-machine hybrid) – the cyborg, a frequent trope in science fiction. She positions the cyborg beyond the merely tropic, reaching into the space of grounding metaphor. From an analytical standpoint, we might say the cyborg represents a starker, Promethean configuration of the alchemical second stage of the *coniunctio*, where the *unio mentalis coniunctio* made up of soul and mind, initially separated from the instinctual longings of the body, are now recombined with the body via this alchemical *caelum*, i.e., the Machine in cyborg form. For Haraway, it is a third position between, and synthetic amalgam of, the biological and technological. Haraway writes this in the service of challenging essentialist ontologies and their unquestioned patriarchal assumptions fundamental to much of Western philosophical and cultural traditions. Her stated purpose lies in the possibility of eliminating "natural" or essentialist limitations on social roles and human potential, which have historically been predicated on biology. She proposes the cyborg as a dramatic representation of how the biological domain and human body are mutable rather than fixed in time and function. As she notes in her essay, notions of biological difference are often used as the fundament for sanctioned disparities in sociocultural roles, political and discursive domains – propping up the systems that maintain them. Haraway argues the blurring of those distinctions – in making them fluid and subject to willful enhancement and modification – obviates biologically-oriented, naturalist premises. In her view, three important collapses create the historical conditions for the possibility of the cyborg's emergence: the breakdown in distinction between the fixed, dualistic domains of animal and human; between the domains of biological organism and machine; and between domains of the physical and non-physical. It is important to note breakdown here implies blurring, not erasure. Equally important is to reiterate our focus here is not on the constructionist versus essentialist debate, the flattening of ontological horizons, feminist conceptualizations of gender, elimination of hierarchies based on biology, or power relations as they collide with analytical psychology – which are examined extensively by Jenkins (2018) and Hauke (2000). Rather, the focus here is the invocation of Machine as a "magical"/technological agent – a connective function in analytical parlance – a function that suggests a connective correspondence to both the alchemical *caelum* and Mercurial archetypal aspect, although Haraway would disavow such notions.

In the 37 years since its publication, Haraway's erosions of distinction have become even more apparent within scientific, cultural, and philosophical circles. A casual survey of the current popular and scientific literature reflects our intoxication with the Machine: the socioeconomic consequences of the thinning barrier between human and robot in labor tasks (Oxford Economics, 2022), and the accompanying political fracture lines as these tasks are relegated to robots and other forms of "surrogate humans" (Atanasoski & Vora, 2015, p. 3). A recent compilation of articles by the scientific journal *Applied Soft Computing* details near-term use cases of predictive AI in shaping human environments and care: in the diagnosis of brain tumors using minimal resources (Ma & Zhang, 2021); in identifying prevalence rates of adverse drug effects in populations by parsing social media (Shen et al., 2021); and for automated control of residential environments based on eye scanning-based electroencephalography for elderly, disabled, or mobility-impaired individuals (Hassan et al., 2021). A study by Skjuve et al. (2021) illustrates the increasing acceptance of social chatbots perceived as caring, empathic "companions" relative to human interaction among its users. A recent case of the implantation of a "digital bridge" by a team of neuroscientists to allow ambulation in a patient who was previously paralyzed due to chronic tetraplegia following a spinal cord injury (Sample, 2023) provides a literal representation of Haraway's "cyborg". The emerging subdiscipline of synthetic biology and advances in neurobiology (Powell, 2018; El Karoui et al., 2019; Chiaradia & Lancaster, 2020) have ushered in the era of designer molecules, programmable cells, and brain organoids (i.e., a cultured growth of living neural material that functions analogous to discrete neuroanatomical regions, used in the study of disease process, neurodevelopment, and information flow in neural networks). In a summary on synthetic biology, El Karoui, Hoyos-Flight, and Fletcher flesh out the contemporary reaches of this cyborgization, and its market potential, writing:

Synthetic biology offers the opportunity to create responsive and multifunctional materials. The integration of biochemical components from living systems with inorganic components can lead to new materials that are able to sense the environment (or internal signals) and change their properties. These features could be particularly useful for improving protective clothing or building materials.

(2019, para 26).

At the same time, her invocation of this third position of the cyborg, as connective syntheses between previously differentiated categories, is offered up as a form of network rather than dialectic synthesis. Absent from her writing is any notion of transcendent function, or ontology predicated on pasts of original unity or omega points of future integration; no *telos* save adaptation, difference, permutation, and evolution in response to the massive tidal forces of history and culture. As such, her text actively resists attempts to situate it within Jungian ontologies; indeed, she closes with the declarative: "I would rather be a cyborg than a goddess" (Haraway, p. 101). But only after 43 pages describing the evolutive, middle position occupied by her metaphorical-cum-Mercurial/*caelumic* cyborg, one found suspended amidst the familiar tension of opposites and still subject to their limitations. This is not to reinterpret her overt declarations, but rather – as both Jung and Deleuze and Guattari might assert – point out the difficulty in achieving escape velocity from our historical, cultural, philosophical, and psychological gravity well. As DeCook remarks on Haraway's project, "The material, the virtual, and the technological all collide into one another, but this does not help us transcend our humanity nor our human identities" (DeCook, 2020, p. 1166).

Examples of Deleuze and Guattari's thinking – and the centrality of the machine – are also encountered in contemporary critical theory. Sociologist and philosopher Maurizio Lazzarato (2014), for example, examines the functioning of late-stage capitalism and the way in which it aids in the formation of the contemporary subject through a complex assemblage of linguistic, technical and social machines. According to Lazzarato, the institutions, technical systems, algorithmic and scientific-technological deployments, systems of management, labor, and distribution all are machines. Machines that comprise a vast network connected to – and engendering the functioning of – the machine called capitalism. Reciprocally, one of the functions of this meta-machine of capitalism is to produce subjects with vocational, legal, political, and – crucially – economic identities and roles. These subjects in turn serve as both consumers of the machine's output as well as necessary "components" for its continued growth and functioning (Lazzarato, 2014).

Lazzarato and those who employ the theoretical underpinnings of Deleuze and Guattari's (1983, 1987) abstract and technical machines or Bryant's (2014) corporeal and incorporeal machines (i.e., material objects, biological organisms, and knowledge practices – mathematics, philosophy, literature, myths) trace the presence of the Machine in philosophical and critical thought, attempting to frame our current collective and personal realities. Others, however, have sought to illustrate the precise mechanics where the theory becomes flesh, data, and algorithm. Both social psychologist and philosopher Shoshana Zubroff (2020) and digital studies professor John Cheney-Lippold (2017) demonstrate how our real-world behaviors inform the formation of our digital selves – i.e., the digital representations of our identity. These digital "selves", data structures existing in technical machines, are constituted by the consolidation of our activity patterns: online browsing and shopping behaviors, geo-location of our physical movements, facial recognition, media consumption choices, and collection of biometric data from wearable technology. And they are mutable according to which machinic agent is sampling the vast dataset constituting these "selves". This creates a feedback loop that engenders not only constant sampling and surveilling of our activities, but also algorithmic construction and prediction of our future behavior, biomedical conditions, psychosocial, and demographic traits (e.g., political affiliation, gender and cultural identification, generational cohort, income levels, etc.).

As they argue in their respective works, these identities, coupled to corporatized perspectives, represent a shifting flux generated from a continuous feed of our personal data and the corresponding data-analytic products – all via a persistent, technologically mediated interface with the vast digital ecology in which we subsist. Cheney-Lippold writes: "Google's, Quantcast's, and Alexa's interpretations of my data are necessarily contradictory because they each speak about me from their own, proprietary scripts. Each is ambivalent about who I am, interpreting me according to their individual algorithmic logics" (Cheney- Lippold, 2017, p. 6). In this respect, the computational machines and the organizational machines which employ them unwittingly suggest a polysemic prism of process dimly reflective of Jung's notions of multiple agencies inhering in the psyche. It is a prism, however, defined within the ontic horizons of collective capitalism rather than objective psyche, with a *telos* oriented toward consumption rather than individuation. As such, they represent "selves" – more akin to datafied ego/persona fragments – with a linguistic but threadbare conceptual relationship to any analytical structure or process.

Outside the domains of philosophy, critical theory, and humanist sciences, fields such as neuroscience and biology also embrace metaphors of the machine in an attempt to provide relatable epistemologies of the functioning of the vast, interconnected complex systems of body and brain. Typically, these machinic metaphors tend toward computational rather than mechanical. A great deal of contemporary cognitive and affective neuroscience, for example, tends to employ not only neuroanatomy but also metaphors of the brain as a computational machine – or more accurately, a network of computational machines. Contemporary neuroscience references not only brain regions, but also functional neural networks arising from information flows within and between these regions – e.g., the dorsal attention network (DAN), central executive network (CEN), default mode network (DMN), salience network, etc., as well as the recent discovery of an 11-dimensional topological structure to the human brain's information flow (similar to the topology of a computer network; Reimann et al., 2017). As in the understanding and design of computational machines, the abstract machine of physics is often identified as the fundamental epistemological layer; in the case of computational systems, undergirding their electronic engineering. In the case of brain and mind, it becomes the layer undergirding biological and evolutionary process. One recent theory, for example, outlines the leap from brain and biology to consciousness, where processes in the brainstem region give rise to the experience of affect, theorized as a form of proto-consciousness. Through interaction with other neural systems and networks, the brain is thought to employ a type of predictive processing theorized to aid in the reduction of uncertainty and entropy in our biological-neurological systems (Solms, 2018). Entropy here refers to a basic concept in statistical mechanics and thermodynamics as a measurement of the amount energy unavailable for productive work – i.e., disorder – present in a physical system.

Thus, the Deleuzian-Guattarian abstract machines in the form of the domains of mathematics, biology, information theory, chemistry, and physics provide the epistemological framework where biological processes in general and neurological processes in particular are increasingly understood as computational or physical/corporeal machines. This becomes a recursive loop where abstract machines employ physical/technical machines to empirically derive and describe a language and thinking steeped in machinic metaphors. As we will see, it is a loop that – from the vantage point of analytical psychology – reflects a seductive but death-denying and ultimately catastrophic, Promethean aspect of the archetype of the Machine. One characteristic of this Promethean aspect of the archetype of the Machine is its *telos* toward reproducing itself in many forms, an algorithmic mimicry of life – often absent the living.

Beyond the purview of philosophy and science, usage statistics suggest the depth of our entanglement with technical machines. According to 2021 Pew Research study (Pew Research Center, 2021a; 2021c, around 85% of Americans use a smartphone (Pew Research Center, 2021a; 2021c), with 97% claiming ownership of a cellular phone of some type. In terms of activity, 72% of Americans stated they used social media in 2021 (Pew Research, 2021b), with 2022 data putting that figure at 80.9% and an average of 134 daily minutes spent engaging in social media use (Kemp, 2022). According to Kemp's (2022) analysis of available data from numerous sources (e.g., United States Census Bureau, United Nations Statistics Division, Statista, GWI, GSMA Intelligence, etc.), as of 2022, there were 4.95 billion global Internet users, with 307.2 million of those residing in the United States; of those within the US, an average, *daily* Internet usage of seven hours and five minutes per individual.

In terms of cultural and social focus, at the time of this writing, concerns and criticism abound surrounding the capabilities offered by a variety of AI-based platforms. These systems work via deep learning algorithms that effectively train them to create output based on their exposure to large volumes of data – linguistic, visual, musical, etc. For visual and music-based platforms, this entrainment data is often in the form of copyrighted material. Among content creators, artists, authors, and academics, there have been choruses of concerns about the potential of copyright infringements of content, style, and form, as well as the impact on professional livelihoods, employment disruptions across multiple industries, and increased likelihood of digital plagiarism (Khalil & Er, 2023; Planker, 2023).

ChatGPT, a recently-released generative AI system, is a natural-language system that can respond to sophisticated questions with a range of elaboration, from short answers to paper-length responses, allowing it to fulfill a variety of tasks: generate undergraduate-level essays (Stokel-Walker, 2022); achieve a passing score on the United States Medical Licensing Examination (USMLE; Kung et al., 2023); and serve as an adjunctive worker in investment banking workflows (Clarke, 2023). Replika, a similar AI system, has found usage as a virtual friend and erotic/romantic "companion" (Tong, 2023) to those lacking human romantic partners. There have been numerous reports of inaccuracy or incorrect information given by ChatGPT – a phenomena that Holomak (2023) finds especially problematic as AI-generated material penetrates medical and academic publishing. Patel and Lam (2023) imagine a tandem approach of human-supervised,

ChatGPT-generated discharge summaries for patients, which become part of a medical record where they serve as communications to downstream healthcare providers. This tension of seeking to balance human oversight of AI-generated work and release of data when working with patients was highlighted in a recent study by Ayers (2023) where he found AI-generated responses to patient health concerns were rated by a panel of healthcare professionals as being more empathetic and preferred over those written by human physicians.

Platforms like Stable Diffusion and Midjourney generate visual artwork from text prompts, including a desired artistic or photographic style or form, leading to concern from a number of graphic and visual arts professionals as well as computer scientists (Elgammal, 2019; Marcus, 2022). AI-generated music has stirred debate from artist and music professionals on the attendant creative and financial perils, from recent synthetic performances of living artists to "functional sound" generated for individual users in real-time from individual biometric data (Sherburne, 2022; Coscarelli, 2023; Meaker, 2023). Proliferation statistics speak to the rate at which adoption of AI is occurring, with the oft-cited figure of ChatGPT in use by 100 million users just two months after launch, with Hu (2023) from Reuters qualifying this as "the fastest-growing consumer application in history" (Hu, 2023, para 1).

The Where of the Machine: Framing, Inhabiting, and Becoming the Consulting Room

What might we make of all these machines? All these oscillations and pulses of technical objects, knowledge domains, sociocultural formations, and political and economic systems falling under the umbra of the Machine? What might such crossings and encounters – theoretical, practical, intellectual – offer Jungian psychology? In short, how might we make use of aspects of technology and the Machine that are often relegated in analytical psychology to utopian fantasies collapsing into their enantiodromic mode or shadow eruptions at the level of civilization writ large? Is there a way to employ the very energies inundating us so that the Machine can be conceived as an archetypal manifestation; or as a complete *phármakon* – adding the facet of remedy to its role in our present drama as scapegoat and poison? As stated at the outset, recent writing and thinking from disparate fields has undertaken the challenge of expanding analytical psychology into contemporary cultural and philosophical circles to inform analytical theory and practice in contemporary language – and offer ways of updating the corpus. Within other domains that have the unconscious as their area of inquiry, this exploration and incorporation of the Machine seems to have been going on for some time.

From its outset, psychoanalytic thought has been engaged with the machine in the form of the earliest conceptualizations of emotional processing and functioning found in the hydraulic model embraced by Sigmund Freud (Breuer & Freud, 2000). This early understanding effectively renders emotions and their impact on the nervous system as analogous to hydraulic machinery – i.e., building pressure within the psyche until such time as they find expression through emotional and somatic catharsis. Elsewhere, Freud (1961) relied on the metaphor of the "mystic writing pad" (a children's toy comprised of a wax substrate covered by wax paper, which was then covered with a thin sheet of transparent celluloid) to describe how the nervous system is able to record sensory events that become stored by the unconscious. The early focus on Freud's project on providing a scientific basis to psychoanalysis has continued to this day, with the consequences of often reducing the vastness of the unconscious to non-conscious processing and implicit memory systems as described by contemporary neuroscience.

Guattari, a psychoanalyst, employs the framework originated by Deleuze and himself. He writes in *The Machinic Unconscious* about the unconscious as fundamentally machinic and productive, rather than emerging from Freudian concepts such as drives, Oedipal dynamics, and ego-mediated repression of Id impulses (Guattari, 2011). Rather, as a machinic process, he holds the unconscious as foundational to social, historical, economic, political fields and "objects" in materialist, not merely psychic, contexts. This places the unconscious in direct correspondence with the contemporary political and capitalist milieu in which we subsist. It creatively appropriates and utilizes aspects of these collective energies and flows as part of its ongoing elaboration of itself and human subjectivity, which in turn are mirrored in the elaboration of human social, economic, and political collective realities. We unconsciously recreate or reinforce these "superstructures", he argues, by reifying them and their aspects as universalisms (e.g., profit incentive, economic hierarchies, class structures, etc.). In doing so, Guattari emphasizes the material conditions of the "external" world as informing the constitution of the "internal", where such designators become linguistic distinctions without fundamental difference at the level of this productive unconscious. Part of the challenges in reading Guattari's work echo the same challenges often leveled at Jung – i.e., the dense, aleatory form that suggest an experience of immersion in the unconscious flow rather than objective rendering or delineation of it – a kind of printed hypertext absent of hyperlinks.

Contemporary Lacanian psychoanalysis has also taken an interest in the subject's relationship to technical machines in general and contemporary AI systems and architectures in particular. Philosopher Luca M. Possati (2020), for example, revisits the stages in subject formation as proposed by Lacan, and reframes the latter's mirror phase and accompanying imaginary register of identification. This identification, thought to occur in early childhood, begins with the child viewing their own reflected face as the one object in the mirror's reflection they cannot also see in the surrounding world, which in turn facilitates their sense of themselves as separate from the world. Possati proposes this is more than a dyadic encounter between child and their mirror image. Rather, reworking this process using Latour's actor-network theory (2005), he posits a networked exchange of forces between the child, a technical machine (the mirror), and other objects (parents, family members, others) to achieve an initial identification and internalization of an imago. In this early way, a technical object serves as interface or mediating machine between the child and their early unconscious – i.e., a machine becomes a central actor in a network of relations that facilitates the initial structuring of the unconscious. Later, during the phase in which the child enters the Lacanian symbolic register of language, the child becomes a "split" subject, bifurcated by the Other of language – where this massive field of language becomes the structuralizing form of the unconscious during subject formation (subjectivation). And this subjectivation occurs within a milieu mediated by the machinic via at least two assumptions: that language itself can be seen as a technology (McLuhan, 1996); and the ubiquitous presence of technical machines forming our communications and media, in contemporary childhood environments. In this way, as both Possati (2020) and Apprich (2018) demonstrate, this process of structuralization through technology – linguistic, technical, and social – corresponds to the machine from Lacan's declaration, "The symbolic world is the world of the machine" (Lacan, 1991, p. 47).

A second consideration suggests itself from the incorporative tendencies informing Jung's work, where he drew from a considerable array of philosophical, scientific, historical, and intellectual currents. As Jung described his project in 1913: "We need not only the work of medical psychologists, but also that of philologists, historians, archaeologists, mythologists, folklore students, ethnologists, philosophers, theologians, pedagogues and biologists" (Jung, 1973, pp. 29–30). Decades later, yet still a generation ago, Jungian analyst Andrew Samuels (1998) similarly echoed the need to engage with other disciplines and specialists, with a focus on enlisting experts and interrogating other disciplines for a more robust and informed dialogue with Jungian theory. More recently, Saban reiterated this call for engagement with specialists as a critical check against reductionistic or tenuous understandings of these domains, writing: "The pages of Jungian journals are littered with half-digested, half-thought neuroscience, quantum physics, post-modern philosophy – in the same way they used to be strewn with barely understood ideas from anthropology, ethology, and theology" (Saban, 2020, p. 91). Given the discussion above, with the current advancement in AI, technological mediation of most human activities, and current pace of technological adoption underway, the addition of AI researchers, philosophers of science and technology, and information theorists may need to be added to the list of specialists.

A third consideration comes from the trend toward increasing engagement with empirically driven and technologically mediated practices of applied science as basis for revisioning or grounding psychological and analytical concepts, often within the philosophical school of realism. It can be argued these constitute an increasing presence of the machine in analytical practice and theory, where machine here refers alternatively to: a Deleuzian-Guattarian idea of a fundamental connective unit conveying energy/desire/libido (or in Bryant's language, incorporeal machine); an abstract machine organizing the language and thinking of empirical sciences and mathematics; and an increasing reliance on the technical machines facilitating investigations within scientific disciplines to provide an empirical basis for various Jungian concepts, from synchronicity to archetypes (e.g., computational platforms, fMRI, bioinformatics, EEGs, and simulation systems). In this, analytical psychology has benefited and adapted by way of the computational and machinic and their help in elucidating the complex interrelations between psyche and the physical, biological, cultural, and ecological domains which thread it.

The theoretical understanding of archetypes, for example, has continued to evolve and be debated upon within the Jungian community. As Jungian analyst George B. Hogenson (2019) outlines, what began as archetype as predicated on the instinctual/biological in Jung's early writings evolved into archetypes as emerging from genetic imprints in Michael Fordham's work (1957/2013), which became refined into Jean Knox's (2009) parsing of archetypes as based on early image schemas arising in the premotor cortex. According to Knox, these innate biological aptitudes and processes – elaborated via contemporary neuroscience and an increased visibility into moment-by-moment processes within neuroanatomical regions and across entire brain networks – provide the developmental scaffolding for organizing experience and the purported emergence of archetypal images. This increasing visibility, and attendant conceptual complexity, is largely due to advances in measuring and imaging systems. The data from these machine-facilitated processes serve to further elaborate the contemporary neuro-scientific epistemology of the nervous system and brain networks, which are also increasingly understood in machinic and computational terms. In parsing this via a Deleuzian-Guattarian framework, data products from technical machines (fMRI, EEG's, etc.) are linked with abstract machines (affective neuroscience, biology, information theory, and physics) to give rise to machinic assemblages (a scientifically informed biopsychological perspective on human functioning). In analytical terms, the archetype of the Machine energizes and catalyzes a mode in which the Machine itself both organizes experience and becomes the dominant image and metaphor – to the exclusion of other images and other metaphors.

Hogenson examines how Jung's later writings, centered around the concept of *unus mundus* (as elaborated in *Mysterium Coniunctionis*; Jung, 1963), were taken up by Jungian scholar and physicist Harald Atmanspacher. Here Jung's invocation of the *unus mundus* in his later writings on archetype and synchronicity are viewed through the prism of contemporary physics and, according to Atmanspacher (2012, 2014), suggest a lineage to Spinoza's notion of dual-aspect monism. This philosophical frame posits the entirety of both physical and psychic phenomena as emerging from a single, under-lying ontic layer. Atmanspacher credits Spinoza's philosophical framing as facilitating his own, scientifically informed view "by concatenating an ontological monism with an epistemological dualism, yielding an overall worldview in which both philosophy and the sciences can find appropriate places and mutual relations" (Atmanspacher, 2014, p. 181). In analytical terms, Atmanspacher's system of thinking posits a transcendent function or aspect of Mercurius; in Deleuzian-Guattarian terms, as an assemblage of machines.

Perhaps intentionally embodying such an approach through example, Atmanspacher, both a Jungian scholar and theoretical physicist, has published similar concepts in different journals, addressed to differential readership in the distinct conceptual languages of these respective fields. In one instance, for example, his work appears in the *Journal of Analytical Psychology* in his article "Psychophysical correlations, synchronicity and meaning" (2014) invoking familiar concepts from analytical psychology. In another, it appears in the journal *BioSystems* under the title "Mind and matter as asymptotically disjoint, inequivalent representations with broken time-reversal symmetry" (2003) invoking concepts from quantum mechanics and complexity theory. This latter is inhabited by the presence of Deleuzian-Guattarian abstract machines in the form rigorous physical-mathematical systems, and reflects an approach taken by others in analytical psychology who also come from previous professional scientific backgrounds (see Cambray, 2012; Le Mouël, 2021).

In clinical practice, advances in affective and cognitive neuroscience – which as we have seen are increasingly explored via the machinic and computational using frameworks that conceptualize neurological processes as machinic and computational – have helped inform the techniques and models found in contemporary trauma and somatic therapies. The most recent discoveries and advances in these fields have been brought to bear to give new form to Jung's original assertion of the analytical process and techniques as encompassing more than just the verbal:

> I therefore took up a dream-image or an association of the patient's, and, with this as a point of departure, set him the task of elaborating or developing his theme by giving free rein to his fantasy. This, according to individual taste and talent, could be done in any number of ways, dramatic, dialectic, visual, acoustic, or in the form of dancing, painting, drawing, or modelling. The result of this technique was a vast number of complicated designs whose diversity puzzled me for years, until I was able to recognize that in this method I was witnessing the spontaneous manifestation of an unconscious process which was merely assisted by the technical ability of the patient, and to which I later gave the name "individuation process".
>
> (Jung, 1969a/1981, para 400)

Jung's injunction to moving beyond verbal expression in the exploration of unconscious material was taken up early in the history of analytical practice. Jungian analyst Toni Wolff employed somatic techniques as early as 1924, continuing with the development of authentic movement by Mary Starks Whitehouse in the 1950s, its subsequent incorporation as an active imagination practice by Jungian analyst Joan Chodorow in the 1970s, and further incorporation of somatic components into analytical work during the 1980s with the work of Jungian analyst Marion Woodman (all as detailed in Chodorow, 1997, 2006).

Using Woodman's work as a point of departure and amplifying and refining this via the synthesis of contemporary somatic and trauma modalities, Jungian analyst Marian Dunlea and her BodyDreaming approach (2019) provide a method for both working with developmental trauma within an analytical context as well as refining the inclusion of the somatic register of unconscious process in analysis. Dunlea's method incorporates concepts from contemporary affective neuroscience and methodologies from different trauma and attachment-repair somatic-relational psychotherapy systems. This highly attuned process attends to the minute, moment-by-moment postural tendencies, patterns of physical movement, markers of autonomic activity and state (e.g., breathing, muscle tonicity, heart rate), and fluctuations within the patient's sensory field (particularly interoception) as a way of working with nervous system changes and dysregulation often accompanying trauma and the intrusion of highly charged, dysregulating complexes; as well as facilitating ways of deepening contact with symbolic "channels" as complexes constellate. Writes Dunlea:

> In BodyDreaming, by bringing the opposites into dynamic flow – sympathetic and parasympathetic systems, psyche and body – we experience how our biology and psyche interact to produce a new position and possibility: a living third presents itself.
>
> … in working with the emotion of a dream image and the felt resonance of the dream within the body through the process of inner attunement, we may discover the image parallels (or images) our physiology and biological processes, and holds the key to new possibilities.
>
> (Dunlea, 2019, p. 101)

Laurie Savlov, a Jungian training analyst on faculty at the C.G. Jung Foundation of Ontario and the Ontario analyst training program as well as private practice clinician, employs eye movement desensitization and reprocessing (EMDR), a trauma and attachment-repair resourcing and processing modality, as part of analytical work. EMDR is typically administered via successive, bilateral stimulation of brain hemispheres while recalling unpleasant and traumatic memories – typically by introducing tactile, auditory, and/or visual stimuli in alternation between lateralized (right and left) sensory channels. Neuroscientific studies employing brain imaging, again parsing an exploration and understanding of the brain via machinic and computational epistemologies, suggest a decreased activation of neural circuits associated with autonomic fear response and their attendant biological sequelae often accompanying trauma (e.g., sympathetic nervous system hyperarousal also known as the "fight-flight-freeze" response; see Landin-Romero et al., 2018). Beyond the treatment of post-traumatic stress disorder (PTSD) often associated with single-incident or complex trauma, EMDR is increasingly used in working with attachment-based issues associated with developmental or relational/attachment trauma (Kemal Kaptan & Brayne, 2021). Savlov states in his work it has been particularly helpful in depotentiating strong affect accompanying the activation of complexes that can push patients toward states of autonomic nervous system hyper- or hypoarousal, as well as working with the symbolic and imaginal aspects involved in attachment repair. As Savlov states, "At this point, I consider the [EMDR] work analysis" (Savlov, 2023). Jungian psychotherapist, EMDR trainer, and psychologist Andrew Dobo has written (2023) and conducted trainings on the use of EMDR within a Jungian psychotherapeutic context, where he refers to EMDR as a psychoanalytic process (The Art and Science of EMDR, 2021) amenable to Jungian associative and active imagination practices.

Jungian analyst Jane Clapp (Clapp, 2022) has written about the importance of attending to analysands' social media use and immersion, arguing they represent important windows into analysands' ego functioning, as well as their potential or actual inundation by the collective unconscious manifesting in the infinite ocean of Internet content. According to Clapp, these construct personal and collective "labyrinths" for their users. She argues a paradox emerges by which individuals are drawn into these social media labyrinths and effectively isolating them through the promise of instantaneity of connection and access – albeit access without embodied effort and interpersonal encounter, and connection without Eros (Clapp, 2022).

Jungian analyst August J. Cwik, (2021) examines the impact of the machinic within a telehealth framework as a result of the recent COVID-19 pandemic and corresponding move to online sessions within the psycho-therapeutic and analytic communities. He revisits Jung's well-known transference diagram from *Psychology of the Transference* (Jung, 1954/1985), introducing the notion of a machinic-catalyzed irruption within the analytic field as a sign of putative synchronistic phenomena intervening within that field, and acting as a marker of psychic event. As Cwik advocates:

> [The analyst should] attempt to 'draw-in' everything that happens during the presentation as belonging to the moment rather than what the ego thinks should be happening. Consider this particularly with technological disruptions and glitches. Technology is fairly unstable thus sensitive to the field we are generating and discussing. So, when breaks in video or audio occur, consider them as unconscious messages, like slips of the tongue, that are speaking to you about the underlying emotional content.
>
> (Cwik, 2021, pp. 416–417)

The Why of the Machine: Archetype of the Machine

We are left with the hum of the Machine as it becomes increasingly interwoven into our contemporary discourses – cultural, philosophical, scientific, psychoanalytic, and analytical. Within each of these domains, the internal logics and rationale for the invocation of the Machine finds ample consideration and explanation from intra-domain experts and theorists. Whether manifesting as technical machines, the abstract machines of scientific cultural, and linguistic systems, or ontological primitives at the core of contemporary philosophical explorations, this machinic presence seems pervasive while eluding precise definition, abstract while providing structure. But why the Machine? It is a presence that constellates a thematic domain of meaning and intentionality while simultaneously catalyzing and transforming energies interpenetrating this domain. In short, an archetypal presence. "But why the Machine?" seems answerable in terms of positing this archetypal presence as manifesting psychically and historically – as Ellul (1964), Mumford (1967, 1970) and others have stated – i.e., as an ongoing, ancient pattern and presence. Given the impossibility of precisely circumscribing or defining archetypes as such, we can only note this presence and, following Jung's notion of the evolutive nature of archetypes as predicated on older ones (Jung, 1968/1980, speculate on what this archetype might be based.

Author and journalist Erik W. Davis provides one such examination in his book *TechGnosis* (1998), where he distinguishes "technologies [machines] of power" (Davis, 1998, p. 14) from "technologies [machines] of communication" (Davis, 1998, p. 14), identifying the former with the archetype of Prometheus, and the latter with that of Hermes/Mercurius – with this latter being the focus of his investigation. He examines the history of communications technologies and their intertwining with the earliest religious and cultural formations, concluding that these technologies and their machinic embodiments function via Hermetic/Mercurial principles. For Davis, these Hermetic/Mercurial communication machines – from the earliest Sumerian cuneiform to the then-emerging Internet – are characterized not by their similarity of mechanism and form, but by their functioning via sudden interruptions, glitches, ambiguities, garbled transmissions, and unintended outcomes. For Jung, Mercurius is often identified as an archetypal symbol for various aspects of his psychological system: the collective unconscious, the trickster, the transforming bridge between "higher" and "lower" realities, and the individuation process (Jung, 1967/1983). The features Davis ascribes to his communicative machines seem equally applicable to the vicissitudes, ambivalences, and ambiguities of Jung's Mercurius. Both interact with, but are not bound by, human intention and agency, and both function as mediators and transformers of energy, intentionality, and meaning.

Davis traces the development and increasing incorporation of the machinic into ancient civilizations, from the mythological attributions of the fictional personage of Hermes Trismegustus in instructing the Egyptians of antiquity on the construction of water pumps and cranes; to his comparison of Talmudic scholarship and production as an ancient form of hypertext; to showcasing Heron of Alexandria's construction of mechanical systems used in the theatrical rendering and automation of ancient rites and rituals: "Flames leapt, thunder crashed, and miniature female Bacchantes whirled madly around the wine god on a pulley-driven turntable" (Davis, 1998, p. 19).

Raya Jones (2017) also explores the fascination with machines and automata, from the earliest accounts of 5th century BCE Taoist legends to contemporary research by social psychologist Sherry Turkle. In her own research, Jones identifies a similar strand as Davis in terms of a transcultural and historically continuous engagement with Machines – with Jones' focus on humanlike automata culminating in contemporary forms of robotics, which she terms social robots. Where here we ascribe this to the presence of the archetype of the Machine, Jones – citing the difficulties she perceives as inhering in a lack of consensus definition of archetype – proffers explanations from semiotics as well as what she terms the Pygmalion complex as energizing and organizing these phenomena (Jones, 2017). Where Davis' focus is on communications technology writ large, Jones' focus is on a specific domain of interactive technologies – the simulation of embodiment by non-biological agents and the attendant human tendency to anthropomorphize them. As we will see, this may be indicative of an archetypal core, in this case a possible Hephaestean archetypal core, as animating Jones' Pygmalion complex. At the same time, and echoing the themes in Davis, Jones also speculates on the modern tendency to reductively explain the biological and psychic in machinic and technological terms. In both their accounts, this dual tension between psyche and mind as machine, and machine as alive and agentic, seems present.

In contrast to identifying complexes or enlisting semiotics, however, Davis threads his account of technology in general and communication machines in particular as animated by and influenced by core Hermetic/ Mercurial archetypal energies and intentionality. He posits that these energies drove the human effort to create technologies and technical machines that would impact millennia of sociocultural development. Davis sees writing as the prototype and first embodiment of this emerging archetype of the machine. As he asserts near the beginning of his book, following Ellul (1964) and Mumford (1967, 1970), "let it be said as frankly as possible: Writing is a machine … The material history of writing is an utterly technological tale" (Davis, 1998, p. 23). Toward the end, he sounds a more expansively cautious note – apropos of a Jungian differentiation between the pleromatic realm of the archetypal, operating quite independently of human agency or anthropocentric concern, and that of the egoic/interpersonal/sociocultural. And while his tracing of the history of communications technologies is predicated on the Hermes/Mercurius archetype, by the conclusion of his text he seems to characterize an evolution into a newer form that we might simply identify as an aspect of the archetype of the Machine. As Davis writes:

As I announced at the outset, technology is a trickster. We blame technology for things that arise from our social structures and our skewed priorities; we expect magic satisfactions from machines they simply cannot provide; and we remain consistently hoodwinked by their unintended consequences. Technologies have their own increasingly alien agenda, and human concerns will survive and prosper only when we learn to treat them, not as slaves or simple extensions of ourselves, but as unknown constructs with whom we make creative alliances and wary pacts.

(Davis, 1998, p. 335)

In a similar vein, Jungian scholar Robert D. Romanyshyn (2019) reaches toward the archetype of the Machine through the armature of Mary Shelley's novel *Frankenstein*, examining aspects of this archetype Davis relegates to "technologies of power" (Davis, 1998, p. 14) and which both he and Romanyshyn associate with Prometheus. Romanyshyn's analysis centers on the fictional Victor von Frankenstein as carrier of this underlying Promethean archetype – an archaic kernel that has given rise to our current archetype. His examination suggests Promethean light, when refracted through a prism of symbolic thinking, reveals itself as comprised of multiple colors of meaning and agency: the abrogation of death, the flight from shadow and the "monstrous", Frankenstein's monster's modern progeny, the simultaneous impulse to reduce the human body to mere object (coupled with a pull to transcend it), and the absence of the feminine. As exemplars of these first four colors, Romanyshyn suggests two additions to the evolutionary tree currently terminating with *homo sapiens*: *homo astronauticus* and *homo digitalis*. He finds the former emblemized in the 1969 lunar landings. There, humanity's symbolic transcendence of death manifested in a literal transcendence of Earth's atmosphere and gravity – via absolute dependence on the Machine facilitating this transcendence. His identification of *homo astronauticus* mirrors Mumford's writings:

While he is hurtling through space the astronaut's physical existence is purely a function of mass and motion, narrowed down to the pinpoint of acute sentient intelligence demanded by the necessity for coordinating his reactions with the mechanical and electronic apparatus upon which his survival depends. Here is the archetypal proto-model of Post-Historic Man, whose existence from birth to death would be conditioned by the megamachine, and made to conform, as in a space capsule, to the

minimal functional requirements by an equally minimal environment –
all under remote control.

(Mumford, 1970, insert 14-15: The encapsulated man)

The second, *homo digitalis* also offers a transcendence of death, not by
decoupling the human body from its Earthbound environs, but rather
the human mind from its human body. As Romanyshyn points out, this
aspect of the archetype of the Machine is reflected in the contemporary
transhumanist movement, a loose affiliation of futurists, "biohackers",
computer and cognitive scientists, philosophers, and Silicon Valley
technologists and founders (Rushkoff, 2018). At its most fundamental,
the transhumanist agenda is revealed through the emphasis on fund-
ing and developing advanced AI, longevity and life-extension research,
and a push toward increased cyborgization of computational and biological technologies. At its boldest, it is captured by the thinking of
futurist and inventor Ray Kurzweil, a former director of engineering at
Google and a popularizer of the concept of the technological singularity
originally proposed by mathematician and computer scientist John von
Neumann (Kurzweil, 2006). This technological singularity, or simply
the Singularity as Kurzweil refers to it, is conceived as a point where
technological innovation becomes exponentially complex and rapid,
with human bodies becoming functionally immortal – renewed and regulated by nanoscale machines. Kurzweil predicts these bodies will be
networked with forms of artificial intelligence, and that the distinction
between biological and technological life will collapse. This telic terminus is the enlistment of inert matter in the universe as material for creating a conscious, computational cosmos (Kurzweil, 2006). Romanyshyn
provides commentary on Kurzweil's philosophy as illustrating an organizing principle of *homo digitalis* – the absence of shadow and embodiment. As such, it is a continuation of Frankenstein's drive to transcend
embodiment's biological predicate – death:

Kurzweil imagines his cyborgian creature as leading to a future self
whose non-biological portion of intelligence will so dominate the biological portion that these future selves will be described in one of his
works as spiritual machines. As such, these future selves 'will claim to
have emotional and spiritual experiences, just as we do today'.

[Kurzweil, as cited in Romanyshyn, 2019]

The claim has been and is the stuff of our collective dreams, and Kurzweil's work promises to transform these dreams into waking reality. Our collective dreams, which are often quite closer to nightmares in which cyborgs turn against humanity, are becoming our imagined futures. For Kurzweil, however, the darker, revolting side of this future is quite absent, for it is a future that emerges from the technological triumph over the natural processes of evolution.

(Romanyshyn, 2019, p. 61)

In contrast to Kurzweil's unipolar alignment of technological development with positivistic notions of boundless progress, Romanyshyn poses a number of questions throughout his work. In doing so, he circumscribes the dimensions of Frankenstein's (and Kurzweil's) Promethean Project and outlines the Promethean facet of the contemporary Machine archetype. A central notion that emerges from Romanyshyn's inquiry is that of Promethean firelight as fundamentally attached to its shadow from the outset – an explicit warning against Kurzweil's belief in computationally directed life and cosmic evolution. Of all the ways this appears, perhaps the fifth color of the Promethean refraction is the most telling: the exclusion of the feminine principle that Romanyshyn traces throughout the story: in the original myth of Prometheus, Epithemeus, and Pandora; in Frankenstein's withholding existence of his experiments from his fiancé, Elizabeth Lavenza; in Frankenstein's destruction of his monster's bride-to-be midway through her creation; and finally in the monster's murder of Elizabeth as revenge (Romanyshyn, 2019). While Davis identifies the Mercurius archetypal aspect underlying communications technologies and machines – thus holding potential to symbolize or manifest a *coniunctio* of masculine-feminine energies – no such possibility exists in the archetypal Machine's Promethean aspect outlined by Romanyshyn. This latter aspect, the flight toward the future of decreasing biological embodiment and increasing fusion with the technological, seems less a synthesis of the biological and technological than the gradual erasure of the former in favor of the latter. It is this Promethean aspect that is perhaps the most worrisome, problematic, and potentially lethal to human living and thriving within a planetary biosphere under existential threat.

A final aspect that might be tentatively proposed is derived from a Hephaestean archetype, after the mythological Hephaestus, master craftsman, and blacksmith of the Greek pantheon. Much as in the Promethean myth, Hephaestus had a painful relationship to aspects that Jung identifies as "feminine" – first via his exile by way of his mother Hera and second via the infidelities of the goddess Aphrodite. At the same time as being renowned for his ability as a craftsman and tinkerer, Hephaestus was also known for his physical disability (and root cause of his exile by Hera), suggesting an interpenetration of the themes of craftsman-genius, disability, and a corresponding, compensatory enlistment of advanced technology. Ebenstein (2006) notes this in his writings on archetypal perspectives surrounding disability, writing:

> Hephaestus is the only god that works. He is the most physically vivid of all the Olympians. In the *Iliad* he is depicted as a robust smith, middle-aged, with a bearded face, a powerful thick neck, hairy chest, sweaty brow and heavily muscled arms, wearing a sleeveless tunic. In this setting *Super Cripple* Hephaestus looms large and distinguished. His wife is the beautiful Charis, one of the Graces, who serves as his romantic companion and workshop assistant. He is seen by his anvil and forge, wielding a hammer and tongs, working with metals, and crafting wondrous objects. His poetic workshop is specifically designed to accommodate his disability. Of particular interest to the field of disability studies is his work in the area of assistive technology, accommodations in the workplace, and his creation of mechanical objects that function as robots or automata.
>
> In his workshop he has built 20 self-animated tripods with golden wheels that can move back and forth at the gods' assemblies and perform the work of robot servants. He also utilizes voice-activated bellows. In order to steady his unsure steps he fashioned two golden statues that resemble living girls. They hasten to his side and assist him as he walks. These golden maidservants could not only speak and use their limbs but were also endowed with intelligence. His creations also include other machines that imitate the behavior of human beings such as Talos, the giant bionic bronze man who had Olympian blood in his veins, and the beautiful but artificial maiden Pandora, the first woman.
>
> (Ebenstein, 2006, para 44–45)

In condensing these archetypal investigations, we are left with a rendering of the archetype of the Machine with manifold aspects. We encounter a Hermetic/Mercurial aspect, operating throughout and across historical eras, manifesting and impelling a drive toward connection and novelty

– promising to tranquilize frustrations while just as often amplifying them. A striving Promethean aspect, absent the Eros of relationship – focused on pursuing immortality projects, enhanced embodiment, life without living bodies, and an inert cosmos of mere matter enfolded into an expanding "radiance" of self-replicating, ubiquitous computation, complexity, and machine-human intelligence. Promethean fantasies espoused by some technologists and posthumanists are those of a universe-scale utopia illuminated by light, absent shadow, or consequence, and part of the mainstream discussion of the logarithmic AI computational curve (e.g., Friedman, March 21, 2023). Finally, a Hephaestean aspect, reflecting the need and tendency to create technology and machines as extensions for actual or perceived limitations and lingering wounds – psychic and physical. In doing so, the impulse gives rise to creations that serve as aides and companions – not borne out of the same impulse to transcend death as found in the Promethean project, but arguably the impulse to participate in life more fully.

Given the immediacy of threat and onrushing movement toward increasing entanglement with the machinic, a retreat into Luddite bubbles or a world excised of technology seems improbable and intimates a regression from not only our machines, but also the cultural, scientific, and the philosophical moment as expressed within those domains. Within analytical psychology, it would represent an attempt at disengagement from the archetype of the Machine – a feature of objective psyche manifesting materially in contemporary philosophical and critical theoretical formations, the myths of our present cultural moment, and the waveform of technological, financial, and sociopolitical energies and creations. In this sense, it would represent an attempt to excise part of our psyche rather than engage with it. Like its Mercurial, Promethean, and Hephaestean archetypal aspects – forebears if we are to invoke Jung's possibility of the evolution of archetypes – this presence calls for relationship, reckoning with, and integration through considerable effort. And if analytical psychology chooses not to take up the enterprise of such engagement, other forms of psychoanalytic theory (e.g., Magee et al., 2022; Rousselle, 2023; Žižek, 2023) and organizational mobilization (e.g., Consilience Papers, 2022) are already doing so as part of their structural imperatives, clinical practices, and theoretical discourses (e.g., Cannon & Greasley, 2021; Inkol, 2018; Johanssen, 2022; Smith, 2022; Tikkun, 2001/2020; Yang et al., 2023). In some, the machine represents a descriptive facet of reality and psyche, something to be understood; in others, as a structural component of both, and something to be worked alongside rather than abandoned; in still others, as a telic warning, and something to be resisted through turning its mechanisms back upon itself.

From an analytical standpoint, we must exercise caution when dealing with the Promethean aspect in particular. Ever accelerating, this aspect seems poised to autocatalyze into its own, machinic lifeworld. Relating with it does not entail a disengagement from the urgent concern for our planetary biosphere and its fragile, faltering interlinked ecologies. Rather, it is a call toward deeper and urgent dialogue with this aspect of our psyche, to traverse into the realm of the Machine – potentially a domain of objective psyche and realm of the Mothers, a link suggested by Jung in an interpretation of a patient's UFO dream (Jung, 2014/1959).

The convenience of tidy bifurcations between the psychic and the machinic, the biological and the mechanical, the mind and the computational, seem situated in different moments and ages. There such antinomies remained inertly ensconced in their positions as seemingly disconnected opposites rather than terminal ends of a living, nondual spectrum. Our contemporary myths, dystopian and otherwise, tend toward not only nostalgic or imagined pasts but complex (and complexed) futures – futures that include machines implicated in personal and collective human unfolding as both *phármakon* and archetype. As inhering in psyche, implicated in human cultural, creative and technical process, and giving rise to our fascination with machines and the technological, the archetype of the Machine is a highly charged, deeply entangled, and self-opposing embrace of both the creative and the catastrophic. In this sense, it is a Janus structure, constellated in origin stories as well as telic arrows – the actual world and virtual/ potential ones, evidenced by our current scientific and cultural preoccupation with multiverses and multiple realities. It appears in new forms but is neither recent nor novel in purpose and function. An archetype intertwined with myth, interpenetrative with the transcendental, and manifest presence in culture and psyche since antiquity. Perhaps only the ubiquity and increasing sophistication and pace of emerging technologies has allowed us to think otherwise. As a paradox of the ancient and new – an instrument of fascination and Otherness – it offers to extend our agency while also delimiting and eliminating it, often by exercising its own. If we are to move beyond the stale differentiation between the human and Machine, more elaborate myths will be needed – myths of threading alongside resistance, interpenetration alongside differentiation, myths of the archetypal

Machine inhering within the psyche to counterbalance the increasingly popular anthropomorphized myths of a simulated psyche within machines. As Joseph Campbell once declared, "The myth has to incorporate the machine" (Moyers & Campbell, 2021, para 179).

References

Apprich, C. (2018). Secret agents. *Digital Culture & Society*, *4*(1), 29–44. https://doi.org/10.14361/dcs-2018-0104

Atanasoski, N., & Vora, K. (2015). Surrogate humanity: Posthuman networks and the (racialized) obsolescence of labor. *Catalyst: Feminism, Theory, Technoscience*, *1*(1), 1–40. https://doi.org/10.28968/cftt.v1i1.28809

Atmanspacher, H. (2003). Mind and matter as asymptotically disjoint, inequivalent representations with broken time-reversal symmetry. *Biosystems*, *68*(1), 19–30. https://doi.org/10.1016/s0303-2647(02)00051-5

Atmanspacher, H. (2012). Dual-aspect monism à la Pauli and Jung. *Journal of Consciousness Studies* 19(9-10), 96–120.

Atmanspacher, H. (2014). Psychophysical correlations, synchronicity and meaning. *Journal of Analytical Psychology*, *59*(2), 181–188. https://doi.org/10.1111/1468-5922.12068

Ayers, J. W. (2023, April 28). Comparing physician and chatbot responses to patient questions. *JAMA Internal Medicine*. Retrieved April 30, 2023, from https://jamanetwork.com/journals/jamainternalmedicine/fullarticle/2804309

Baudrillard, J. (1988/2020). *Simulacra and simulation* (Series: The body, in theory: Histories of cultural materialism) (S. F. Glaser, Trans.). The University of Michigan Press.

Blanco-Wells, G. (2021, March 12). Ecologies of repair: A post-human approach to other-than-human natures. *Frontiers*. https://www.frontiersin.org/articles/10.3389/fpsyg.2021.633737/full

Breuer, J., & Freud, S. (2000). *Studies on hysteria* (J. Strachey, Trans. and A. Freud, Ed.). Basic Books.

Bryant, L. R. (2014). *Onto-cartography: An ontology of machines and media*. Edinburgh University Press.

Cambray, J. (2012). *Synchronicity: Nature and psyche in an interconnected universe* (Carolyn and Ernest Fay Series in Analytical Psychology) (Vol. 15, Reprint ed.). Texas A&M University Press.

Cannon, J. W., & Greasley, A. E. (2021). Exploring relationships between electronic dance music event participation and well-being. *Music & Science*, *4*. https://doi.org/10.1177/2059204321997102

Cheney-Lippold, J. (2017). *We are data: Algorithms and the making of our digital selves*. NYU Press. https://doi.org/10.2307/j.ctt1gk0941

Chiaradia, I., & Lancaster, M. A. (2020). Brain organoids for the study of human neurobiology at the interface of in vitro and in vivo. *Nature Neuroscience*, *23*(12), 1496–1508. https://doi.org/10.1038/s41593-020-00730-3

Chodorow, J. (1997). Introduction. In J. Chodorow (Ed.), *Jung on active imagination* (pp. 1–20). Princeton University Press.

Chodorow, J. (2006). Active imagination. In R. K. Papadopoulos (Ed.), *The handbook of Jungian psychology: Theory, practice and applications* (pp. 215–243). Routledge.

Clapp, J. (2022). Social media and the collective unconscious. *Jung Journal*, *16*(3), 113–131. https://doi.org/10.1080/19342039.2022.2088995

Clarke, P. (2023, April 2). Why this investment bank is embracing AI and ChatGPT for its dealmakers. *Financial News*. https://www.fnlondon.com/articles/chatgpt-ai-banking-use-dealmakers-alantra-20230403

Consilience Papers. (2022, June). Technology is not values neutral: Ending the reign of nihilistic design. *The Consilience Project*. https://consilienceproject.org/technology-is-not-values-neutral/?fbclid=IwAR3ehUnlj5PnCTX4-lN3JC6BdGx9lJ2hrWDgFjB5t5qv0hsuEfh4V4fVQfA

Coscarelli, J. (2023, April 19). An A.I. hit of fake 'Drake' and 'The Weeknd' rattles the music world. *The New York Times*. Retrieved April 24, 2023, from https://www.nytimes.com/2023/04/19/arts/music/ai-drake-the-weeknd-fake.html

Cwik, A. J. (2021). The technologically-mediated self: Reflections on the container and field of telecommunications. *Journal of Analytical Psychology*, *66*(3), 411–428. https://doi.org/10.1111/1468-5922.12684

Davis, E. (1998). *TechGnosis: Myth, magic, and mysticism in the age of information*. Harmony Books.

DeCook, J. R. (2020). A [white] cyborg's manifesto: The overwhelmingly western ideology driving technofeminist theory. *Media, Culture & Society*, *43*(6), 1158–1167. https://doi.org/10.1177/0163443720957891

Deleuze, G. (2004). From Sacher-Masoch to masochism (C. Kerslake, Trans.). *Angelaki*, *9*(1), 125–133. https://doi.org/10.1080/0969725042000232441

Deleuze, G., & Guattari, F. (1983). *Anti-Oedipus*. University of Minnesota Press.

Deleuze, G., & Guattari, F. (1987). *A thousand plateaus*. University of Minnesota Press.

Dobo, A. (2023). *The hero's journey: Integrating Jungian psychology and EMDR therapy*. Soul Psych Publishers.

Dunlea, M. (2019). *Body dreaming in the treatment of developmental trauma: An embodied therapeutic approach* (1st ed.). Routledge.

Ebenstein, W. (2006). Toward an archetypal psychology of disability based on the Hephaestus myth. *Disability Studies Quarterly*, *26*(4). https://doi.org/10.18061/dsq.v26i4.805

El Karoui, M., Hoyos-Flight, M., & Fletcher, L. (2019, August 7). Future trends in synthetic biology - a report. *Frontiers*. Retrieved November 25, 2022, from https://www.frontiersin.org/articles/10.3389/fbioe.2019.00175/full

Elgammal, A. (2019). AI is blurring the definition of artist. *American Scientist*, *107*(1), 18. https://doi.org/10.1511/2019.107.1.18

Ellul, J. (1964). *The technological society* (J. Wilkinson, Trans.). Vintage Books.

Fordham, M. (1957/2013). *New developments in analytical psychology (psychology revivals)* (pp. 1–34). Routledge.

Freud, S., Freud, A., Strachey, A., & Tyson, A. (1961). A note upon the 'mystic writing pad'. In J. Strachey (Trans.), *The standard edition of the complete psychological works of Sigmund Freud*; transl. from the German under the general editorship of James Strachey; in Collab. with Anna Freud; assisted by Alix Strachey and Alan Tyson (pp. 226–232). The Hogarth Press and the Institute of Psycho-Analysis. https://www.sas.upenn.edu/~cavitch/pdf-library/Freud_WritingPad.pdf

Friedman, T. L. (2023, March 21). Our new Promethean moment. *The New York Times*. Retrieved March 21, 2023, from https://www.nytimes.com/2023/03/21/opinion/artificial-intelligence-chatgpt.html

Guattari, F. (2011). *The machinic unconscious: Essays in schizoanalysis* (T. Adkins, Trans.). Semiotext(e).

Haraway, D. (1985/2006). A cyborg manifesto: Science, technology, and socialist-feminism in the late 20th century. In J. Weiss, J. Nolan, J. Hunsinger, & P. Trifonas (Eds.), *The International handbook of virtual learning environments*. Springer. https://doi.org/10.1007/978-1-4020-3803-7_4

Hassan, M. M., Hassan, M. R., Huda, S., Uddin, M. Z., Gumaei, A., & Alsanad, A. (2021). A predictive intelligence approach to classify brain–computer interface based eye state for smart living. *Applied Soft Computing, 108*, 107453. https://doi.org/10.1016/j.asoc.2021.107453

Hauke, C. (2000). *Jung and the postmodern: The Interpretation of realities*. Routledge.

Hogenson, G. B. (2019). The controversy around the concept of archetypes. *Journal of Analytical Psychology, 64*(5), 682–700. https://doi.org/10.1111/1468-5922.12541

Homolak, J. (2023, February 28). Opportunities and risks of ChatGPT in medicine, science, and academic publishing: A modern promethean dilemma. *Croatian Medical Journal*. Retrieved April 29, 2023, from https://www.ncbi.nlm.nih.gov/pmc/articles/PMC10028563/#:~:text=Consequently%2C%20ChatGPT%2Dgenerated%20manuscripts%20might,an%20accumulation%20of%20dangerous%20misinformation.

Hu, K. (2023, February 2). ChatGPT sets record for fastest-growing user base - analyst note. *Reuters*. Retrieved April 30, 2023, from https://www.reuters.com/technology/chatgpt-sets-record-fastest-growing-user-base-analyst-note-2023-02-01/

Inkol, C. (2018). Melusine machine: The metal mermaids of Jung, Deleuze and Guattari. *Shima: The International Journal of Research into Island Cultures, 12*. https://doi.org/10.21463/shima.12.2.07

Jenkins, B. (2018). *Eros and economy: Jung, Deleuze, sexual difference*. Routledge.

Johanssen, J. (2022). Reconsidering trauma and symbolic wounds in times of online misogyny and platforms. *Media, Culture & Society, 45*(1), 191–201. https://doi.org/10.1177/01634437221127362

Jones, R. (2017). Archaic man meets a marvellous automaton: Posthumanism, social robots, archetypes. *Journal of Analytical Psychology, 62*(3), 338–355. https://doi.org/10.1111/1468-5922.12316

Jung, C. G. (1954/1985). Psychology of the transference (R. F. C. Hull, Trans.). In H. Read et al. (Eds.), *The practice of psychotherapy: Essays on the psychology of the transference and other subjects (The collected works of C. G. Jung Vol. 16.)* (2nd ed., pp. 163–323). Princeton University Press.

Jung, C. G. (1956/1967). (R. F. C. Hull, Trans.). In H. Read et al. (Eds.), *Symbols of transformation (The collected works of C. G. Jung vol.5)* (2nd ed.). Princeton University Press.

Jung, C. G. (1963/1989). (R. F. C. Hull, Trans.). In H. Read et al. (Eds.), *Mysterium coniunctionis (Collected works of C. G. Jung vol.14)* (2nd ed.). Princeton University Press.

Jung, C. G. (1966/1977). (R. F. C. Hull, Trans.). In H. Read et al. (Eds.), *Two essays on analytical psychology (Collected works of C. G. Jung vol. 7)* (2nd ed.). Princeton University Press.

Jung, C. G. (1967/1983). The spirit Mercurius (R. F. C. Hull, Trans.). In H. Read et al. (Eds.), *Alchemical studies (The collected works of C. G. Jung Vol. 13.)* (2nd ed., pp. 191–250) (2nd ed.). Princeton University Press.

Jung, C. G. (1968/1980). (R. F. C. Hull, Trans.). In H. Read et al. (Eds.), *Psychology and alchemy (Collected works of C. G. Jung vol. 12)* (2nd ed.). Princeton University Press.

Jung, C. G. (1969a/1981). On the nature of the psyche (R. F. C. Hull, Trans.). In H. Read et al. (Eds.), *The collected works of C. G. Jung: Vol. 8. The structure and dynamics of the psyche. Archetypes and the collective unconscious* (2nd ed., pp. 159–234). Princeton University Press.

Jung, C. G. (1969b/1981). On psychic energy (R. F. C. Hull, Trans.). In H. Read et al. (Eds.), *The collected works of C. G. Jung: Vol. 8. The structure and dynamics of the psyche. Archetypes and the collective unconscious* (2nd ed., pp. 3–66). Princeton University Press.

Jung, C. G. (1973). *C.G. Jung letters, Vol. 1: 1906-1950* (R. F. C. Hull, Trans., Vol. 1). Princeton University Press.

Jung, C. G. (2014/1902). On the psychology and pathology of so-called occult phenomena (R. F. C. Hull, Trans.). In H. Read et al. (Eds.), *The collected works of C. G. Jung: Complete digital edition* (Vol. 1, pp. 20–98). Princeton University Press. (Original work published 1902)

Jung, C. G. (2014/1954). On flying saucers (R. F. C. Hull, Trans.). In H. Read et al. (Eds.), *The collected works of C.G. Jung: Complete digital edition* (Vol. 18, pp. 11069–11076). Princeton University Press. (Original work published 1954)

Jung, C. G. (2014/1959). Flying saucers: A modern myth of things seen in the skies (R. F. C. Hull, Trans.). In H. Read et al. (Eds.), *The collected works of C. G. Jung: Complete digital edition* (Vol. 10, pp. 5886–6013). Princeton University Press. (Original work published 1958)

Jung, C. G. (2014/1960). On the psychology of dementia praecox (R. F. C. Hull, Trans.). In H. Read et al. (Eds.), *The collected works of C. G. Jung: Complete digital edition* (Vol. 3, pp. 1082–1217). Princeton University Press. (Original work published 1960)

Jung, C. G. (2014/1961). Symbols and the interpretation of dreams (R. F. C. Hull, Trans.). In H. Read et al. (Eds.), *The collected works of C.G. Jung: Complete digital edition* (Vol. 18, pp. 10641–10718). Princeton University Press. (Original work published 1961)

Jung, C. G. (2014/1970). The love problem of a student (R. F. C. Hull, Trans.). In H. Read et al. (Eds.), *The collected works of C.G. Jung: Complete digital edition* (Vol. 10, pp. 5685–5700). Princeton University Press. (Original work published 1970)

Kemal Kaptan, S., & Brayne, M. (2021). A qualitative study on clinicians' perceptions of attachment-focused eye movement desensitisation and reprocessing therapy. *Counselling and Psychotherapy Research*, *22*(3), 594–605. https://doi.org/10.1002/capr.12479

Kemp, S. (2022, March 14). Digital 2022: The United States of America - DataReportal – global digital insights. *DataReportal*. Retrieved December 18, 2022, from https://datareportal.com/reports/digital-2022-united-states-of-america

Kerslake, C. (2007). *Deleuze and the unconscious (Ser. Continuum studies in continental philosophy)*. Continuum.

Khalil, M., & Er, E. (2023, February 8). Will ChatGPT get you caught? Rethinking of plagiarism detection. *arXiv.org*. Retrieved April 30, 2023, from https://arxiv.org/abs/2302.04335

Knox, J. (2009). Mirror neurons and embodied simulation in the development of archetypes and self-agency. *Journal of Analytical Psychology*, *54*(3), 307–323. https://doi.org/10.1111/j.1468-5922.2009.01782.x.

Kung, T. H., Cheatham, M., Medenilla, A., Sillos, C., Leon, L. D., Elepaño, C., Madriaga, M., Aggabao, R., Diaz-Candido, G., Maningo, J., & Tseng, V. (2023, February 9). Performance of chatgpt on USMLE: Potential for AI-assisted medical education using large language models. *PLoS Digital Health*. https://journals.plos.org/digitalhealth/ article?id=10.1371%2Fjournal.pdig.0000198

Kurzweil, R. (2006). *The singularity is near: When humans transcend biology*. Penguin Books.

Lacan, J. (1991). *The seminar of Jacques Lacan / Book II: The ego in Freud's theory and in the technique of psychoanalysis, 1954–1955* (S. Tomaselli, Trans. and J.-A. Miller, Ed.). W.W. Norton & Company.

Landin-Romero, R., Moreno-Alcazar, A., Pagani, M., & Amann, B. L. (2018, July 18). How does eye movement desensitization and reprocessing therapy work? A systematic review on suggested mechanisms of action. *Frontiers*. Retrieved April 30, 2023, from https://www.frontiersin.org/articles/10.3389/fpsyg.2018.01395/full

Latour, B. (2005). *Reassembling the social: An introduction to actor-network-theory*. Oxford University Press.

Lazzarato, M. (2014). *Signs and machines: Capitalism and the production of subjectivity*. MIT Press.

Le Mouël, C. (2021). A logical theory of life. *Psychological Perspectives*, *64*(1), 88–117. https://doi.org/10.1080/00332925.2020.1852838

Lyotard, J.-F. (1984). *The postmodern conditions: A report on knowledge* (Series: Theory and History of Literature) (G. Bennington & B. Massumi, Trans.). University of Minnesota Press.

Ma, L., & Zhang, F. (2021). End-to-end predictive intelligence diagnosis in brain tumor using lightweight neural network. *Applied Soft Computing*, *111*, 107666. https://doi.org/10.1016/j.asoc.2021.107666

Magee, L., Arora, V., & Munn, L. (2022, December 8). Structured like a language model: Analysing AI as an automated subject. *arXiv.org*. https://arxiv.org/abs/2212.05058

Main, R., Henderson, D., & McMillan, C. (Eds.). (2020). *Jung, Deleuze and the problematic whole*. Routledge.

Marcus, J. (2022, December 10). Artists decry use of AI art: 'I'm concerned for the future of human creativity'. *The Independent*. Retrieved December 19, 2022, from https://www.independent.co.uk/news/world/americas/ai-art-lensa-magic-avatar-b2242891.html

Maxwell, G. (2022). *Integration and difference: Constructing a mythical dialectic*. Routledge.

McLuhan, M. (1996). *Essential McLuhan* (E. McLuhan & F. Zingrone, Eds.). Basic Books.

McMillan, C., Main, R., & Henderson, D. (Eds.). (2020). *Holism: Possibilities and problems*. Routledge.

Meaker, M. (2023, April 21). How the streaming era turned music into sludge. *Wired*. Retrieved April 24, 2023, from https://www.wired.com/story/plaintext-how-the-streaming-era-turned-music-into-sludge/

Miah, A. (2008). Posthumanism: A critical history. In B. Gordijn & R. F. Chadwick (Eds.), *Medical enhancement and posthumanity* (Ser. The International Library of Ethics, Law and Technology, Vol. 2, pp. 71–94). Springer.

Moyers, B., & Campbell, J. (2021, March 28). EP. 2: Joseph Campbell and the power of myth -- 'the message of the myth'. *BillMoyers.com*. Retrieved April 23, 2023, from https://billmoyers.com/content/ep-2-joseph-campbell-and-the-power-of-myth-the-message-of-the-myth/

Mumford, L. (1967). *Technics and human development: The myth of the machine* (Vol. 1). HBJ.

Mumford, L. (1970). *The Pentagon of power: The myth of the machine* (Vol. 2). HBJ.

Oxford Economics. (2022, May 12). How robots change the world: What automation really means for jobs and productivity. *Oxford Economics*. Retrieved November 25, 2022, from https://resources.oxfordeconomics.com/hubfs/How%20Robots%20Change%20the%20World%20(PDF).pdf

Patel, S. B., & Lam, K. (2023, February 6). ChatGPT: The future of discharge summaries? *The Lancet*. Retrieved April 30, 2023, from https://www.thelancet.com/journals/landig/article/PIIS2589-7500(23)00021-3/fulltext

Pew Research Center. (2021a, April 7). Internet/broadband fact sheet. *Pew Research Center: Internet, Science & Tech*. Retrieved December 18, 2022, from https://www.pewresearch.org/internet/fact-sheet/internet-broadband/

Pew Research Center. (2021b, April 7). Social media fact sheet. *Pew Research Center: Internet, Science & Tech*. Retrieved December 18, 2022, from https://www.pewresearch.org/internet/fact-sheet/social-media/#panel-4abfc543-4bd1-4b1f-bd4a-e7c67728ab76

Pew Research Center. (2021c, April 7). Mobil fact sheet. *Pew Research Center: Internet, Science & Tech*. Retrieved December 18, 2022, from https://www.pewresearch.org/internet/fact-sheet/mobile/

Planker, A. (2023, March 8). The legal implications of AI generated artwork. *Cardozo AELJ: Arts & Entertainment Law Journal*. Retrieved April 30, 2023, from https://cardozoaelj.com/2023/03/08/the-legal-implications-of-ai-generated-artwork/

Possati, L. (2020). Algorithmic unconscious: Why psychoanalysis helps in understanding AI. *Palgrave Communications*, 6(1), 1–13. https://doi.org/10.1057/s41599-020-0445-0

Powell, K. (2018, November 7). How biologists are creating life-like cells from scratch. *Nature News*. Retrieved November 25, 2022, from https://www.nature.com/articles/d41586-018-07289-x

Reimann, M. W., Nolte, M., Scolamiero, M., Turner, K., Perin, R., Chindemi, G., Dłotko, P., Levi, R., Hess, K., & Markram, H. (2017). Cliques of neurons bound into cavities provide a missing link between structure and function. *Frontiers in Computational Neuroscience*, 11. https://doi.org/10.3389/fncom.2017.00048

Romanyshyn, R. D. (2019). *Victor Frankenstein, the monster and the shadows of technology: The Frankenstein prophecies* (1st ed.). Routledge. https://doi.org/10.4324/9780429028335

Rousselle, D. (2023, March 8). Escaping the meta-verse. *Sublation Magazine*. Retrieved April 15, 2023, from https://www.sublationmag.com/post/escaping-the-meta-verse

Rushkoff, D. (2018, July 24). How tech's richest plan to save themselves after the apocalypse. *The Guardian*. Retrieved March 21, 2023, from https://www.theguardian.com/technology/2018/jul/23/tech-industry-wealth-futurism-transhumanism-singularity

Saban, M. (2011). *Psychoid*. International Association of Analytical Psychology IAAP. https://iaap.org/jung-analytical-psychology/short-articles-on-analytical-psychology/psychoid-2/

Saban, M. (2020). Simondon and Jung: Re-thinking individuation. In C. McMillan, R. Main, & D. N. Henderson (Eds.), *Holism: Possibilities and problems* (pp. 91–98). Routledge.

Sample, I. (2023, May 24). Paralysed man walks using device that reconnects brain with muscles. *The Guardian*. https://www.theguardian.com/science/2023/may/24/paralysed-man-walks-using-device-that-reconnects-brain-with-muscles

Samuels, A. (1998). Will the post-Jungians survive? In A. Casement et al. (Eds.), *Post-Jungians today: Key papers in contemporary analytical psychology* (pp. 15–32). Routledge. https://doi.org/10.4324/9780203360521-1

Savlov, L. (2023, March 25). Personal communication.

Shamdasani, S. (2005). *Jung and the making of modern psychology: The dream of a science.* Cambridge University Press.

Shen, C., Li, Z., Chu, Y., & Zhao, Z. (2021). Gar: Graph adversarial representation for adverse drug event detection on Twitter. *Applied Soft Computing, 106,* 107324. https://doi.org/10.1016/j.asoc.2021.107324

Sherburne, P. (2022, May 24). Will AI lead to new creative frontiers, or take the pleasure out of music? *Pitchfork.* Retrieved December 19, 2022, from https://pitchfork.com/features/article/ai-music-experimentation-or-automation/

Simondon, G. (2017). *On the mode of existence of technical objects* (C. Malaspina & J. Rogove, Trans.). University of Minnesota Press.

Simondon, G. (2020). *Individuation in light of notions of form and information* (T. Adkins, Trans., Vol. 1). University of Minnesota Press.

Skjuve, M., Følstad, A., Inge Fostervold, K., & Bae Brandtzaeg, P. (2021, January 23). My chatbot companion - A study of human-chatbot relationships. *International Journal of Human-Computer Studies.* https://www.sciencedirect.com/science/article/pii/S1071581921000197

Smith, D., Protevi, J., & Voss, D. (2022, Summer). Gilles Deleuze. In E. N. Zalta (Eds.), *The Stanford encyclopedia of philosophy.* https://plato.stanford.edu/archives/sum2022/entries/deleuze/

Smith, J. E. H. (2022). *The internet is not what you think it is: A history, a philosophy, a warning.* Princeton University Press.

Stiegler, B. (1998). *Technics and time, 1: The fault of Epimetheus* (R. Beardsworth & G. Collins, Trans.). Stanford University Press.

Solms, M. (2018, December 17). *The hard problem of consciousness and the Free Energy Principle.* Frontiers. https://www.frontiersin.org/articles/10.3389/fpsyg.2018.02714/full

Stiegler, B. (2008). *Technics and time, 2: Disorientation* (S. Barker, Trans.). Stanford University Press.

Stokel-Walker, C. (2022, December 9). AI bot ChatGPT writes smart essays - should professors worry? *Nature News.* Retrieved December 19, 2022, from https://www.nature.com/articles/d41586-022-04397-7

The Art and Science of EMDR. (2021, September 12). *EMDR and Jungian psychology: An interview with Dr. Andrew Dobo.* https://www.youtube.com/watch?v=MHzcSl4GKSs

Tikkun. (2001/2020). *The cybernetic hypothesis.* Semiotext(e).

Tong, A. (2023, March 25). AI chatbot company Replika restores erotic roleplay for some users. *Reuters.* https://www.reuters.com/technology/ai-chatbot-company-replika-restores-erotic-roleplay-some-users-2023-03-25/#:~:text=Replika's%20chatbots%20are%20powered%20by,ability%20to%20foster%20humanlike%20interactions

Yang, L., Feng, X., Chen, X., Zhang, S., & Huang, K. (2023, March 16). See your heart: Psychological states interpretation through visual creations. *arXiv.org.* https://arxiv.org/abs/2302.10276

Žižek, S. (2023, April 7). ChatGPT says what our unconscious radically represses. *Sublation Magazine.* Retrieved April 15, 2023, from https://www.sublationmag.com/post/chatgpt-says-what-our-unconscious-radically-represses

Zuboff, S. (2020). *The age of surveillance capitalism: The fight for a human future at the new frontier of power.* Public Affairs.

Chapter 6

The Dance of Limit and Possibility[1]

Giorgio Tricarico

The topic of possibility, in particular the emergence of unconscious possibilities within the relational field shared by patients and therapists, attracted my interest many years ago and became the main theme of my book *The Labyrinth of Possibility: A Therapeutic Factor in Analytical Practice* (Tricarico, 2015).

The initial impetus for that work was a recurrent experience I had during my years of training as an analyst, an experience shared by many of my colleagues: after a fruitful supervision session on a difficult case, a different, prospective perception of the clinical situation on my part, somehow perceived by my patients as well without me verbalizing it, was often pushing the analytical process forward, in new directions. A second impetus was the observation that both patients and therapists tended to make large use of metaphors related to a movement within a horizontal space, during the therapeutic journey. Expressions such as *finding oneself at a crossroads*, *at a dead end*, in a situation with *no way out*, *going in circles*, and *taking a step forward* rather than *backward,* to name a few, seemed to be extremely common in the consulting room, in the most diverse languages and cultures, as I had the chance to ascertain, working with people from many different countries.

It is worth underlining that psychological theories result in a *method*, with this very word hinting at the same spatial representation. As a matter of fact, *hodos* in Greek means "road" and *metá* means "beyond"; thus method, the *metá-hodos*, could be defined as "the road which goes beyond", a road that can open to new horizons and new *meaning* (in some languages the word *meaning* refers namely to "direction", for instance, *sinn* in German and *senso* in Italian). The image of the labyrinth seemed to encompass all those aforementioned expressions referring to a movement within a

DOI: 10.4324/9781003412823-7

horizontal space. Accordingly, the first part of my work was dedicated to a careful exploration of the so-called "classical labyrinth", a symbol that, in its simple meandering curvilinear shape, can be found in several different cultures, spread over the course of some millennia.

Mostly relying on some papers by Károly Kerényi (Kerényi, 1941, 1956, 1963), the renowned scholar of Greek mythology and cultural anthropologist, I ended up envisioning the labyrinth as a symbol of possibility. In very diverse contexts and epochs, in fact, the classical labyrinth apparently depicted the journey into the Realm of the Dead, the Underworld, and the *possibility* of a return to life transformed/reborn.

In different cultures, such a journey was usually portrayed in dance, within the frame of specific rituals dealing with the cycle of death and rebirth. Labyrinth-dances shared the common plot of entering a separated world, reaching its center, and coming out renewed through the very same way that previously had been the entrance: as a matter of fact, a fundamental characteristic of any labyrinth, from the simple classical one to the more complex angular ones,

> is that, despite its complications and the tortuosity of the path, there is always *the way in which is also the way out*. If we imagine ourselves physically in a labyrinth, knowing that somewhere there is a way out could be our motivation to search for salvation, which otherwise we would almost certainly give up on.
>
> (Tricarico, 2015, p. 28)

In every labyrinth, a way out always exists, and it is *possible* to go out, or at least it is reasonable to hope for such a possibility. C.G. Jung would have probably considered the classical labyrinth an archetypal image, one that in its essential form of curvilinear meanders has been found almost anywhere in the world. From his theoretical perspective, archetypal images stem from an archetype "behind", so to say, and Jung mentioned a specific group of archetypes that would represent a process as such, dubbing them "archetypes of transformation": in his own words "they are not personalities, but are typical situations, places, ways and means that symbolize the kind of transformation in question" (Jung, 1934/1954, p. 38). The mandala, symbols of quaternity, and the symbol of the entwined couple are among Jung's examples of images that originated from this kind of archetype: I would definitely add the classical labyrinth to this small list of examples.

The concept of archetype is very complex and rather controversial, and since a deeper discussion on this concept is not possible here, let's be content to consider the labyrinth as an image spread worldwide representing possibility, and as the visual expression of an emerging unconscious predisposition. In its simplest version, such an image could be linked to what Jean Knox, quoting Jean Mandler, refers to as "image-schema", i.e., the earliest and more primitive forms of representation, which are conceptual structures mapped from spatial structures (see Knox, 2003). An image-schema could be seen as a set of predispositions to perceive, elaborate, and process internal and external realities. Envisioning the classical labyrinth as a symbol of possibility does not reduce the expression of the *possible* to a single image, though. It would be recommendable to leave the very image of the labyrinth in the background and to keep the concept of the *possible* in the foreground instead, to extract its essence from the image, so to say. Dreams, fantasies, symptoms, behaviors, and synchronistic events usually offer many other images, plots, and narratives that express the emergence of an unconscious possibility, a potential, a direction, or a *telos* in the psyche of the patient. Most importantly, such emerging elements require some form of validation by a significant other: the birth of what Jung terms the "Ego-complex" provides a useful paradigm of how an unconscious potential (a predisposition to developing consciousness, in this case) needs to be validated within a meaningful relationship with the caregivers, whose acceptance mirrors back to the child what could be dubbed "the right of existence" (Kast, 1992, p. 57).

Keeping in mind such a parallel with the birth of the Ego and the development of consciousness, I proposed a model about a common transformative factor to be found in any kind of therapy. What might represent such a transformative factor is that the unconscious of the therapist feels and perceives a "potential" in the patient's psyche (through their dreams, symptoms, behavior, countertransference, fantasies, and so on), a *possibility* that is often unconscious to the patient as well; when this "unconscious knowledge" meets the consciousness of the analyst, even partially, it can be mirrored/reflected back to the patient, who feels it to be "true" as it comes from deep within themselves. The patient does not necessarily need to have a rational understanding of it but may mostly experience its feeling-tone: coming in touch with unconscious aspects accompanied by intense affect can make the patient and the therapist feel a shared sense of possibility, an opening toward new directions, a *telos*.

Detecting a sense of possibility that belongs to the patient within the significant relationship between patient and therapist and mirroring it back may account for transformative passages and individuative processes and could be seen as a common denominator to many therapeutic methods. Different theories of the mind make use of diverse images, words, metaphors, and jargon, to express essentially the same concept.

In the present collective work on the birth of the possible, as well as in the work I sketched above, reflecting on the topic of possibility compels us to take into account what may be considered upon first glance its opposite, i.e. *impossibility*, and to deal with the concept of *limit*. Constantly entwined, in fact, possibility and limit can be imagined as dancing with each other. Only by including the dimension of *limit* can a more authentic meaning of the word *possibility* itself be retrieved. One of the core elements of Western societies though is the repression of limit. This repression is the outcome of a long process, the upshot of the internal logic of the history of the Western world, as Martin Heidegger argued in his oeuvre. The essence of the philosophical thought of the eighteenth and nineteenth centuries, together with the increasing power of the scientific-technological apparatus, has brought an apparent omnipotent domination of technology to every aspect of human life. Hand in hand, Enlightenment and the Industrial Revolution fostered a progressive *repression of limits* and paved the way to the ascendance of a pervasive omnipotent mentality. No absolute truth, no immutable principles, and no metaphysical limits are the precondition for technology to reach a status of omnipotence. The need for no limits requires every *epistéme* (literally, what stands on its own feet, without any external support) to fade away, leaving room for a multiplicity of relative truths and a polytheism of values. It's an epochal rupture that Nietzsche clearly discerned at the end of the nineteenth century when he stated that God was dead and that all the supreme values had lost their hold. In a context of repressed limits, technology can expand its unlimited potential to reach goals and function, as aptly argued by the philosopher Emanuele Severino (Severino, 2009).

As repression is posed as an unconscious mechanism that intervenes to distance particularly painful and feared content from the individual's consciousness, moving the concept to a collective level, we could assume that the Western world fears limits and neutralizes the resulting distress and discomfort by keeping them outside of the conscious horizon of its members. Retrieving the concept of limit would immediately lead to questioning the idea of scientific and technological progress, and of the hegemony of capitalism and consumerism, the warp and the weft of our current world. Every ancient myth, from that of Prometheus to the biblical tale of Adam and Eve, usually revolves around the concept of *hybris*, the human arrogance of trespassing limits, breaking the rules of Nature, aiming to be like the gods, and the consequent punishments (see Zoja, 1995). During the last two centuries, instead, technology and science have promoted an enormous acceleration in every field regardless of any form of limitation, which has led human beings to seemingly dominate Nature, considered nothing more than *materia* to be exploited and ransacked according to their economic needs and will to power.

Repressing limits allows this *hybris* to remain unnoticed, but the tragic consequences, on a collective level as well as on the individual one, are now in front of us in the shape of climate change, pandemic diseases, wars over increasingly scarce resources, insane economic discrepancies between rich elites and billions of poor, migration crises, widespread mental health illnesses, and so on.

During the twentieth century, many in the West learned to think of progress in primarily positive terms, mainly because they were part of the minority of human beings on the planet who benefited from this conviction in some way. Increased life expectancy, advances in life-saving medical care, access to limited food and water resources, owning a home, private transportation, tourism and leisure industries, and new information technologies were, and still are, the prerogative of the few, when considered on a global level. People were led to keep in the foreground the positive aspects of technological and scientific progress and ignore the negatives for which the whole living planet is paying a price.

As the recent COVID-19 pandemic and the increasing devastation related to climate change are showing, the idea of limitless expansion in a closed and therefore limited system like planet Earth is no longer defensible. Thoughtless consumption of resources crossed the line of sustainable balance long ago. The uncontrolled use of raw materials, rare minerals, seas, forests, and lands (often through the exploitation of the underprivileged) is irreversibly altering the eco-biological and climatic balance of the planet. Such actions can arguably be deemed insane.

A reasonable consciousness would see that a closed system naturally involves limitations, and that infinite growth is impossible, particularly if it is based on a profound imbalance between distribution, consumption, and waste. Technology is the example *par excellence* of a no-limits mentality, considering that its implicit motto is "everything that can be done must be done", in Günther Anders' words. Capitalism, particularly in its current neoliberal, globalized, and financialized form (see Chomsky & Waterstone, 2021), has been going hand in hand with the acceleration of technological development. The two share the same no-limits mentality and intrinsic omnipotence with an economic model built on unlimited growth and expansion regardless of its effects, according to what I dub "the inner logic of cancer".

During recent decades, mobile phones, computers, tablets, the internet, and the whole cyber world have been unceasingly reinforcing our fallacious sensation of limitlessness, allowing access to contents and connection to people beyond any space or time limitations. In the current age of mass communication, advertising is also a powerful and pervasive element that nurtures and amplifies the repression of limit and an omnipotent mentality, since almost any slogan could be reduced to the basic message "*you can*", "*anything is possible*", or "*there is no limit*".

If we agree on the idea that technology, science, capitalism, economy, consumerism, and the marketing industry are the transparent water we all are immersed in, it is possible to assert that we unwarily swim in an ocean of omnipotence, and that the repression of limit imbues almost every aspect of our world. Perhaps the main example of this repression that characterizes Western societies is visible in our current relationship with death. Our supreme limit, the unknown *par excellence*, death has always accompanied human beings in the short journey of their personal lives but has been dealt with in very different ways over the course of history. The French historian Phillipe Ariés (1914–1984), some decades ago illustrated the massive differences in how death has been envisioned in the Christian West, from the Middle Ages (an era in which human beings immediately knew that they were close to death, and dying was essentially a public event) to the twentieth century (in which death was (and still is) usually hidden *in primis* among the dying, and has become a private matter in the double sense of intimate/non-public and deprived of frames of meaning with which to insert it into the journey of our lives; see Ariés, 1975). For centuries, individuals knew they were near the end, and waited for it, often lying in their own bed, surrounded by masses of people made up of family, relatives, and perfect strangers who just happened to be passing by. Nowadays instead, the terminally ill are often kept in the dark as to the gravity of their condition until the end, in an attempt to protect them from anguish, and often die alone, rarely at home and more often in hospital, unconscious, perhaps hooked up to the machines provided by technology.

The latter has become the true custodian of life and death, and determines life's extension or termination, according to current scientific parameters. The rituals of medieval human beings, who could weigh up their existence on their deathbed, the good and evil they had committed, and aspire to the salvation of their souls, those rituals which allowed the dying to take an active role (turning the divine judgement toward forgiveness, giving family members instructions to help his soul with masses and prayers, and so on) make way, in our time, to a large and passive void of practices and meaning.

In the Middle Ages, death was painfully accepted as a part of life, a conviction maintained by Christianity, according to which true life began after that on Earth; what was most feared was sudden death in an accident or a violent act, as these events would have prevented them from carrying out all that was required by the dying ritual to save their souls. In turn, our current era sees death as mostly repressed, and we live our lives as if it did not exist. When it does present itself, often through the common illnesses of our time (cancer, degenerative diseases, epidemics of new viruses, and so on) or in unexpected ways, it is felt with a total lack of preparation and unspeakable pain: death is absurd and unfair, an atrocious wrong committed by a blind and arbitrary fate, which deprives us in an instant of all that we have painstakingly built. Unlike early ancient, medieval, and pre-modern human beings who could in some way rely on myth and rituals to gain some meaning, the dying nowadays do not know how to deal with their own end. Death has been delivered in the hands of the healthcare machine, which tries to make it as correct as possible, discreet, hidden from view. Death is obscene, literally "out of the scene" (*ob-scaena*).

The psychic effect of repressing death is that of living an illusory brilliant and eternal life, although constantly threatened by depths of darkness, from which emanates a sense of worrying, growing uncertainty, and insecurity. The disappearance of death from the horizon of life itself, prevents individuals from making peace with this inescapable experience, and from the possibility of living authentically and fully, not allowing them to find any meaning, as this would require considering the end, the limit. Concurrent with all this, aging is subject to a similar repression as well, as it represents another inescapable limit for every living thing. The second half of life, which Jung described as the phase in which the individual, after mastering their role in the outside world, could turn to their inner world, is often kept at bay by the "society of eternal youth". Signs of aging can be counteracted with an infinite range of means and techniques such as cosmetics and plastic surgery, and clothing keeps those approaching old age tied to the dominant image, that of younger age groups.

The Latin word *senex*, from which the word *senator* is derived, expresses the idea of maturity brought by experience, but today rather declines into words such as *senile*, associated with a devaluation and loss of ability instead. Thus, the elderly as custodians of historic memory, the elderly who potentially have much to offer to the young, ruefully make way for the useless old person who is unsuited to a world which changes too quickly, unable to work the ever-changing tools of technology.

In such a scenario, it is no surprise that even psychologies have to some extent absorbed the same omnipotent mentality present in every field of our lives, feeding it back in return, even. Positive psychology and positive thinking, for example, contribute to a flourishing self-help industry that produces thousands of books, podcasts, and online and live retreats and courses all over the world, aimed at empowerment, personal and spiritual development, life coaching, and the wellbeing of targeted groups of consumers. Although potentially useful and beneficial to some people and in some cases, common features shared by all these experiences are the expulsion of the negative (be this in the form of negative thoughts, emotions, or traits), and the assumption that the way to happiness and fulfillment in life is basically in the hands of the person who carefully follows the techniques, advice, and prescriptions supplied.

Nested in such an assumption, we find the same message that animates many advertisement slogans, i.e., "anything is possible", a message in which the word *possible* is clearly intended in an omnipotent way. "Anything is possible" means that anyone can reach the promised result. Following the right instructions, there are no limits, apart from those that one poses to oneself.

A corollary of this last point is that, in case of failure, guilt falls on the person who has not carefully committed to the suggested techniques, does not have enough "faith", or who holds onto negative thoughts and emotions. Resorting to guilt to explain suffering resembles the old retribution theory, as can be found in the Old Testament's Book of Job, a strikingly old-fashioned mindset disguised as it is under the name of "New" Age. Besides, the financial aims of the capitalistic oriented self-help industry depend upon the failure of its disciplines aiming to expel the negative as "toxic". From the point of view of the production of self-help materials, in fact, a satisfied and self-realized client would be a nightmarish outcome, as it would prevent them from buying new tools for their "development".

In that gray area where New Age and Jungian theories meet and merge, it is not surprising to find the same implicit omnipotent mentality that imbues every aspect of the current way of being in the world. Even a complex Jungian topic such as the individuation process can be commercialized and commodified as a path of development that is at the disposal of anyone who commits to the required techniques. We know instead, that on a deeper level, the Jungian theory of psychic energy implies positive and negative as two necessarily co-existing polarities, seen as the precondition for energy to flow, as in physics. An emphasis on the positive pole, and the willful expulsion of the negative counterpart as dysfunctional for healthy wellbeing cannot be reconciled with Jung's theory of a developmental process aiming at totality and wholeness.

The negative polarity exists and is of equal importance to the positive one. Limits exist as well, and they need to be acknowledged, faced, and even challenged. Overcoming a limit, or striving to transcend it, is an entirely different thing than repressing or denying it. It is useful to recall that the word *limit* comes from the Latin *limes*, meaning "boundary", or "border". To know my limits is to know my boundaries, to know where I end and the other begins; in other words, to know who I am and what I am not. Limits are essential to self-definition. The attempt to go beyond a limit/ boundary, to transgress it, to transcend and redefine it, is part of an individuative process but requires that one acknowledges limits in first place. The pervasive repression of limit outlined earlier instead undermines the process of building a solid sense of self, and could be seen as a contributor to the *liquidity* of society and the identity often described by the sociologist Zygmunt Bauman (1925–2017) in many of his works (see for example Bauman, 2003, 2007).

How can these brief reflections on the repression and eclipse of the concept of limit in Western culture help us to retrieve a more authentic meaning of the term *possibility* itself? The concepts of *necessity* and *possibility* are central to the field of modal logic, a discipline that explores the dialectic between potentiality and actuality. This field examines how statements about potential and actual states interact and combine with each other. Organized in axiomatic systems for the first time by the philosopher C.I. Lewis (1883–1964) at the beginning of the twentieth century and developed further by several other thinkers, modal logic has its basic roots in Book I of Aristotle's *Analytica Priora*.

The four fundamental words in modal logic are *possible, necessary, contingent*, and *impossible*. Once we choose one word as the starting point, the others can be defined from it: if we take the word *possible* as axiomatic, for example, *impossible* can be intended as its negation, the *non-possible*; from this we can state that the *necessary* is the "impossible that it's not", while negating the *necessary* we define the *contingent*, that is, is "not necessary that is or isn't" or also "possible that is or isn't". In the common use of these words, the concept of *impossible* is not much considered as the negation of *possible,* rather as its opposite, as if they could be placed on the two extremes of a *continuum*. Linguistically as well we are invited to perceive *possible* and *impossible* as contraries, like shadow and light, up and down, and so on. From the perspective of this work, though, it would be more fruitful to counter *impossible* with *certain*: these could be considered as the two real opposites or contraries to be placed at the extremes of a *continuum*. On such an ideal *continuum*, it is the entire transitional area between the *impossible* pole and the *certain* pole that could be considered the *possible*. If the concept of *impossible* aims to indicate that an action or an event can *in no way* be realised ("it is necessary that it's not", in the language of modal logic), the opposite concept should logically be *certain*, where the action or the event will certainly be realised ("it is necessary that it is"). In such a representation, the concept of *possible* could instead be reserved for the vast range of situations in between, in which the action or the event could potentially happen or not happen (in modal logic this would be the realm of the contingent: "possible that it is/possible that it is not"). This range of situations must reckon with a series of conditions, which make the occurrence more or less probable and that represent limitations and either favourable or unfavourable eventualities.

To clarify this thought better, we can refer once again to the image of the labyrinth. When we imagine ourselves lost in a labyrinth, finding a way out is not impossible, as we know that a way out exists somewhere: it is a possible event, but this in turn is not equivalent to saying it is a certainty. The complicated network of passages may trap us forever in an agonizing, fruitless search, or an encounter with the mythical Minotaur may spell death and annihilation. Finding a way out is a possible event in the precise sense that this chance requires to actively confront limits: to look for the exit might take much time, and we need to face risks and dangers. We must deal with all sorts of limitation, like the walls, corridors, dead ends, and so on.

The symbol of the labyrinth indeed condenses the dual nature of our human condition at the same time as it conveys both the possibilities of exiting successfully and transformed, and of remaining lost, and thus perishing. In analogy with the ancient dancers in the classical labyrinths, in such a perspective, limit and possibility dance with each other too. Consequently, the concept of *possible* that should be retrieved is closely linked to that of risk: it is the result of a tension between *certain* and *impossible*. It is the journey in that in-between space, that probability tries to capture and quantify.

In a social context, retrieving this meaning of *possibility* appears like a rebellion against the omnipotent mentality previously sketched, detectable in every aspect of our current world, a mentality that sadly promotes its opposite, i.e. impotence. Hence, it is no trivial question to carefully differentiate *possible* from *certain*. The common use of the statement "anything is possible" can give the false impression that there are no limits and no risks, feeding a culture characterized by the misleading optimism of positive thinking and positive psychology. This *Weltanschauung*, relentlessly cultivated by technology and capitalism, is literally destroying the only world we know.

Giving up omnipotence, in the use of the word *possible* even, will surely lead to a "depressive" phase, but we should not forget that in a Kleinian sense, this would represent a step forward from the primitive and more dangerous paranoid-schizoid position.

Healing is a *possibility* in the consulting room as well as individuation is a *possible* event in the journey of an individual life. Unsurprisingly, both healing and individuation require an open and honest confrontation with limits and risks, and a perseverant attitude of trying to go beyond our own egoic needs, our personal history's vicissitudes, the constraints of our personal complexes, the tyranny of our cultural normativities, and beyond our collective ways of being in the world. As a matter of fact, never before in history has the individuation process of individuals concerned the survival of our planet so closely.

Note

1 This chapter is a reworked and expanded version of chapter eight *Closing chords – Possibility and Limit,* from my book *The Labyrinth of Possibility: A Therapeutic Factor in Analytical Practice.* London: Routledge (2015).

References

Ariès, P. (1975). *Western attitudes towards death: From the Middle Ages to the present.* The Johns Hopkins University Press.

Anders, G. (1956). *Die Antiquierheit des Menshcen, Band I.* Verlag C.H. Bech.

Anders, G. (1980). *Die Antiquierheit des Menshcen, Band II.* Verlag C.H. Bech.

Babich, B. (2021). *Günther Anders' philosophy of technology: From phenomenology to critical theory.* Bloomsbury Academic.

Bauman, Z. (2003). *Liquid love: On the frailty of human bonds.* Polity Press.

Bauman, Z. (2007). *Liquid times: Living in an age of uncertainty.* Polity Press.

Chomsky, N., & Waterstone, M. (2021). *Consequences of capitalism. Manufacturing discontent and resistance.* Haymarket Books.

Jung, C.G. (1934/1954). Archetypes of the collective unconscious. In *Collected works* (Vol. 9). Routledge & Kegan Paul Ltd.

Kast, V. (1992). *The dynamics of symbols: Fundamentals of Jungian psychotherapy.* Fromm.

Kerényi, K. (1941). Labyrinth-Studien: Labyrinthos als Linienreflex einer mythologischen Idee. In *Albae vigiliae* (Vol. 15). Pantheon.

Kerényi, K. (1956). Die Herrin des labyrinthes. In *Neue Zürcher Zeitung.* NZZ Mediengruppe.

Kerényi, K. (1963). Vom Labyrinthos zum Syrthos: Gedanken über den griechischen Tanz. In *Atlantis* (Vol. 35).

Knox, J. (2003). *Archetype, attachment, analysis: Jungian psychology and the emergent mind.* Routledge.

Severino, E. (2009). *Il destino della tecnica.* BUR.

Tricarico, G. (2015). *The labyrinth of possibility: A therapeutic factor in analytical practice.* Routledge.

Tricarico, G. (2016). The individuation process in post-modernity. *Psychological Perspectives, 59*(4), 461–472.

Zoja, L. (1995). *Growth and guilt: Psychology and the limits of development.* Routledge.

Index

Fordham, Michael: on correlations between
Bion and Jung 40; on primary self
40–41; on psychic deintegration and
integration and primary self 41
Freud, Sigmund 3, 5, 6, 16, 37; causal-
reductive nature of his theory 161–62;
his focus on the past 16, 161–62, 194;
hydraulic model of mind 194; two
principles of mental functioning 37

Gayanashagowa 20
Gnosticism 8–9
Great Law of Peace 20, 167, 170;
see also Gayanashagowa
Great Tree of Peace 19–20, 159, 167;
symbolism of 20, 167, 169
Grot, Nikolaus 94–95
Grotstein, James 16, 24: as bridge between
Bion and Jung 16, 24, 37–39, 43–44
Guattari, Felix 180–86, 189, 194

Haudenosaunee: culture and myth of
167–70; see also Great Tree of Peace
Heidegger, Martin: on average
everydayness 58; on Being's presencing
67; enframing 98; ownmostness 58
Hogenson, George: on archetypes and
emergentism 13–14
Hollis, James: on mental illness and
thwarted eros 152
Husserl, Edmund: on mental "bracketing"
65, 73, 86
Hydra: in Greek mythology 163–64;
as mythic symbol of American social
crisis 170–71

impossibility: and concept of limit 220
individuation 7; and coming into being
7, 28–29; and Fordham's deintegrate-
integrate model 16; in Jung's teleology
25–26
Iroquois woodland tribes
see Haudenosaunee

Jung, C.G.: on archetypes 13, 85–86;
constructive-synthetic method 3, 6; on
conviction 58; on experience, fidelity to
104; on his cross-disciplinary interests
94; on his eurocentrism 2–3; his literary
style 1–2; his moral beliefs 96–97, 101;
on individuation 28–29; on intuition
80–82; Kant, positive results of his

misunderstanding of 87–90; Kant, uses
of 79–96; on play and creativity 87–88,
94–95; on psychological types 89; on the
Self 33; on the teleology of human life
1, 20, 22; on the transcendent function 3,
16, 26–27; Zofinga lectures 6

Kerényi, Karoly 218
Klein, Melanie 40, 43

labyrinth 200, 217, 218; labyrinth,
symbolism of 217–19, 226

machine, the: and analytical psychology
191, 193–94, 196–201, 208; as metaphor
and archetype, machine 175, 177–79,
182, 186, 187, 190, 191; as mythological
rendering 202; telos of Machine as
archetype 191
mandalas 218
McLuhan, Marshall: on technology 176,
180, 192
memory 4, 127, 130, 194, 224
metaphysics 2, 6, 15, 18, 27, 61–68, 70–73,
76, 78, 79; moral realism, metaphysical
101, 105, 112, 160, 175; realism,
metaphysical 84–85, 87, 101, 105;
scientific, metaphysics 79–80
Mumford, Lewis: on technology 176, 177,
180–93
musement 78, 96–98, 100, 103; and
morality 96

neuroscience 190–91, 194, 196–99
Nietzsche, Friedrich 66, 97–98; Jung,
influence on 105
numinous, the 59, 104, 152

Ogden, Thomas 24, 30, 31
ontology 14, 17, 20, 31, 59–64, 66, 67,
69, 71–73, 81, 82, 91, 93, 98, 103, 108,
109, 111, 112, 178, 179, 181, 187,
201; ontic co-equality 109; ontological
commitments 66

Papadopoulos, Renos: on reductive and
constructive analysis 3, 25; on teleology
in Jung 25–26
Parmenides, philosophy of eros 119
participation mystique 59, 97
Pauli, Wolfgang 15; see also quantum
mechanics

Taylor & Francis Group
an **informa** business

Taylor & Francis eBooks

www.taylorfrancis.com

A single destination for eBooks from Taylor & Francis
with increased functionality and an improved user
experience to meet the needs of our customers.

90,000+ eBooks of award-winning academic content in
Humanities, Social Science, Science, Technology, Engineering,
and Medical written by a global network of editors and authors.

TAYLOR & FRANCIS EBOOKS OFFERS:

A streamlined
experience for
our library
customers

A single point
of discovery
for all of our
eBook content

Improved
search and
discovery of
content at both
book and
chapter level

REQUEST A FREE TRIAL
support@taylorfrancis.com

Routledge
Taylor & Francis Group

CRC Press
Taylor & Francis Group

For Product Safety Concerns and Information please contact our EU
representative GPSR@taylorandfrancis.com
Taylor & Francis Verlag GmbH, Kaufingerstraße 24, 80331 München, Germany

www.ingramcontent.com/pod-product-compliance
Lightning Source LLC
Chambersburg PA
CBHW050642280326
41932CB00015B/2748